D1164458

Empire

KEY CONCEPTS

Published

Barbara Adam, Time
Alan Aldridge, Consumption
Alan Aldridge, The Market
Colin Barnes and Geoff Mercer, Disability
Darin Barney, The Network Society
Mildred Blaxter, Health
Harry Brighouse, Justice
Steve Bruce, Fundamentalism
Margaret Canovan, The People
Alejandro Colás, Empire
Anthony Elliott, Concepts of the Self
Steve Fenton, Ethnicity
Michael Freeman, Human Rights
Russell Hardin, Trust
Fred Inglis, Culture
Jennifer Jackson Preece, Minority Rights
Paul Kelly, Liberalism
Anne Mette Kjær, Governance
Ruth Lister, Poverty
Jon Mandle, Global Justice
Micheal Saward, Democracy
John Scott, Power
Anthony D. Smith, Nationalism
Stuart White, Equality

Empire

by Alejandro Colás

polity

Copyright © Alejandro Colás 2007

The right of Alejandro Colás to be identified as Author of this Work has been asserted in accordance with the UK Copyright, Designs and Patents Act 1988.

First published in 2007 by Polity Press

Polity Press
65 Bridge Street
Cambridge CB2 1UR, UK

Polity Press
350 Main Street
Malden, MA 02148, USA

All rights reserved. Except for the quotation of short passages for the purpose of criticism and review, no part of this publication may be reproduced, stored in a retrieval system, or transmitted, in any form or by any means, electronic, mechanical, photocopying, recording or otherwise, without the prior permission of the publisher.

ISBN-10: 0-7456-3251-3
ISBN-13: 978-07456-3251-3
ISBN-10: 0-7456-3252-1 (pb)
ISBN-13: 978-07456-3252-0 (pb)

A catalogue record for this book is available from the British Library.

Typeset in 10.5 on 12 pt Sabon
by SNP Best-set Typesetter Ltd, Hong Kong
Printed and bound in Great Britain by MPG Books Ltd, Bodmin, Cornwall

The publisher has used its best endeavours to ensure that the URLs for external websites referred to in this book are correct and active at the time of going to press. However, the publisher has no responsibility for the websites and can make no guarantee that a site will remain live or that the content is or will remain appropriate.

Every effort has been made to trace all copyright holders, but if any have been inadvertently overlooked the publishers will be pleased to include any necessary credits in any subsequent reprint or edition.

For further information on Polity, visit our website: www.polity.co.uk

Contents

To Ishani

Preface and Acknowledgements

This is a small book on a big subject. Writing it has proved to be a bit like managing an empire with limited resources: I have faced a constant pull between focusing my energies quite narrowly on defining the concept's core features and the recurring temptation to range more widely over the historical and theoretical terrain which makes the study of empires such a fascinating (but perilously limitless) subject. The only way of dealing with this tension, I have found, is to write a book which is both synthetic and selective. I have drawn extensively from specialist (mainly anglophone) literature on the history of empires and the study of imperialism, and sought to put it to work in explaining the meaning and significance of the concept. Similarly, I have been fairly selective in the choice of historical illustrations, and indeed the range of theoretical debates addressed. There are, therefore, inevitable gaps in the book, which I hope result from the constraints of space and expertise, rather than from indifference towards such histories and theories.

I have incurred many debts in writing the book, some untraceable and a few difficult to repay. Louise Knight bravely encouraged me to write a title on empire for the Polity series and, with the able assistance of Emma Hutchinson, has led the project through to publication with an enviable combination of grace and steely professionalism. Friends and colleagues at the University of London and elsewhere –

Jason Edwards, Laleh Khalili, Ray Kiely, Alfredo Saad-Filho, Benno Teschke and Sami Zubaida – gave up their time and energy in offering comments on the manuscript. Rick Saull has, as ever, been a most reliable sparring partner in thinking through American empire and related issues, while other friends working outside academia (you know who you are) have indulged me in talk on empire, providing much insight and inspiration when we were meant to be out having fun. Two anonymous readers provided very helpful comments on the draft manuscript. I am grateful to all of the above and, as seems to be customary, should state that I am solely responsible for any recommendations I have chosen to ignore or errors I have failed to correct.

I wish, finally, to thank my parents, my sister Sofía and, on the other side of the family, Malika, Pani and Lasantha for their steadfast support in all kinds of ways which they may not have recognized as being relevant to finishing the book. My greatest debt, however, is to my wife Ishani. I started writing the text as our daughter Lalini was born, and have only been able to complete it over the past couple of years because of the care, love and attention Ishani has lavished on us both. I therefore dedicate this book to her, as a first instalment in repaying my dues.

1
Empires in History

In November 2003, the British poet Benjamin Zephaniah received a letter from the office of the then Prime Minister, Tony Blair, recommending his appointment as an officer of the Order of the British Empire (OBE). Zephaniah declined the offer and made his response public, starting an opinion piece with the following explanation:

> Me? I thought, OBE me? Up yours, I thought. I get angry when I hear the word 'empire'; it reminds me of slavery, it reminds me of thousands of years of brutality, it reminds me of how my foremothers were raped and my forefathers brutalised. It is because of this concept of empire that my British education led me to believe that the history of black people started with slavery and that we were born slaves and should therefore be grateful that we were given freedom by our caring white masters. It is because of this idea of empire that black people like myself don't even know our true names or our true historical culture. I am not one of those who are obsessed with their roots, and I'm certainly not suffering from a crisis of identity; my obsession is about the future and the political rights of all people. Benjamin Zephaniah OBE – no way Mr Blair, no way Mrs Queen. I am profoundly anti-empire.[1]

This statement is worth quoting at length simply because it expresses very eloquently what many people around the world feel and think about the word 'empire'. But it is also noteworthy in that it implicitly raises a number of broader issues relating to empire which are the focus of this book. In this short paragraph, Zephaniah alludes to the violence of empire, its modes of exploitation, and the racialization of power as a means of subjecting whole populations in the name of other, generally very distant populations. He talks of history, culture, freedom, identity, suffering and, crucially, the future (and present, one assumes) of 'political rights of all people'.

Empires – not just the British one of course – bring to the fore all these aspects of human political, socio-economic and cultural experience across both time and place. In many respects, studying the origins, dynamics, evolution and decline of empires offers the shortest route to identifying and understanding both the enduring hierarchical structures and the powerful forces of change across human societies, ranging from our forms of government to the creation and distribution of wealth and poverty, and still further to the myriad expressions of individual and collective identity. Analysing empires also allows us to register the long history of struggles against political oppression, racial domination and socio-economic exploitation which, through war, revolution, protest and mass mobilization, have constructed the world in which we now live, and arguably set the standards for the contemporary use of concepts such as justice, equality, rights, solidarity or democracy.

The word 'empire', however, can also conjure up more positive emotions and experiences. Imperial structures and processes have fostered significant advances in natural and human sciences; they have enriched languages, cuisines and art-forms as well as producing new, dynamic societies through the miscegenation of cultures and traditions. They have furthermore governed over diverse ethnic, religious and national groups, often respecting and protecting their customs and beliefs in ways that presage and inspire contemporary understandings of 'multiculturalism'. (Contrast, for instance, the violently exclusive and parochial expressions of nationalism or religiosity in the modern Middle East with the relatively peaceful coexistence of Jews, Christians and Muslims under the Abbasid and later Ottoman empires, or the emblematic modernist culture which was forged in the polyglot capitals of the Austro-Hungarian empire with narrow conceptions of, say, German or Slovak identity.) Empires have offered many of their subjects the kind of prosperity, stability and sense of belonging which to this day can still muster support across the globe from both elites and subaltern populations, metropolitan and post-colonial, young and old alike.

It is clear, then, that the notion of empire is mixed up with all sorts of conflicting political sentiments and social processes. It is not the purpose of this book to draw up a balance sheet of the costs and benefits of empires, or to condone or defend such forms of rule. While recognizing that imperial experiences, right up to present ones, are necessarily politically and emotionally charged – and without for a moment positing a normative or analytical equivalence between arguments for and against empire – this text nonetheless offers no explicit critique of empire or its more active derivation, imperialism. My objective, instead, is to delve into the various contradictory aspects of imperial rule across the (mainly Western) world during different historical periods, with the aim of giving the notion of empire some categorical identity. The study therefore presupposes that any useful understanding of what empire involves requires a strongly historical, indeed historicist, approach to concept-formation. That is, I shall assume throughout that, like other key concepts in the social sciences – democracy, power, race, the state, class – empire is a category the meaning of which carries considerable historical baggage: it is constantly contested and reaffirmed in the present with reference to the past. Thus, rather than discard this historical load and approach the term from a purely analytical standpoint in order to deliver a neat typology, I start from the premise that, not only does the meaning of empire vary throughout time and space (that much is obvious), but its deployment as an explanatory concept requires being especially sensitive to the historical particularity of different imperial experiences – their unique structures of political rule, their specific modes of social reproduction and their correspondingly singular forms of cultural self-understanding.

This emphasis on the historicity of empires signals a second starting-point of the book. And that is the simple recognition that, since for the better part of our civilized existence humans have lived under imperial rule of one description or another, our contemporary division into close to 200 territorially exclusive and politically independent national states requires some explanation. The current absence of formal empires and the corresponding disappearance of emperors and empresses (the Japanese exception aside) is not only of symbolic significance: it also drives home how different our own epoch is to the most recent Age of Empire (1875–1914) which immediately preceded it, and by the end of which '[m]ost of the world outside Europe and the Americas was formally partitioned into territories under the formal rule or informal political domination of one or other of a handful of states: mainly Great Britain, France, Germany, Italy, the Netherlands, Belgium, the USA and Japan.'[2] Much of this book is therefore concerned with identifying different ways in which empires have organized political space in order to exercise authority and reproduce societies which fell within their rule. By extension, it also recurrently contrasts these diverse imperial experiences with the contemporary organization of the world into an international system of states.

The rest of this introductory chapter will expand on these themes in the following order. A first section briefly considers the semantics of empire and its various derivations by way of introducing the diverse meanings of the concept and its important cognates. In contrast to other contemporary studies of empire – some of which will be surveyed shortly – I offer neither a historical reinterpretation nor a conceptual history, even less a political-scientific comparison of administrative systems of empires, but rather a historical sociology of the changing imperial structures and processes which make this concept a useful social-scientific tool.

Because of its signal role in inspiring later (mainly Western) empires and setting a benchmark against which they measured their own power and world-historical standing, particular attention is dedicated in the chapter to the Roman empire. A second section explores in greater detail the forms of political authority and social reproduction which sustained the early Roman empire and one of its contemporaries, the Later, or 'Eastern', Han empire in China. Both these empires left enduring ideological and material legacies not only in their respective geographical zones of influence, but also for later imperial experiences across the world. Indeed the Roman and Han experiences demonstrated how much of what defines particular empires is imported and reconstituted from competing imperial formations; empires are built as much on the traffic in ideas, goods and people with other, rival polities as they are on claims to cultural and political uniqueness or economic and military superiority over other empires. It is this assumption – that imperial entities are generally defined and constituted through their mutual interaction across both time and space – which informs the investigation of empire in the rest of the book.

A final section of the chapter re-emphasizes how the particularity of imperial rule, both vis-à-vis any other given empires and in relation to alternative forms of government (national states, tribal federations, leagues of city-states), can be discerned through the examination of three of its facets (which serve as headings for successive chapters): the imperial organization of political space, the role of markets in sustaining imperial rule, and the contradictory expressions of imperial culture. In each of these arenas we can establish differences among empires themselves, but also contrast imperial polities to other forms of political community. One commonplace contrast, for instance, between the contemporary international system of states and imperial rule is that between autonomy and domination. In principle at least, what distinguishes an imperial from a non-imperial world order is the degree to which peoples can freely determine their own collective socio-economic and political future as opposed to having it constrained or imposed from the outside by a dominant power. The key to understanding empires, then, lies in identifying the specific combination of territorial organization, modes of wealth-creation and distribution, and dynamics of cultural self-understanding specific to each imperial experience.

The meanings of empire

The English word 'empire' is derived from the Latin *imperium*, meaning 'command', 'authority', 'rulership' or, more loosely, 'power'. In Republican Rome, the term referred to specific powers invested in magistrates to declare war and enforce the law.[3] With the territorial expansion of Rome, reference was increasingly made in public debates to the *imperium populi Romani*, or empire of the Roman people, and so by the end of the Republican period the abstract noun 'imperium' had turned into a proper noun, denoting not only the civil and military authority wielded by magistrates and commanders, but also the specific socio-political and geographical entity known as the Roman empire.[4] This gradual shift in meaning is conventionally marked with Octavian's appointment as *Princeps* (first citizen) in the 'first settlement' of 27 BC, his adoption of the auspicious name Augustus and its accompanying honorary title of *Imperator* – chief commander of Roman legions. By the turn of that century, one notable scholar of empire indicates,

> The proud Republican term 'Imperium Populi Romani' was transformed by the Augustans into Imperium Romanum. Both expressions referred to a world-wide dominion built up in the course of a long history. . . . The Romans remained the 'imperial' people . . . but imperial policy had become the prerogative of the *princeps*, and the imperial authority of the Senate and the People could never again be asserted in an effective system of collective action.[5]

Three important dimensions of later imperial experiences can be gleaned from the shifts in the Roman definition of empire. The first is quite obviously that empires are built on expansion. Their histories invariably entail a relatively small political community (in the Roman case, a modest city-state by the Tiber) conquering other peoples and territories, often settling among them, and always absorbing them through a combination of coercive, legal, cultural and economic mechanisms into a larger socio-economic and political entity – an empire. The Romans adopted the Greek term *oikoumene* (the known world) to describe the universal ambition of their rule. From Virgil's celebrated rendition of Rome as 'sine fine' (not only eternal in time, but also boundless in space) to the definition by its Grand Chancellor Mercurino Gattinara of Spain's early sixteenth-century *imperium* as the exercise of limitless power, through to Britannia's empire of the open seas, the imperial organization of political space has assumed the absence of permanent and exclusive borders.[6] This persistent boundary-extension is what today we might call imperialism: a policy and a process, guided in large measure by an ideologically constructed sense of superiority, which seeks to assimilate foreign regions and populations into an expanding polity. As we shall see in later chapters, some claim that this incorporation need not be territorial or juridical: it is possible for a given state to be imperialist without formally becoming an empire by, for instance, controlling key global markets and resources. Others still suggest that 'imperialism' as a relatively new arrival to the modern lexicon is a mere term of abuse which ascribes far too much congruence and purpose to an often involuntary or unintended expansionism. Made famous by the Victorian historian Seeley, this claim that empires can be acquired through a fit of absent-mindedness finds sympathy among some contemporary scholars who note the absence of a clearly discernible imperialist 'grand strategy' in many past empires.[7]

What few historians of empire can deny, however, is that such political expansion and incorporation (empire-building for short) is a hierarchical process. Expanding social formations proclaim and generally enforce their political, cultural and military superiority by codifying the subordination of subject peoples, and thereby leaving no doubt as to where power and authority reside. As Napoleon's foreign minister Talleyrand would have it, 'Empire is the art of putting men in their place.'[8] A second key feature of empires, therefore, is the hierarchical rule over a periphery from a metropolitan centre or 'motherland'. Put differently, empires spatialize power along geographical lines of super- and subordination. All empires have a capital which, however tenuously, concentrates the institutions of imperial power and wealth, and thereby aim to command diverse and distant populations from a geographical centre. In many cases, such capitals become imperial microcosms, displaying in their customs, demography, architecture and markets the wealth of empire. Similarly, imperial outposts – from Havana to Sarajevo, Algiers to Lhasa – bear the imprint of their peripheral status in the superimposition of imperial forms upon existing social, political and economic structures. Much of the world's toponomy reflects this imperialist subordination of foreign lands and peoples: for what else but imperial hubris can explain the renaming of a vast archipelago as 'The Philippines' or the declaration of a large chunk of southern Africa as belonging to 'Rhodesia'? Likewise, the actual burying of the Mexica temples at Tenochtitlán under the Spanish imperial Zócalo also serves as a concrete metaphor of the broader process of grafting metropolitan ways of life – from work patterns and the law to recreation and clothing – upon the everyday existence of colonial populations. This structural relation between the imperial centre and its subaltern periphery is neatly expressed by Alexander Motyl when, drawing on Johan Galtung's theory of structural imperialism, he describes an empire as 'an incomplete wheel, with a hub and spokes but no rim'.[9] The critical feature of such a relation is the absence, indeed the structural impossibility, of independent relations among peripheral entities.[10]

Empires, then, are about expansion and subjection. In exchange they offer a third quality, namely 'order'. Like beauty, the meaning of order is in the eye of the beholder: it was and is, of course, still used as a self-serving assertion of legitimacy by imperial ideologues in formulations ranging from the *Pax Romana*, the Chinese notions of harmony between Earth and Heaven (*yin* and *yang*) mediated by the imperial 'Son of Heaven', or the more contemporary invocations of the 'new world order'. But it is possible to employ a relatively objective conception of imperial order as the condition of stability, legitimate authority and sense of belonging which empires have fostered. Public infrastructure, the law, *linguae francae*, shared cultural-religious institutions and customs, common currencies and, not least important, imperial armies, navies and constabularies have in this respect all propped up imperial orders. The reproduction of a vast and disparate polity over an extended period of time requires the allegiance, or at least acquiescence, of its subjects. This is something which many political communities have achieved through a combination of coercion and consent. But perhaps what marks out the imperial from other forms of political rule is the pervasiveness of coercion in this equation. War and violence (or the threat thereof) are intrinsic to imperial rule in a way which is not true of other political orders. This is why imperialism – the active policy and process of empire-building – always involves the use of force against other peoples and polities – be they imperial rivals or conquered subjects.

The links between militarism and imperial orders need not always be nakedly coercive: possessing unrivalled military power is a very good way of eliciting collaboration without actually exercising force.[11] It was their very belonging to an expansive and hierarchical political entity, for instance, that arguably motivated volunteers from across the British empire to sacrifice their lives on the front lines of two world wars which were essentially European in origin, in the name of that greater political order. Similarly, it was the prospect of being on the side of the victorious power – with all its promises of glory and material wealth – which must account in large measure for the phenomenal spread of the Ottoman empire across three continents. Plainly, such orders have been periodically challenged by forces of 'disorder' – revolts, revolutions, invasions, migrations, occupations, civil wars and internecine conflict – many of which presaged or sealed a terminal decline of imperial rule. Metropolitan life has at regular intervals been subject to radical political, socio-economic cultural upheavals with colonial origins – from Quintilius Varus's defeat in the Teutoburg Forest to the collapse of the French Fourth Republic in the course of the Algerian War. But the fact remains that we can only make historical sense of such disruptive moments in the context of imperial commitments to reproducing stability, prosperity and legitimate rule within a vast and diverse territory, often through the accommodation and cooperation of subject populations.

Expansion, hierarchy and order are therefore features common to most historical empires. The central question which animates this book is how to distinguish one form of imperial rule from the next with regard to these common denominators. What, in other words, have been the expansionary forces behind different empires? How have they organized their respective hierarchical institutions? And through what mechanisms have they sustained an imperial order through time? The rest of this book addresses some of these questions, but offers no single response, nor an over-arching theory of empire. In fact, the core claim of this book is that empire is, both conceptually and empirically, parasiti-cal on other categories and phenomena such as power, the state, territory, class or the market. Different forms of empire combine these various social relations in diverse ways, and the only way to arrive at a definition of empire that allows for both its categorical unity and its manifold phenomenal expressions is by identifying patterns of historical change and continuity of empires. Much of this study is therefore concerned with charting the social structure and processes associated with empire as they emerge and disappear in time. It also assumes that, because the contemporary deployment of the term 'empire' and its cognate 'imperialism' are neces-sarily connected to their past meanings, we cannot but bring these meanings to bear in present usages.

Such an historicist approach to the category and phenom-enon of empire contrasts to most existing engagements with the concept. The various branches of social sciences have certainly explored the historical development of specific empires and compared their diverse socio-economic, political and cultural manifestations through time and place. Yet there are few comprehensive studies of 'empire' as a distinct category of social science, and even fewer explicit *theories*, that is, explanatory accounts, of this phenomenon as a whole. Samuel Eisenstadt's monumental analysis *The Political Systems of Empires* relies, as its title indicates, on a purely political definition of empires as centralized, bureaucratic forms of rule which should be contrasted to modern states characterized, *inter alia*, by the 'greater differentiation of political activities', the 'distribution of political rights' or the 'weakening of traditional hereditary patterns of legitimation of rulers'.[12] A contemporary of Eisenstadt, Robert G. Wesson, also offers an analysis strongly influenced by a Cold War concern for the historical origins of bureaucratic totalitarian-ism. He identifies empires with 'vast and noncompetitive' concentrations of political power to be contrasted with a 'divided system' of independent states: 'If the divided system is conducive to individualism, inquiry, political freedom and variety, the unified order favors a rigid and conformist social system, an unassailable ideology, autocratic government, and general uniformity.'[13] As the rest of the book will indicate, such static understandings of imperial rule, and their associated overemphasis on political structures at the expense of other socio-economic and cultural sources of imperial domination, deliver a very poor guide to historical experience of empires, let alone explaining the dynamics of the concept.

Richard Koebner's book on the subject and a volume edited by Maurice Duverger help to redress such a political-scientific bias in analysing empires. But even these two invaluable sources shirk from identifying the features of empires through a systematic comparison of imperial experiences.[14] It is to more recent contributions that we must turn when seeking a comprehensive historical sociology of empires. Thus, the work of David B. Abernethy, Michael W. Doyle, Michael Mann and Paul Kennedy offer the kind of historically informed examinations of empire as changing forms of rule and exploitation.[15] Alas, all but Michael Mann concentrate their energies on modern empires and imperialism. All four, however, combine compelling narratives of empire with explanations as to the rise and decline of such polities. Doyle's analysis in particular delivers a definition of empire which highlights the changing configurations of imperial power: 'Empire', he says, 'is a relationship, formal or informal, in which one state controls the effective political sovereignty of another political society. It can be achieved by force, by political collaboration, by economic, social or cultural dependence. Imperialism is simply the process or policy of establishing or maintaining an empire.'[16]

I take my cue from such a definition and the challenge it throws up in understanding empire of teasing out the particular combinations of coercion and consent, formal and informal rule, economic and military power. By way of a preliminary response to the question of continuity and change, particularity and universality of empires, the following section considers briefly an imperial experience different to that of the Romans. For central as it is to the history of the Western world, the Roman case is in many respects unique in the wider global history of empires, and recognizing this begins to drive home the inherently historical character of our subject.

Contrasting empires

As we have seen already, the turning point in Rome's trans-formation from Republic to empire is conventionally dated in January 27 BC, when Julius Caesar's adopted son Octavian was granted *imperium* or command over the three key Roman provinces of Gaul, Spain and Syria and garlanded with the honorary title of Augustus – a notion etymologically derived from *auctoritas* ('influence' or 'prestige'). To mark the occasion, 'wreaths of bay-leaves and the civic crown ("for having saved the citizens") were attached to his door, and a golden shield was placed in the senate house awarded, as the citation read, for *virtus* (courage), *clementia* (clemency), *iustitia* (justice) and *pietas* (piety).'[17] The choice of offerings made here is not without interest for our purposes. Bay leaves are indigenous to the lands bordering the Mediterranean and had for centuries been used to decorate victorious commanders after battle. But wreaths, crowns and shields were symbols of power imported from the more distant polities of Greece, Egypt and Persia. Bay leaves are likely also to have accom-panied spices such as clover, traded from the East via the silk routes, as part of fragrant chaplets used in triumphal pag-eants like those which marked Octavian's momentous victory over Antony and Cleopatra at Actium in 31 BC.[18] Other empires – both contemporaneous and antecedent – were therefore present, however anecdotally, at the very birth of Rome's own 'enunciation' as an imperial power under Augus-tus.[19] Far from representing what one specialist has called 'Empire as Cosmic Domination', where imperial authority is self-ascribed to unique Roman qualities of virtue and piety and a manifest destiny to rule over the known world, the seemingly innocent use of crowns and spices in the affirma-tion of its ecumenical powers in fact points to Rome's devel-opment within a wider world of (generally Eastern) empires and civilizations.[20]

Among the most notable of these was the Later Han empire, which from AD 25 to AD 220 ruled over close to 60 million people and stretched across a territory of 1.5 million square miles – pretty much the extent of the Roman empire over the same period.[21] Like its Roman counterpart, the

Later Han empire is associated with the restoration of order and stability across much of China after a brief but intense period of social and political crisis. The Later Han empire was, logically enough, the successor of the Former, or Western, Han empire (202 BC–AD 9). These two dynasties were in turn built on the foundations of the Ch'in (or *Qin*) empire (325 BC–202 BC), which centralized, standardized and has since then given name to the lands, peoples and languages of what today we know as China. Unlike the contemporaneous Roman empire, however, Later Han relied on two institutions to reproduce its imperial rule which were largely absent in Roman lands: an extensive and centralized bureaucracy and a highly elaborate system of social gradation which sustained the bureaucratic empire. These instruments of power, Sinologists have argued, were not only fairly unique to China but have furthermore survived into the modern period to shape contemporary politics and society in the region.

The first singular aspect of Later Han was its large and rationalized administrative system. Mirroring the Confucian emphasis on cosmological harmony, the Han system of government was premised on the idea of hierarchy and balance. At the apex of the hierarchy sat the 'sovereign emperor' (*Huang-ti*) himself. As the bearer of 'Heaven's Mandate' to extend and sustain Han civilization across China, the emperor had a principally ritualistic authority which only acquired meaning in relation to the officers of his court at the capital Loyang and the provincial reach of his imperial bureaucracy. The organization of the imperial palace under Later Han had undergone several modifications since its move from the eastern capital of Chan'an, but essentially it comprised three echelons: a grand tutor (*t'ai-fu*) with a largely symbolic function of moral adviser to the emperor; three excellencies (*san kung*) responsible for finance, the military and public works, respectively; and nine ministers (*chiu-ch'ing*) who superintended areas of imperial power ranging from palace security to transport and justice.[22]

By the turn of the first millennium the vast territory covering 'China proper' was ruled from the imperial court at Loyang through a pyramid-like administrative division that left no doubt about the centripetal sources of power. Later

Han comprised thirteen regions (*chou*) including the capital. Each of these was in turn subdivided into various provincial commanderies (*chün*) or kingdoms (*wang-kuo*), the latter being hereditary territories granted as fiefs to imperial sons and their heirs. By AD 140, there existed ninety-nine such commanderies and kingdoms, once more broken down, in descending order, into prefectures or counties (*hsien*), districts (*hsiang*), communes (*t'ing*) and hamlets (*li*).[23] Chiefs and prefects were appointed by the palace at these first two levels and organized into bureaus with responsibility over, *inter alia*, collecting revenue, upholding law and order, compiling a census, supervising public works and undertaking rituals. In order to perform these tasks, prefects and chiefs relied on the assistance of hundreds of local officials. A further bureaucratic layer was imposed on the provinces from the metropole in the key figure of the regional inspector or commissioner (*tz'u-shih*), who in the course of Later Han became a resident governor or grand administrator (*t'ai shou*). The subordinate administrative units – counties, districts and communes – were inspected twice a year by the governor and his assistants and an annual report delivered to the palace every new year.

Like all organizational charts, the administrative structure of Later Han just outlined was an ideal type subject to all sorts of socio-economic crises, political rebellions and courtly intrigue. As Samuel Finer has noted, the 'Benthamite symmetry' of Han bureaucracy operated more as a model than as a reality: 'For all the government paperwork flowing up and down the ministries and localities, the actual delivery of services – taxation, justice, conscription, and the like – was rough and ready.'[24] Nevertheless, whether symmetric and efficient or rough and ready, Han bureaucracy survived over several centuries and indeed inspired later Chinese dynasties. On one calculation, the overall number of officeholders employed by the Han bureaucracy in AD 140 was anything between 300,000 and 500,000 – in proportion, roughly twenty times the number of civil servants employed by imperial Rome during the same period.[25] This was, then, a formidable experiment in territorial domination of a widespread population from a geographical centre. The question remains, however, of how this vast expanse of peoples and territories managed to sustain its imperial integrity. Part of the answer must refer to the other original pillar of Han imperialism: the rigid system of stipendiary offices.

The Han empire essentially reproduced itself by taxing a largely independent peasantry through the extensive body of officeholders identified above. The intimate connection between agrarian surplus extraction and the imperial bureaucracy is encapsulated in the unit of account employed in ranking bureaucratic offices – the *shih*, or a bushel of grain, which originally would have constituted payment in kind but gradually came to act as a cash equivalent. By the time of Later Han, bureaucratic offices were divided into eighteen ranks, ranging from 10,000 *shih* at the top to the lowliest 100 *shih*. Once more, these figures did not correspond directly to the salary in cash or kind (both of which were used in payment), but rather acted as measures of relative standing in the rank order. Consequently, salaries were not proportionate to the difference in *shih* ranking, nor was there a necessary progression from one rank to the next. What is noteworthy for our purposes is that Han China represented an archetypal instance of a redistributive agrarian polity: the state levied land and poll taxes on a free peasantry and then reinvested part of this surplus in public works, education, security and institutions of law and order. An extensive bureaucracy acted as the intermediary between rulers and subjects, as we saw above, by both directly extracting taxes and then disbursing, and indeed administering and auditing, them on behalf of the palace. The Han state certainly extracted surplus through other means – excises, monopolies in salt and iron, corvée labour – but these were relatively insignificant sources of wealth. Similarly, merchants, iron-founders, salt-producers and, not least important, the land-owning 'Great Families' closely linked to the palace all accumulated considerable wealth in private property. But tellingly, their ambition was generally to access officialdom by way of either recommendation or examination, both of which were facilitated through attendance at elite educational institutions in Loyang or the provincial capitals. In sum, although the Han state often sought to undermine the private access to wealth of landlords and industrialists, this was in many respects redundant, for, as one comparative historian of empires has put it, 'office was itself a route to wealth.'[26]

Another striking feature of the Later Han empire was the predominant role of civilians in upholding these monumental structures of rule and exploitation. Both Han dynasties and indeed the foundational Ch'in empire emerged as victorious polities in the wake of protracted military conflict and could not therefore easily dispose of their martial origins. Yet by the time of Later Han, the army had been firmly subordinated to the political authority of a civilian bureaucracy, with all but two of the 'Grand Commandants' (the Third Excellency responsible for the military) during this period being civilians. Later Han had no standing army, aside from the relatively small body of palace guards and the mere 4,000 men responsible for the protection of the empire's capital and its northern frontier (the so-called Northern Army). Conscription was obligatory for all able-bodied men aged twenty-three to fifty-six but, after a two-year military service, conscripts were discharged to form local militias which were only mobilized at times of political emergency generated by the threat of barbarian invasion or domestic rebellion. It was only on such (relatively infrequent) occasions that military officers were appointed on an *ad hoc* basis to command over a proportionately modest army of about 100,000 soldiers.[27] Once emergencies were over, both officers and soldiers were released from duty and so, uniquely for an empire of such dimensions and power, no permanent or extensive body of military officials emerged in the course of Later Han history.

The Han experience of empire is significant on its own terms – certainly for the ensuing history of China and its neighbours. But it is also extraordinary when contrasted to its contemporary Western Eurasian counterpart. Whereas Rome's empire was built on a structural connection between an extensive and pervasive army and the wealth created through tribute, slavery and private property in land (what Michael Mann in his *Sources of Social Power* termed a 'legionary economy'), the Han empire was, as we have seen, reproduced through a largely civilian body of officeholders responsible for extracting and administering taxes through a complex bureaucratic infrastructure. Similarly, while the

Augustan revolution placed the emperor and his entourage at the centre and pinnacle of imperial authority, even the most proactive Han emperors were unable to mobilize the kind of personalized authority associated with the *Princeps* and *Imperator*, relying instead on the depersonalized and rationalized power of the state's mandarins. Finally, as the next chapter will illustrate in greater detail, the Han empire's organization along a (however imperfectly) symmetrical, hierarchical and centralized bureaucracy delivered something closer to a modern state: a territorially delimited and standardized polity. In contrast, Rome's mixed constitution (again, however ideal-typically) produced a land-based, aristocratic and chiefly tributary polity which, despite being more territorially ambitious than Han China, operated through a 'heteronomous' and relatively decentralized imperial administration heavily reliant on local clients: that is, something closer to our contemporary understanding of empire. In short, while China had no standing army and a vast bureaucracy, in Rome the inverse was true; while the Roman emperor became an independent source of imperial power, in China his authority was dependent on the workings of a greater courtly and bureaucratic whole; while Roman imperialism adopted a predominantly extensive character, conquering afresh new lands and peoples, Later Han concentrated on intensifying its authority within the territories inherited from its Former Han and Ch'in predecessors.

For many observers, this distinction between the centralized, bureaucratic and stipendiary form of empire in China and Rome's decentralized, militarized and tributary command marks the start of the subsequent divide between Western and Eastern forms of rule. Despite its frequent invocation by successive Western empires, the *Pax Romana* was never revived. Instead an unstable, amorphous and unruly succession of feudal states, dynastic kingdoms, city-states, leagues and republics were to jostle for European supremacy in later centuries. From all this upheaval and disaggregation, many have argued, emerged a distinctive social dynamism associated with capitalism and a political suspicion of absolute authority linked to Western liberalism and democracy. Eastern political history, particularly that of China, has in contrast been presented as a series of footnotes and amendments to the social and political structures established by the Ch'in and Han empires. Here the continuity and relative stability in the forms of rule and social reproduction delivered more static and hierarchical societies and polities.

It is beyond this book's remit to investigate the validity of this distinction between Western freedom and mobility and Eastern despotism and stagnation. Certainly any absolute and transhistorical rendition of this contrast cannot hold historical or conceptual water. But it does bring into focus the legacy of ancient empires for contemporary social formations, and how far empires can be contrasted to other forms of political community.

The distinctiveness of empire

The working definition of empire developed thus far suggests that it is an expansive polity which, with the assistance of military, economic and cultural instruments of order, dominates and exploits a subordinated population from a metropolitan centre. The immediate problem with such a definition is that polities other than empires share some of these characteristics. A further stumbling block is that the common denominators of empire identified earlier – expansion, hierarchy and order – have often combined in very different ways in diverse imperial experiences. This latter concern is the subject of the rest of the book, so in this closing section of the introduction I concentrate on the former issue surrounding the distinctiveness of empires vis-à-vis other forms of rule and, in doing so, also canvass some contending notions of empire.

The first thing to note about empires is that they are also states – that is, enduring political communities where a ruling class possesses the administrative capacity to extract and redistribute wealth, as well as the means of violence to impose such forms of authority.[28] This is at first sight obvious enough, but it has important implications for the distinction between empires and other polities – most obviously the territorially exclusive, sovereign, national state (I henceforth use these terms interchangeably). A useful starting-point in this endeavour is to consider the respective organizations of political space in these two forms of rule. As will be discussed at greater length in the following chapter, empires – both ancient and modern – have been unwilling or unable to close their frontiers. They have claimed to be, and often succeeded in being, literally boundless. Most empires, certainly the two ancient ones surveyed earlier, have plainly delimited their internal administration in all kinds of ways. They have furthermore developed sophisticated conceptions of 'inside' and 'outside' or 'civilized' and 'barbarian', and enforced these external boundaries through law, war, custom and culture – often in response to metropolitan anxieties over the corrupting effects of unchecked expansion on domestic political life. But such imperial boundaries have rarely been permanently fixed and exclusive. An expansive polity such as an empire is almost by definition constantly seeking to extend the reach of its frontiers and absorb fresh populations into its ecumenical order. To use a distinction common in political geography, empires have frontiers and boundaries, but no external borders.[29] National states on the other hand are built on territorially exclusive borders. A sovereign state may have internal boundaries – ethnic, religious or even national – but its very existence is threatened by an open or shifting frontier – that is, by the absence of a fixed and exclusive demarcation between its own territory and that of neighbouring states. This is why empires tend to be multinational entities which, at their height, thrive on this centripetal diversity, while national states always seek to unify their populations under the banner of a single, standardized and often homogenizing cultural or constitutional identity.

Predictably, complications and qualifications arise when considering actual historical illustrations of these differences between empires and territorially bounded states. We have seen already that, in the important case of the successive Han empires, the intensive bureaucratic rule over a population increasingly subjected to cultural homogenization and living within a fairly well-delimited territory has made of China one of the oldest continuously existing states in the world. Here an empire appears gradually but irreversibly to crystallize into a national state. This is of course the kind of transhistorical permanence cherished by nationalists everywhere in sustaining their political claims to national uniqueness and exclusivity and thereby also (perhaps inadvertently) blurring the lines between imperialism and nationalism. Yet even in this peculiar Chinese case, the persistence of shifting frontiers across much of the north and west of the imperial territory, coupled with the later contribution of non-Han elites such as the Manchus or Mongols to the construction of the modern Chinese state (let alone the prolonged bouts of internal strife), suggests that such a tidy narrative of continuity needs at the very least to be qualified by paying due attention to the many ruptures in the forms of rule across Chinese history. Looked at through the lens of spatial organization, for instance, a unified and territorially exclusive national state emerged in China only after 1949. In this respect, while allowing for the obvious fact that successive Chinese empires built the political, socio-economic and cultural foundations for the current People's Republic, the distinction between empire and nation-state can be sustained on the basis of their different organizations of political space – the one amenable to open frontiers, the other incapable of surviving without fixed and exclusive borders.

Perhaps the more common experience is one where states become empires. Here, as later chapters will once more indicate, processes of nation- and state-building coincide with moments of imperial expansion usually linked to trade and markets. Notable examples in the West include the Spanish and British construction of a national identity and territorial sovereignty while extending their frontiers by conquering and colonizing foreign lands and peoples. Further east, the case of Muscovy might be cited as an instance where a distinctive cultural identity at least was being forged in the process of imperial expansion. This interrelation between empire and nation- or state-building further challenges the neat distinction between these two forms of polity and has led some scholars to argue that the 'imperial moment' continues into the post-colonial era of national states.[30] Yet once again, while recognizing and exploring this interconnection is crucial to the study of empires and nations, it is equally important to insist on the structural differences between imperial and territorially exclusive organizations of political space. From this perspective, the telling feature of Spanish and British imperialism is not so much that it contributed to the construction of territorial sovereignty at home, but rather that it violently denied this very sovereignty abroad. In other words, what made Britain and Spain empires as opposed to merely national states was precisely that they were willing to recognize territorial borders in Europe while seeking to extend their imperial frontier overseas.

These experiments in simultaneous state-formation and empire-building were fraught with all sorts of contradictions – some of which, later chapters will show, proved to be fatal. But in order to understand and explain such contradictions it remains imperative to differentiate states and empires conceptually according to their dominant mode of territorial organization. Indeed, this has been for some years a major concern among scholars investigating the origins and development of territorial sovereignty – that very peculiar form of political space which underpins the modern international system of states. Within the field of international relations, this transition from a world of empires to one of national states is generally presented as a shift from hierarchy to anarchy, that is, from a political order where a supreme authority governs hierarchically over a diverse and functionally differentiated range of communities to a 'pluriverse' of functionally identical sovereign states without any superior authority. There is no space here for a detailed account of the various explanations for this shift from hierarchy to anarchy, or from empire to system of states.[31] Moreover, as the rest of the book will endeavour to show, any sharp and absolute contrast between imperial hierarchy and international anarchy is historically and conceptually untenable. Not only was this a protracted and highly uneven shift, it is also in many respects unfinished, as imperial forms of power find continued expression in many socio-economic, political and cultural arenas of today's world. Two broad approaches, however, can be identified to the question of how and why this transition from empire to international system of states took place – first in Europe during the course or the 'long' sixteenth century (1450–1650), and subsequently across other regions of the globe.

The first approach focuses upon the competition between rival forms of political authority arising from the disintegration of the Carolingian empire after the tenth century. Drawing on the writings of Max Weber and Otto Hintze, this broad school of historical sociology emphasizes the role of war and violent conflict in the emergence of the modern territorial state. On this account, the 'heteronomous' and expansive territoriality of imperial rule gives way to the exclusive sovereignty of the modern state in the course of military confrontation between competing polities. Such military competition encouraged technological and operational innovations in the modes of warfare, including the professionalization of armies and state-led investment in arms procurement. This in turn meant that ruling classes were forced to rationalize and intensify their modes of revenue-collection as well as develop the necessary bureaucratic infrastructure to administer such military–industrial–fiscal complexes. The outcome in Charles Tilly's famous rendition was that 'war makes states, and states make war'. The Peace of Westphalia which closed the Thirty Years' War in 1648 is thus presented as the historical marker of this new organization of political space in Europe.

In a variant on this kind of explanation, Hendrik Spruyt suggests that the sovereign, territorial state was only one among a number of institutional forms of rule emerging from the collapse of European feudalism – the other two main kinds of unit being city-leagues such as the Hanse or city-states in the shape of the Italian republics. The sovereign state imposed itself as the dominant territorial unit in the course of a protracted process of competitive selection from the late Middle Ages where war, economies of scale and, crucially, domestic social alliances rendered other forms of rule – leagues, city-states, feudal lordships, the Church or empires – less efficient or effective in administering power both internally and vis-à-vis competing polities.[32]

A second set of theorists acknowledge the place of competition, war and violence in the emergence of the modern territorial state, but choose to emphasize the 'vertical' class antagonisms which underpinned such 'horizontal' confrontation between states. Inspired by the work of Karl Marx and his followers, these scholars suggest that what gradually emerged from the general crisis of European feudalism in the fourteenth century was less a modern system of capitalist sovereignty than a collection of dynastic monarchies which continued to reproduce themselves through absolutist and personalized mechanisms of surplus extraction – chiefly the sale of offices. The spatial logic accompanying this mode of social reproduction remained tied, as under feudalism, to the territorial expansion via inter-dynastic unions or violent conquest in war. Continental Europe had on this account moved away from imperial territoriality, but had not yet entered the world of modern, sovereign territoriality. This form of spatial organization instead first emerged in the one state absent at the Westphalian settlement – England. There, the feudal crisis was resolved with the introduction of agrarian capitalism, and the rise of a new class of landed capitalists who in the course of the seventeenth century challenged the existing hegemony of merchant classes based in the City of London. The political outcome of this intra-ruling class antagonism was encapsulated in the formula of 'Crown-in-Parliament' emerging out of the Glorious Revolution of 1688. This arrangement codified a formal separation between state and civil society in capitalist societies which remains the dominant expression of sovereignty today. And it is this division between juridico-political authority of the state and economic power of the market which, as later chapters indicate, allows us to distinguish contemporary forms of capitalist hegemony from pre-capitalist forms of imperial rule.

This latter understanding of modern state sovereignty opens up a second arena of dispute over the difference between empires and other forms of authority, this time relating to the place of the economy in the definition of empires. For the eminent historical sociologist Immanuel Wallerstein, the 'long' sixteenth century witnessed the emergence of a distinctively capitalist world-economy which was 'an economic but not a political entity, unlike empires, city-states and nation-states. In fact, it precisely encompasses within its bounds . . . empires, city-states, and the emerging "nation-states".'[33] World-economies, understood as systems of commodity exchange which transcend particular jurisdictions, had of course existed before the sixteenth century. But, for Wallerstein, such systems had in the past quickly transformed into empires, whereas the new, capitalist world-economy was subverting empires. The implication of this distinction is that capitalist markets and territorial empires make uneasy bedfellows. While in an imperial world-economy, political institutions and economic transactions are fused into one, under the nascent capitalist world-system, the economic logic of the market gradually becomes detached from, and indeed cuts across, the territorial, jurisdictional authority of states. With the possibility of generating and reinvesting surplus through purely 'economic' mechanisms of commodity exchange, the political functions of the state under a capitalist world-economy are circumscribed to providing the legal, administrative and coercive infrastructure necessary for the market to operate legitimately and efficiently. For all kinds of complex reasons touched upon only superficially in the course of this book, national states have established themselves as the dominant expression of political rule under capitalism. Although it should hastily be added that there is no *a priori* reason why other forms of authority – confederations, city-leagues, multilateral governance or indeed empires – might not have carried this burden. The benefit of hindsight, however, allows us to see that there is an historically significant tension between the imperial organization of markets in the quest for geopolitical power and the capitalist logic of ceaseless value-creation and accumulation in the pursuit of plenty.

There is certainly considerable mileage to this distinction between world-economies as empires and the properly capitalist world economy. As we have already seen, ancient empires entangled political authority and economic power in ways that precluded the kind of separation between state and market that obtains under capitalism. The Roman 'legionary economy' tied surplus extraction and distribution – be it through tribute, slavery or private wealth in land – to the military infrastructure of the imperial state. In Han China, the economy was directly regulated by the imperial bureaucracy and wealth accrued through access to the hierarchical system of state-controlled offices. Consequently, the economic organization of empires tends to be built around fairly rigid, relatively centralized and comparatively intensive political control of production, consumption, trade and distribution. In this respect, imperial economies mirror the rimless hub-and-spokes definition of empire referred to earlier. The absence of independent political relations between peripheral polities is compounded by their economic subjection to bilateral systems of exchange and circulation with the metropolitan core. Imperial peripheries are certainly integrated into a larger imperial economy, but economic transactions always bear the imprint of a metropolitan centre: tax and tribute collected from Rome's imperial subjects flowed back to the capital's coffers; gold and silver extracted in the Americas by indigenous labour was carried across the Pacific to the Philippines in Spanish galleons, and exchanged for luxury goods which were traded in the Americas and Europe by peninsular Spaniards. One feature of imperial economies, therefore, is that they tend to preclude autonomous economic relations between subjected peripheries.

Yet this conception of imperial economies begs an obvious question germane to the rest of this study, namely: why, if the capitalist market is so inimical to imperial political organization, has the history of global capitalism been so closely linked to the history of European empires? This is a question which particularly concerned political and economic thinkers at the start of the twentieth century, especially those inspired by the theory and politics of Karl Marx. One response interpreted capitalist imperialism as an atavistic remnant of previous social formations, as a persistence under industrial capitalism of *ancien régime* politics where martial aristocrats imbued with a sense of biological superiority and obsessed with the centrality of land to a nation's prosperity were distorting the peaceful efficiency of free markets. Other perspectives emphasized the inherently expansionist and competitive logic of capitalism, famously seeing European imperial rivalry, and the First World War it engendered, as the 'highest stage' of capitalism. A further influential approach underlined the power of 'informal empire' or the 'imperialism of free trade', that is, the capacity to control markets beneficially, not through conquest and juridical administration, but chiefly through economic mechanisms of trade and investment unencumbered by direct political or military intervention. Chapter 3 will consider in greater detail the content and merits of such explanations of capitalist imperialism. For our purposes in this introduction, all that needs to be noted is the complex but necessary relation between empires and markets. While the one cannot be reduced to the other, later chapters will underscore how the operation of markets, especially the capitalist world market, can sharpen our understanding of the distinctiveness of empires.

Empires, then, are specific types of state and encompass distinctive forms of world economy. They also constitute civilizations with a particular understanding of culture and collective identity. The notion of 'order' conveys this self-representation of imperial authority as one which provides both a literal and a figurative centre of belonging for subject populations. It also offers a narrative of supernatural origins and manifest destinies, with all their attendant myths of military glory, civilizational prowess and cultural superiority, which naturalize and legitimize conceptions of order such as the *Pax Romana*, the Anglo-American 'Empire of Liberty' or the Chinese 'Mandate of Heaven'. Some empires, such as those of the Han, Romans and Ottomans, are open to the cultural assimilation of subject populations, while others, such as the modern European or Japanese empires, remain culturally and indeed geographically aloof from local populations, only occasionally admitting a select number of native *évolués*, *babus* or 'brown Englishmen' into the ranks of the metropolitan society and culture. In both instances, however, a contradictory dialectic of civilization and racialization plays itself out, where certain imperial encounters deliver new, syncretic cultures while other experiences produce rigid racial hierarchies, more often than not leading by outright extermination. Indeed, in the Americas and the Caribbean, hybridization *was accompanied* by the virtual annihilation of local populations. Notwithstanding these often extreme expressions of metropolitan domination, even the most aggressively missionary empires govern over multi-ethnic, polyglot and religiously diverse populations. To this extent, they may be differentiated from national states, which have historically sought to reproduce unified, generally homogenous collective identities.

Paradoxically, it is precisely this cultural drive towards forging a single, shared national identity in the process of state-formation that has led some to argue that many national states are in fact miniature empires. In his book *Internal*

Colonialism, for instance, Michael Hechter suggested that the formation of the British state and national identity involved a process of imperialist absorption of the 'Celtic fringe'.[34] The westward expansion of the American frontier through conquest, purchase or war is also often cited as an instance of empire-building that goes by the name of state-formation. Yet these kinds of conflations obscure more than they illuminate. For one, they ignore the fact that virtually all states, not just Britain, Spain or the USA, are the product of expansion – be it through war, trade, migration or a combination of all three. There are very few, if any, parts of the world that have been permanently settled by the same ethnic group throughout history, still less is there a correspondence between ethnic composition and the territorial limits of states. The distinctive feature of a nation-state in contrast to an empire, then, lies in the unification of the former under a single territorial jurisdiction – such as the federal governments of Germany or the USA – and the coexistence, indeed the promotion, of multiple, often incommensurable, jurisdictions under empires, even if these too are ultimately accountable to a metropolitan authority. More importantly, most regional or demographic divisions within national states assume formal equality of representation between administrative units – once again, as in the US senate or the German Bundesrat – while such arrangements would obviously undermine metropolitan claims to juridical supremacy and political control over diverse protectorates, viceroyalties, residencies or client-kingdoms. (This is also, incidentally, what distinguishes an empire from a commonwealth, federation or indeed union of states such as, for instance, the European Union or the former Soviet Union.)

The assumption that national states born out of imperial expansion can usefully continue to be labelled empires once their territories have been integrated into a single, overarching jurisdiction and their populations unified through national citizenship also fails to consider the central role of so-called peripheral peoples in the construction of empire and nation. As Linda Colley demonstrated some time ago in her classic study on the origins of British identity, the 'Celtic fringe' played a leading role in the construction of the British empire, and the empire returned the favour by forging the union between various peoples of the British Isles.[35] Here again, the conflation of territorial and cultural integration with the enduring hierarchical structures of imperial domination and segregation muddies the distinctiveness of empire. On this account, which of course some petty nationalists are wont to make, Québecois or Catalans could today still be seen as victims of Anglo-Canadian and Castilian imperialism respectively – a perspective which is simply irreconcilable with the reality of cultural, political and socio-economic autonomy in these two regions.

Such historical, cultural and geographical permutations in the relationship between empires and nations beg the final question of how long a state has to expand before it becomes an empire. Once again, given that there are no natural, eternal divisions among the peoples and territories of the earth (let alone sea and outer space) the response to this question must be relative to each case and historical period. Most empires have not recognized themselves as such until long after their most significant expansionary spurts – often, as in the case of Hanoverian Britain or the late Roman Republic, in the context of imperial crisis. Plainly there have been megalomaniac dictators – Bokassa in Central Africa, Reza Shah Pahlavi in Iran – who claimed their states to be empires, as there have also been states which are empires in all but name – Habsburg Spain and, more recently, the USA come to mind. Whether an imperial people or their elites think or proclaim they belong to an empire is not the best way of establishing when a political community has become part of an empire. Rather, in the rest of the book, I shall assume that any single polity that successfully expands from a metropolitan centre across various territories in order to dominate diverse populations can usefully be called an empire.

In presenting the different historical features of empire and charting their particularity in time and place, I will rely on the illustrative experience of specific polities at different junctures in history. Chapter 2 focuses on the political geography in two ancient empires – Han China and Rome – and two early modern empires – Spain and the Ottoman state – by way of tracing the changes and continuities in imperial ordering of space. It is suggested there that imagining and managing space, through both cosmological and territorial means, is a first crucial feature shared by all empires. The place of the frontier, understood as a fluctuating zone of interaction between the imperial centre and its peripheries, will act as a point of departure in examining the complex articulations of imperial geography, and how these inform and condition both the socio-economic exploitation and the cultural domination of subject peoples by imperial powers. It will also serve to underline the distinction used in the rest of the book between empire as an open and expansive territory and other more spatially circumscribed forms of rule.

The early modern empires discussed in chapter 2 already began to display the kinds of tension between the control of peoples and the exclusive sovereignty over territories which increasingly challenged the persistence of imperial rule in a modern world of capitalist markets. This is the subject of chapter 3, where the vexed relationship between markets and empires is considered chiefly with reference to the empire that straddled the historical shift from mercantile to a capitalist world market: Great Britain. Focusing on such a transformation, I argue, brings to the fore the perennial tension between imperial expansion, hierarchy and order – this time through the prism of the modern dynamic between capitalist and territorial logics of power. The assumption here is that the 'long' sixteenth century witnessed the emergence of new forms of social organization in parts of Western Europe – foremost among them the territorially exclusive state and the price-making market – which signalled a substantial rupture with previous social structures, both in Europe and beyond, and which to that extent can be associated with the epochal shift towards a historical period commonly labelled as 'modernity'. Indeed, the final part of that chapter considers how various twentieth-century theories of imperialism have tried to explain the conceptual and political dialectics between two uniquely modern social structures: sovereign states and capitalist markets.

Chapter 4 looks at a different, but related, modern dialectic which empires have fostered: that between 'civilization' and 'racialization'. The spotlight here falls on the New World as the location where modern notions of race were invented in the context of one of the abiding anxieties of empire: the miscegenation of cultures. Once again, the label 'modern' is used here to identify historically distinctive ways of categorizing and dominating 'Others' with reference to physiognomic, cultural and, later, biological understandings of race and ethnicity. I therefore employ the term 'racialization' generically to denote a simultaneous process of cultural differentiation and subordination which found diverse manifestations across different imperial experiences, but which always involved a hierarchical incorporation into imperial civilization through cultural referents. Such an absorption, however, was never entirely one-sided and certainly not uncontested. The chapter therefore also considers the founding of new, syncretic countercultures within empire, at once the product of unique imperial flows and the most immediate challenge to imperial order and hierarchy.

The final chapter considers the meaning of empire today. It surveys three different understandings of empire: American, postmodern and liberal, each roughly corresponding to a set of contemporary theorizations and expressions of empire. The chapter summarizes and renders more explicit some of the implicit claims about empire made in the rest of the book, and concludes by suggesting that, although the legacies of empire are as alive today as they have ever been, we do indeed live in a world where the imperial organizations of space, market and culture along an expansionary, hierarchical order have been sufficiently subverted by the dual processes of capitalist reproduction and state-formation to make empire a thing of the past. This tentative and open conclusion is reiterated and substantiated with different emphasis at the end of each of the three core chapters that form the book, where I briefly consider the legacies and relevance of empire and imperialism in our world today. In the last instance, however, my brief is an analytical one, and so I now immediately turn to the first distinctive facet of empire, namely the organization of political space.

2

Empire as Space

'To establish an empire', the philosopher Eric Voegelin once suggested, 'is an essay in world creation.'[1] What Voegelin implied with this enigmatic statement is that empire-building involves both conceiving of the world and organizing it spatially. Empires tend to develop intricate conceptions of their place in the world, and therefore also attempt actually to model those parts of it under their auspices in this image. Such 'essays in world creation' carry with them plenty of dangers and contradictions, and the nature of these of course varies in time and place, delivering mixed results in actual historical practice. Plainly, not everything imperialists want, imperialists get. Yet, in a number of important ways, the interrelated processes of imagining and managing space are crucial in identifying the distinctiveness of empires, both among themselves and vis-à-vis other forms of rule.[2]

The first of these distinctive features revolves around the conception of imperial space in relation to the wider world and the universe beyond. It was suggested in the introduction that one way of distinguishing empires from other forms of political rule is the degree to which they reproduce themselves through open and shifting frontiers. As expansive social formations, geared towards the absorption of subject peoples and territories, empires have historically been built on ill-defined territorial limits. As will be discussed in chapter 4, they have certainly constructed sophisticated ideologies of domination premised on the distinction between 'inside' and 'outside' or 'civilized' and 'barbarian', but these demarcations have rarely been permanently fixed in space. Instead, imperial conceptions of the world rely on the very existence of an 'outside', a region at the edges of the known world which may still be discovered, conquered or assimilated into an expanding imperial order.

The ancient Greek notion of *oikoumene* perhaps best captures this ambivalent conception of imperial space as both expansive and bounded. The term was first deployed by Herodotus and his contemporaries of the fifth century BC in their assault on the archaic legend that the earth was an island encircled by the river Ocean. Herodotus claimed such a worldview was bogus and proposed instead an 'empirical geography' where territorial limits are set not by natural obstacles such as mythical rivers or oceans, but by an unfixed, man-made space defined by 'the intercommunication of its inhabitants': an *oikoumene*.[3] This conception of the world as an inhabited realm without eternal demarcations but with human boundaries allowed for the possibility of extending the *oikoumene*, of literally expanding the reaches of the known world. It was this idea which informed imperial Rome's understanding of its place in the world (as indeed it had the Macedonians before them and was to inspire Christian empires thereafter) for, as Anthony Pagden has suggested, 'it was relatively easy to think of Zeno's *koinos*, and of the Greek *oikumene* in general, as identical with the Roman *imperium*.'[4]

While the idea of the *oikoumene* as the 'known world' points to spatial ideologies underpinning the territorial expansion characteristic of empires, it also opens up the links between territorial space and two other key features of empire: hierarchy and order. By developing complex cosmological and cosmogenic ideologies empires have placed themselves at the centre of the universe and self-arrogated responsibility for the maintenance of cosmic order. Such creationist narratives and their accompanying tropes of cultural superiority are not merely self-congratulatory conceits. As will be pointed out with reference to the Chinese and Roman experience, they also serve as mechanisms for the concrete distribution and administration of imperial space along centralized and hierarchical lines. Such a strategy of rule is, however, riven with contradictions. For a civilizing mission that constantly pushes outwards the boundaries of empire simultaneously requires a countervailing pull towards the metropolitan centre, thus generating the spatial tensions I have so far suggested are peculiar to empires.

The two early modern imperial polities we shall be discussing below – the Spanish and Ottoman empires – originated in frontier societies driven by a proselytizing and militarized religiosity: the first inspired by Christian crusading, the second by Islamic *gazi* warfare. Conversion or subservience to the dominant faith was an inherent component of the expansion of Spanish and Ottoman civilization and was a precondition of their subjects' incorporation into the emerging imperial order. The Castilians were to face an unprecedented challenge to existing conceptions of space and hierarchy as the westward expansion of their frontier led them to an American world inhabited by 'heathen' peoples previously unknown to Europeans. The Ottomans on the other hand conquered not only fellow Muslims but also other 'peoples of the book', and could therefore draw on Islamic precedent in adopting far more lenient structures of government over their Christian and Jewish subjects than the Spaniards did towards pagan Amerindians. At the same time, both empires, certainly in their sixteenth-century heyday, also offered their subjects 'a place in the world' – a sense of belonging to a larger, powerful and superior political and religious entity. Ottomans and Spaniards drew on the notions of Islamic *ummah* and *respublica christiana* respectively to reconcile imperial order with ecumenical expansion. The Ottomans in particular institutionalized forms of imperial acculturation and assimilation (most notably the *devshirme* – a levy or collection of Christian captives for metropolitan political and military service) which delivered a genuinely cosmopolitan imperial elite.

No matter how universalist their motivation, the extension of imperial frontiers – both geographically and culturally – could ill-disguise the subordination of most of those incorporated into the enlarged *oikoumene*. Once again, it would be a mistake to reject the ideological preconceptions deployed by these two empires in justifying and sustaining their territorial expansion merely as self-serving rhetoric: the exercises in geographical imagination which preceded and accompanied conquest offer deep insights into the modes of spatial administration both empires adopted in their colonies and provinces, and these in turn underline the uniqueness of imperial forms of rule.

The actual historical production of imperial space, of course, rarely corresponds directly to these stylized and abstract conceptions of expansion, hierarchy and order. As in the case of most empires, the Habsburg Court and the Sublime Porte were forced to adapt, reform and often improvise their structures of imperial administration in response to the demands of both natives and settlers, governors and subjects, the barbarian and the civilized. A third broad subject of this chapter thus concerns the ways in which empires institutionalize space in the government of their subjects. Here one of the salient themes to be developed is that of suzerain or 'indirect' rule. For all their claims to universal *imperium* and global domination, empires have historically relied heavily on local collaborators, intermediaries, delegates, clients and assimilated elites to exercise their authority across vast territories and over diverse peoples. They have also faced significant challenges – both human and environmental – to their attempts at direct domination. This dynamic of resistance and accommodation has delivered complex, amorphous and often indeterminate combinations of direct and indirect imperial rule which have in turn generated peculiar forms of spatial organization on the periphery. Here again much of imperial history results from the tensions between centripetal and centrifugal forces, between the tendency of empires, on the one hand, to concentrate power and wealth and, on the other, to redistribute and devolve it more widely so as to maintain that very imperial order.

The conceptions of territorial space adopted by empires, the place of frontiers in this spatial configuration, and the consequences of such territorial organization in the definition of imperial (and indeed post-colonial) worlds are therefore the three major concerns of this chapter. The discussion is organized in the following way. A first section explores the geographical imagination of ancient empires, highlighting the tension between cosmologies that seek to order territory along fixed spatial hierarchies and the relatively open and fluctuating conception of imperial limits displayed by Rome and China. It will be suggested there that such contradictions between the territorial reach and spatial administration are closely related to the modes of social reproduction dominant in these empires. The ruling classes of pre-modern empires generally extracted wealth through tax, tribute and in some cases slavery. This meant that imperial authorities were – in striking contrast to the modern correspondence between political jurisdiction and exclusive sovereignty that dominates the contemporary international system – concerned more with controlling people than territories.

The second section carries the argument forward to the early modern period, suggesting that the Spanish and Ottoman imperial experience in many respects epitomizes this tension between pre-modern, tributary forms of spatial reproduction and modern, market-driven expressions of territorial sovereignty. The role of the frontier in Spanish and Ottoman expansion will act as a foil to illustrate the contradictions and characteristics of early modern territoriality as they were manifested on the peripheries of these two empires. The legacy of these colonial forms of territorial administration is very much alive in today's world, as the contemporary norm of territorial sovereignty and its accompanying institutions of citizenship still struggle to impose themselves universally on the ground. A final section of this chapter therefore considers the implications of this heritage for contemporary international relations, highlighting the problematic sovereignty of post-colonial states in the Middle East and Latin America. It will hopefully become apparent in the course of that discussion how relevant the historical experience of empires is for our understanding of modern world politics.

The spatial imagination of empire: cosmology, cartography and government

Empires, like most other political formations, conceive of order and hierarchy in spatial terms. They legitimize the centrality and superiority of their rule over diverse peoples and vast territories by developing distinctive imperial cosmologies and applying corresponding foundational myths to justify the harmonious relationship between a specific political hierarchy and an eternal universal order. Unlike other polities, however, empires also have to grapple with a third spatial dynamic, that of periodic territorial expansion (or indeed contraction), which tends to unsettle such imperial configurations of hierarchy and order. The geographical imagination of empires can therefore be understood in general terms as an attempt to accommodate expanding territories and assimilated populations into existing or emerging structures of imperial domination. The imperial capital and the imperial frontier have, since antiquity, been two privileged sites in constructing a response to this predicament. A brief consideration of the imperial conceptions of centre and periphery in ancient Rome and China, with reference to the related practices of cosmology and cartography (what Haley arrestingly describes as 'the imprint of power' and 'the handwriting of space' respectively),[5] might help to shed light on the unique role of spatial organization in the reproduction of empires.

At its most plethoric, imperial authority claims to be the sole mediating force between Heaven and Earth. The ancient Chinese notion of the emperor as the 'Son of Heaven' (*T'ien-tzu*) is one famous expression of such imperial cosmology. As was briefly mentioned in the previous chapter, the Ch'in empire and its Han successors drew political legitimacy from their role as reinstators of order and stability in the aftermath of extended periods of tumultuous warfare in China. This they did not only by establishing military supremacy and imposing bureaucratic rule, but also by drawing on creationist myths, heavily influenced by Confucianism, which transferred onto the emperor (or, more precisely, his ritual practices) the function of restoring and protecting cosmological harmony. The understanding of 'harmony' here was both social and geographical, as it entailed the proper, balanced ordering of human and spatial relations along hierarchical lines of father/son, husband/wife, elder brother/younger brother, and concentric tangents radiating from civilized realms of the 'Middle Kingdom' (*Chung-Kuo*) to the barbarian rim lands. 'The established view of China's and the world's geography', one scholar has succinctly put it, 'is a mythical expression of the dominant Confucian ideology.'[6] At the core of the various cosmogonies which detailed the legendary origins of Chinese civilization are the sage-kings, who from the beginning of time, and from the centre of the world (China), judiciously ruled the world. Their legacy to the emperor was a mandate of Heaven to rule over Earth ('All-under-Heaven', *T'ien hsia*) which, if properly administered, would secure the cosmic balance between Heaven, Earth and Man.

Such conceptions of the emperor's place in the world had momentous implications for the actual day-to-day lives of his subjects, for imperial cosmology guided the spatial organization of the polity in areas ranging from the distribution of agricultural lands to the territorial division of provinces, or indeed the positioning of barbarian vassals in relation to the imperial centre.[7] Diverse numerological patterns were employed to impose cosmic order on the Chinese world, of which the most powerful seems to have been the nonary square, or three-by-three check board (derived, legend has it, by the sage-king Yu from the pattern of a turtle's shell). This device informed the so-called well-field system, whereby eight peasant families subsisted from individual allotments surrounding a ninth, central square which they farmed exclusively to pay taxes. It was also used in political prognosis through the *fenye* or 'field-allocation system'. Here court cosmographers divided China into nine terrestrial regions mirroring nine celestial fields. Shifts in the configuration of the stars acted as omens requiring corresponding political changes on the ground. Importantly for our purposes, the nonary system also shaped the urban design and architecture of imperial capitals during the Han period and beyond, thereby reflecting the tight connection between ritual and space in the exercise of imperial power. Sacred buildings or temples known as the *mingtang* or 'luminous hall' were built in the imperial capital and other signal locations following the nonary form, in an effort to reproduce the imperial order within an architectural microcosm. Such constructions were not merely symbolic but acted as spatial frameworks for the unfolding of imperial ritual. As John B. Henderson has suggested,

Debates over the proper form and dimensions of the *ming-tang*, which often arose at court in responses to an imperial commission to construct such a structure, were not merely antiquitarian exercises. For inasmuch as the *mingtang* was supposed to be constructed as an architectural microcosm, the subject of dispute was ultimately the shape and proportions of the cosmos in general, not simply the optimum measurements of a building.[8]

Chinese imperial cosmologies, with their associated foundational myths and numerological patterns, were therefore plainly tools of good or virtuous government. Imperial rule constituted cosmic regulation; a judicious command of space could deliver eternal and universal power. The Mandate of Heaven and its attendant expressions of authority operated simultaneously as material and ideational forms of power, ordering the world according to carefully crafted rituals with deep socio-economic and political consequences for successive Chinese empires and their neighbours. Yet an over-emphasis on the static dimensions of such imperial ordering risks underplaying the important role of movement and change in the maintenance of such cosmic order. For a start, the very premises of imperial cosmology assumed flows and transformation within and across the established boundaries of Heaven, Earth and Man – be they physical or symbolic. As Robin Yates has noted of the founding Chinese empire: 'Careful use of time was one of the principal ways, even the most powerful way, that the Qin sought to differentiate and yet relate, separate yet combine, the actions of Man and the constant movement of the cosmos.'[9] Cosmic balance, it would seem, required a regular readjustment of 'All-under-Heaven' according to the shifts in astrological patterns – an art which only the sage-kings had mastered, and which any skilful emperor would seek to emulate. And it is at the empire's edges where perhaps the dynamic tension between exclusion and assimilation, expansion and retrenchment, upheaval and stability, played itself out most forcefully. For even (or perhaps especially) in a polity so sensitive to the balanced, symmetrical and bounded distribution of space, the question of how to define the limits of empire and relate to those peoples on or beyond its margins became a key concern of empire-builders. 'Dynasty after dynasty', one specialist suggests, 'has faced the question of where China should end, because for most of her history China's northern frontier has not been walled, but rather quite open.'[10] Against the perception of a millennial China, unified and bounded by clearly demarcated borders since time immemorial, a strong case can be made for a more nuanced and dynamic view of China's imperial boundaries as being mobile and indeterminate.

The notion of a distinct ethnicity or civilization delimiting successive Chinese empires is the first example of an imperial domain subject to historical and geographical change. Although, as we have seen, the very notion of a Middle Kingdom and its associated Sinocentric cosmologies had from the beginning assumed Chinese superiority over subject peoples, this did not preclude the possibility of assimilation and absorption into the realm of civilization. Chinese imperial expansion was ordered and hierarchical, but it was at once expansive and transformative. Indeed, the dominant Confucian cultural motif of *wenhua*, denoting virtuous conduct in ritual, language, custom and interpersonal behaviour, translates literally as 'literary transformation'.[11] Non-Chinese peoples, though gradated, as we saw earlier, according to their proximity to the imperial centre, were open to civilization and acculturation. The Confucian hierarchy of big brother–little brother was superimposed – both socio-economically and geographically – upon Han–barbarian relations, so that the process of assimilation could proceed from the centre downwards to the periphery. However, as Stevan Harrell has indicated, 'what seems important here is that who was cultured and who was not depended not so much on race but on moral education, so that the process of acculturation was eminently possible. . . . And that process was legitimized by the ideology that it was behavior, rather than race, that determined civilization.'[12] Chinese institutions were thus from earliest times attuned to processes of spatial transformation and civilizational absorption entailed in imperial expansion. So long as subject populations accommodated to the dominant cultural patterns and institutions of rule, there was little to prevent their successful assimilation into empire, as proved to be the case of southern and eastern barbarians.

Not all neighbouring peoples, however, displayed such pliability. A second zone on the margins of empire where the tensions between expansion, hierarchy and order were played out was on the northern Chinese frontiers. From their very first contact, the agrarian, centralized and bureaucratic Chinese empires looked upon the pastoralist nomads of Inner Asia as the lowest form of barbarian – a sentiment which appears to have been reciprocated. This was one boundary which on the face of it seemed immutable and insurmountable. Indeed, the Great Wall of China is generally presented as the physical representation of this fixed division – a structure which on one classic account stood as the 'most colossal tide mark of the human race'.[13] Yet more recent scholarship casts doubt on the idea that the Great Wall represents such a demarcation; that it was the only or even the preferred Chinese mechanism for relating with the nomadic peoples of Inner Asia; that it is the expression of a coherent and consistent defensive strategy; or even that it constitutes a single, continuous wall in the first place.[14] This is not to say that the distinctions between sown and steppe, cultivator and herdsman, or sedentary civilization and nomadic barbarism were non-existent, but rather that they were never permanently fixed in space. They ebbed and flowed with changing political, cultural, environmental, military–political and socioeconomic configurations between the Chinese and their neighbours. Moreover, the very correspondence between these binary oppositions must also be questioned, for Chinese frontier colonists were not averse to adopting some pastoralist practices, nor were Inner Asian peoples always and everywhere hostile or subservient to Chinese empires: 'While it is conventional wisdom that the nomads of Mongolia prowled like wolves beyond the Great Wall waiting for China to weaken so that they could conquer it, the facts are that the nomads from the central steppe avoided conquering the Chinese territory. Wealth from Chinese trade and subsidies stabilized the imperial government on the steppe and they had no desire to destroy this resource.'[15] For much of their history, the northern frontiers remained zones of exchange and communication as well as exclusion and antagonism, even supplying, as was mentioned earlier, a Chinese dynasty in the shape of the Mongolian Yuan.

Much like their contemporary Chinese counterparts, Roman authorities of the late Republic and early Principate sought to reconcile, both geographically and ideologically, the conflicting aspirations to expansive, ecumenical domination and orderly, hierarchical rule over diverse peoples from a metropolitan centre. Like the Chinese, they did so by combining cosmological myths of origin with a spatial management of their subjects. In one of the more exuberant expressions of this claim to cosmic dominion by the imperial centre, Julius Caesar instructed four Greek scholars to carry out a survey of the known world in order, it is said, not just to represent Rome's majesty over the *oikumene*, but also to measure it for taxation.[16] The most famous result of this enterprise was Agrippa's world map, which contemporary accounts say was displayed on a colonnade in Rome, for the first time representing in cartographic form the empire and its place in the world.[17] Such visual displays of the empire's reach were accompanied by extensive geographical commentaries – both scientific and laudatory – such as Augustus' equally celebrated *Res Gestae* (deeds or acts), all of which point to the Principate's growing appreciation for the power of geography more generally, and cartography in particular. In fact, Agrippa's world map can be seen to encapsulate three aspects of the Roman empire's geographical imagination which are germane to the present discussion of empire as space.

The first of these relates to Roman imperial cosmology. Greg Woolf has suggested that the turn of the first century of our era witnessed a self-conscious refashioning of Roman traditions through the complementary mechanisms of writing and mapping, which he suggests delivered 'a series of cosmological and natural "constants" against which Roman power might be stabilized, justified, explained and understood.'[18] While a distinctively Latin literature, expressed in Virgil's epics or Livy's histories, 'offered new formulations of Roman identity, of the Romans' shared past, of their destiny, and of their special relationship to the gods and the cosmic order', the various geographical representations of ecumenical space mentioned above tied Roman expansion to its civilizational superiority.[19] 'Roman myths', another authority states, 'were in essence myths of place. They recounted the history of the

area of Rome itself, a history that extended without inter-
ruptions or Dark Ages to the Augustan age and of which
were the living tokens in the cults of Rome.'[20] Both myth and
cult were for their part inextricably tied to warfare and, in
particular, Roman triumph in battle, thus generating a close
interaction between imperial cosmology and the extension
and organization of imperial space, both at the centre and
on its peripheries. The development and dissemination across
the empire of the so-called imperial cult and its attendant
festivals, combats, pageants and games became explicitly
associated with territorial conquests and military victories.[21]
These in turn left their mark on the imperial capital in the
shape of new triumphal arches, in Augustus' regeneration of
the area around the Forum Romanum and his reorganization
of Roman wards so as to regulate new cults.[22] In short, cartographic experiments such as Agrippa's world map should
be seen not only as expressions of imperial hubris, but also
as evidence of an emerging imperial cosmology built on the
interconnection of military conquest, mythical histories and
a new organization and representation of space.

Close attention to the cosmological value of Roman cartography should not distract us, however, from the second
and principal role of maps and other spatial registers under
the empire, namely to measure and control the twin socio-
economic pillars of the Roman empire: revenue in tax and
tribute, and private property in land. The two interrelated
geographical instruments employed for this purpose were the
census and the cadastre. While the first broadly concerned
itself with registering the numbers of Roman citizens and
their possessions (including wives, slaves and progeny), the
second was directed towards the delimitation and measure-
ment of private land.

The census had from the early Republic served as a mechanism to establish both rights and responsibilities: it enabled
citizens to claim their distinctive privileges in relation to free
foreigners (*peregrini*) but also allowed Roman authorities to
calculate both the tax levy and the number of troops owed
by different communities outside the capital. The census
recorded not just the number but also the provenance of citizens, thus figuratively if not physically mapping the extent
of the *Populus Romanus*. By the period of the late Republic,

expansion through military conquest exempted Roman citizens from direct taxation. Fiscal arrangements in the provinces were adapted to existing custom and/or were accompanied by the requisitioning of supplies or levying of cash from conquered populations. This decentralized, subsidiary organization of revenue-collection was correspondingly reflected in the forms of provincial administration, which essentially granted governors the geopolitical authority to establish alliances and protect colonies. Thus, at the time of the first settlement in 27 BC, Roman *imperium* was exercised in functionally and geographically uneven fashion: the more urbanized and civilized provinces of the Hellenic East were incorporated into the empire through alliances with existing *poleis* and kingdoms, while the less developed provinces of the Iberian and Gallic West and African South were destined for Roman colonization in the creation of new *civitates* such as Orange in today's France or Cartagena in Spain. In both these instances, Roman provinces acted less as uniform jurisdictions attached bureaucratically to a centralized empire than as loose networks of relatively autonomous communities linked by their tributary relation to a Roman proconsul.

An important component of Augustus' restoration was the reorganization of such loose arrangements by, among other things, granting senate authority over the interior pacified provinces while retaining for himself the power directly to appoint proconsuls in the more troublesome frontier provinces. Yet even after the empire's division into the 'senate's share' and 'Caesar's share', the overarching aims of imperial administration remained the same: to broaden its range through alliances with local aristocracies, protect the interests of Roman colonists and citizens abroad, guarantee the extraction of revenues in exchange for such protection, and secure its territorial acquisitions from foreign encroachment.[23]

The census continued to serve in the provinces as a crucial instrument in this task, not least in extending and calculating the scope of Roman citizenship. A gradual process of assimilation, which had begun with the declaration in 1 BC of all free Italians as Roman citizens, continued with the extension of this status to provincial elites, and culminated in AD 212 with Caracalla's edict proclaiming all free *peregrini* living under the empire as citizens of Rome. Interestingly, the etymology of *civitas* is closer to meaning 'fellow-citizen' rather than simply denoting a legal relation to the state, thereby invoking a sense of common belonging or, to wear down further an already overused phrase, an 'imagined community'. This is the kind of institution which could bring a second-century Greek citizen of Rome to proclaim that,

> In your empire all paths are open to all. No one worthy of rule or trust remains an alien, but a civic community of the world has been established as a free Republic under one, the best, ruler and teacher of order; and all come together as in a common civic centre. . . . What another city is to its own boundaries and territory, this city is to the boundaries and territory of the entire civilized world.[24]

Such ecumenical uses of boundaries and territory were not entirely rhetorical, as the political and legal rights that came with citizenship could indeed be invoked across the different territorial jurisdictions of the empire. St Paul's regular brushes with Roman authority are generally cited instances of how Roman citizens, regardless of their provenance or location, had recourse to 'an appeal to the Roman people in the person of the emperor'.[25] If one adds to this the requirement of citizenship to serve in the Roman legions, the 'Romanization' of local elites and their successive incorporation into the oligarchic institutions of the imperial capital, it becomes clear how Roman citizenship itself became a legal mechanism for the actualization of an imperial space defined by personal status more than by territorial jurisdiction.

While most Roman citizens would have been exempt from the poll tax or *tributum capitis* which applied to the rest of the population, they were subject to a second key tax on agricultural produce, the *tributum solis*. This too was collected with the aid of provincial censuses, but here the source of income was private land appropriated not just by way of conquest and settlement but also through the creation of cadastral surveys. Claude Nicolet has examined in some detail the process of 'centuration' whereby imperial hinterlands were divided into square or rectangular plots (centuries) defined by intersecting roads. Although such agricultural allotments were initially destined for colonization by veterans or civilians, their gradual alienation for profit raised a question over whether the property was private or public, and indeed where its limits lay.[26] Accordingly, a body of specialist land surveyors or *agromensores* emerged not simply to measure the extent of plots and delimit their boundaries, but increasingly also to act as experts in the adjudication of land disputes. What is relevant for our purposes here is how the process of centuration reveals the intimate interconnection between imperial government, surplus appropriation and the organization of land. 'In the cadastral maps recording centuration, just as in geographical maps', one authority suggests, 'the Roman rulers saw a vital tool of government, in this case underpinning an orderly system of land registration.'[27]

The census and the cadastre, then, point to the ways in which property, tribute, citizenship and conquest interacted to produce unique forms of spatial administration within the empire. But what about the outer reaches of the Roman empire? How exactly were the limits to empire defined? Here again there is scope, as in the case of China, to explore the spatial relationship between centre and periphery as one marked by the tension between centripetal and centrifugal forces, which in turn resist a firm and fixed delimitation of the empire's outer boundaries.

There are, in essence, two contrasting responses to these questions: one which stresses the territoriality of imperial rule – that is, the existence of clearly defined borders – and one which focuses on control over populations as the major source of imperial authority. An initial answer to the question of Rome's imperial limits, most famously associated with the military historian Edward Luttwak but also expressed in similar fashion by Arther Ferrill and Derek Williams, argues that, although the territorial limits of the Republic and early empire were in fact quite ill-defined, or at least quite mobile until well into the second century, they began to crystallize into static borders thereafter.[28] Initially, during what Luttwak calls the period of 'hegemonic empire', the prevailing forms of Roman control focused around tribute and the marching camp. Thus the limits of the Roman empire were defined more by flexible boundaries and shifting military frontiers than by fixed borders as we might know them today. So-called client states such as the kingdoms of Mauretania or Thrace were ruled by indigenous authorities and were protected in exchange for tribute, while conquered provinces were placed under the authority of senatorial and, later, imperial proconsuls. With the consolidation of Roman military authority in the outer marches of the empire, the frontier became a defensive boundary – or *limes* – and the mobile marching camp gave way to the administration of fixed, fortified borders of the Roman territorial empire.

Another set of specialists questions whether these lines of forts, garrisons and walls (most notably Hadrian's Wall, the palisades of the Rhine and Danube or the African *fossata*) actually 'marked legal borders between Roman and non-Roman territory'.[29] They emphasize how 'The Romans conquered peoples not land.'[30] In support of this claim, scholars such as Benjamin Isaac, Susan Mattern, Fergus Millar, Peter Wells or Christopher Whittaker argue, *inter alia*, that imperial frontiers acted more as zones of interaction than as fixed and exclusive lines between Romans and barbarians; that Roman diplomacy was personalized in treaties and agreements with client-kings, not kingdoms; that – notwithstanding the discussion above – Roman geopolitical cartography was primitive and used mainly for propaganda rather than for strategic purposes; and, finally, that even those natural and man-made barriers, such as the Danube or Hadrian's Wall, deemed to be defensive frontiers, acted alternatively as regulators of traffic across boundaries or as tactical staging-posts in cross-frontier raids rather than as fixed, strategic borders.[31]

Plainly this is a complex and protracted debate, the details of which lie beyond the remit and expertise of this book. Yet, the fact that such an intense debate exists and, more importantly, that the evidence appears mainly circumstantial and interpretative rather than conclusive indicates that, whatever the nature of Roman *limes* in their various historical and geographical manifestation, there is little to suggest that they were conceived of or were organized along lines similar to the modern system of territorial borders. Even those defenders of the Roman frontier as a system of 'defence in depth' recognize that there are few extant illustrations of Roman strategic thinking or a clearly defined conception of *limes* as borders.[32] They furthermore acknowledge that the empire's territorial limits were marked as much by transgression as by immutable lines, and by a unilateral demarcation rather than some shared notion of discrete sovereignty: 'Even in the second century Hadrian's Wall was no Maginot line – it was intended as a base for forays forward into hostile territory.'[33] It may be more appropriate, therefore, to follow Benjamin Isaac in understanding the Roman *limes* as administrative districts rather than as a military frontier – once again chiefly concerned with controlling peoples, not land – and therefore open to the possibility that 'such districts . . . can co-exist with subject peoples beyond the frontier.'[34]

The spatial organization of empire: frontier, conquest and administration

We have thus far seen how two powerful empires of antiquity developed highly sophisticated notions of space when ruling over their citizens and subjects. They applied cosmological ideologies in the administration and taxation of imperial peoples, thereby generating contradictory expressions of territoriality. The internal organization of political space was highly ordered and hierarchical but it was constantly challenged by periodic bouts of expansion and incorporation at the empire's edges. In both ancient China and Rome, the net result of these tensions was amorphous imperial polities with centralized fiscal systems yet devolved forms of administration; powerful expressions of civilizational supremacy which were nonetheless constantly open to assimilation; and meticulous mechanisms for the distribution of land and extraction of revenue which coexisted with ill-defined territorial limits to empire.

These spatial features of empire were to persist into the modern period, albeit this time increasingly challenged by the twin forces of states and markets. By the middle of the sixteenth century, two new empires, claiming for themselves the ecumenical mantle of Rome, ruled over the bulk of the world's inhabitants west of the Tigris. Armed with the spiritual backing of successive papal bulls, the Spanish crown had by then added the most densely populated regions of America to its European dominions, while its Ottoman rival dominated across European, African and Asian lands that once formed Byzantium and the Abbasid caliphate. Both empires originated as frontier principalities on opposite fringes of the Muslim world, eventually extending their reach across Iberia and Asia Minor, respectively, as surrounding polities collapsed and submitted to Castilian and Ottoman sovereignty. In both cases, too, this expansion was accomplished through a fearsome combination of religious zeal and military prowess fuelled in large measure by the spoils of war. By the end of the fifteenth century the Spanish Reconquest and the Ottoman *gaza* campaigns had produced two formidable dynastic states which became the major early modern empires of the Western world.

Three interrelated aspects of the Spanish and Ottoman imperial experiences will concern us here. First is the key role of the frontier in shaping the dynamics of imperial expansion. For the cultural, political, military and socio-economic institutions of the frontier were to play an instrumental role in the organization of these two empires long after their territorial authority was consolidated in their respective heartlands. Indeed, one of the more fascinating aspects of the Spanish conquest of the Americas is how much the process borrowed – however unwittingly – from Muslim practices on the Iberian frontier, and how these in turn paralleled the *gazi* culture of Anatolian marches. The second issue concerns the essentially tributary nature of both these empires. Despite possessing impressive navies (and using them against each other with some efficacy in the Mediterranean), both empires were land-based polities built on cavalry- and infantry-supported institutions of territorial rule. (Spain was of course an overseas empire, but it never exploited the full potential of transatlantic trade as a source of wealth, instead focusing most of its political–military strength on extracting surplus from American and Caribbean lands and peoples and transferring it directly to the metropole.) As we shall shortly see, both Habsburgs and Ottomans developed complex and pervasive mechanisms of tribute-collection to secure the reproduction of their imperial authority. This in turn leads to the final aspect of the organization of political space in these two polities, namely the key role of suzerain government in the administration of empire. Although they did so in radically different ways, both Madrid and Constantinople learnt to devolve authority to local institutions of rule, be they native or colonist, thereby bequeathing their peripheries a unique political geography marked by variegated and overlapping territorialities.

The fall of Constantinople and Granada in 1453 and 1492 respectively to contending political and civilization forces in many ways marks the culminating shift from state-making to empire-building among Ottomans and Castilians. Cutting across both historical moments was the institution of the frontier, manifested not only in its hostile and exclusionary form as castle, garrison or raiding party but also as a spatial zone that produced military alliances, cultural exchange and commercial traffic between seemingly irreconcilable enemies. The common denominator in all these experiences was the fluctuating nature of the frontier, open as it constantly was to the dynamics of conquest, retreat and reconquest. And it was this promise of continuous expansion which by the turn of the sixteenth century had transformed the Ottoman emirate and the Kingdom of Castile from powerful dynastic states into fledgling empires.

The Ottoman empire

In 1300, the followers of the House of Osman (the Ottomans) formed one of several tribal emirates in northeast Anatolia that survived chiefly off raids across the Byzantine frontier. Legitimated through the notion of *gaza*, or Holy War, the Ottomans inflicted consecutive defeats on their Christian neighbours across the Dardanelles and, despite serious setbacks at the start of the fifteenth century, were in a position by the end of that century to lord over most of Anatolia and the Balkan peninsula from their newly acquired capital in Constantinople. The driving force behind this spectacular expansion was the combination of pillage and warfare peculiar to the reproduction of frontier societies. Turkic nomads had during the thirteenth century been squeezed out of their Central Asian homelands through the twin pressures of Mongol and Seljuk encroachment. It was early Ottoman success in frontier raiding, coupled with the glory derived from defeating both Muslim and Christian rivals, which attracted greater numbers of Turkish migrants to Ottoman Anatolia over the course of the fourteenth century: 'As the other emirates were forced to give up the frontier struggle', one historian indicates, 'and turned to settled and therefore relatively static living, coming under the Ottoman banner remained the only way open to the dangerous but lucrative life in the frontier for newcomers and adventurous brave youth alike.'[35]

If fighting under Osman's banner certainly brought riches, it also offered spiritual solace, for *gazis* were holy warriors bent on extending the reaches of the realm of Islam (*dar al-Islam*) at the expense of the godless abode of war (*dar al-harb*). There is considerable historiographical and, by extension, political controversy in this formulation.[36] Some recent scholarship contests the canonical idea that Ottomans were driven by a religious zeal, arguing in a neo-Khaldunian vein that the *gaza* owes more to the shamanistic culture of Turkic nomadic tribes than to the more sedentary, scriptural legalism of the Muslim *jihad*.[37] They argue moreover that the notion of a coherent *gazi* ideology is very much a product of later Ottoman eulogizing rather than a strategic self-understanding of Osman's raiding bands. Striking what seems to be a more plausible balance between these two poles, Cemal Kafadar has suggested that 'there is nothing we can do about the fact that the people of the marches, including the early Ottomans, chose to retain several of their "shamanistic" notions or, rather, to redefine them within a syncretistic understanding of Islam.'[38] Indeed it is perhaps this marcher syncretism which best explains not only the Ottoman drive for expansion but also their ability innovatively to combine diverse sources and institutions of rule as they absorbed new lands and peoples.

The initial phase of Ottoman conquest over what were to become its imperial heartlands of Anatolia and Rumelia bore the unmistakeable imprint of a frontier polity. During the better part of the fourteenth century Ottoman westward expansion was achieved in one of two ways: on the back of alliances or vassalage agreements with local Christian lords eager to protect themselves from rival princes in the context of a decaying and anarchic Byzantium, or by turning Ottoman frontier raiders (*akinji*) into marcher lords (*uc-beys* or *uc-emirs*) ruling over borderlands on behalf of the House of Osman.[39] In both cases, the existing institutions of rule based on tribute-taking and raiding remained relatively intact under Ottoman suzerainty during this period, as did the dynastic structures of the Christian vassal princes or the kinship ties of the *akinji*.

These arrangements of indirect rule were gradually replaced by a more direct and formalized administration of subject populations in the course of the fifteenth century as the Ottoman state itself developed a formidable military–bureaucratic infrastructure. To the powerful force of cavalry-men (*sipahis*) was added a new elite corps of infantrymen made up of assimilated captives (the *Janissaries*) and a specifically Ottoman administrative body geared towards centralizing and standardizing political and fiscal authority. Territorial conquest thus gave way to political consolidation as the military power of the cavalry and the political author-ity of the palace combined to extract tax and tribute from subject populations. Two interrelated institutions, that of the *dirlik* (literally, 'livelihood' or 'income') and the *sanjak* ('banner' or 'standard'), encapsulate the Ottoman adminis-tration of empire at this time. The term *dirlik* refers to state revenue collected by a class of tax-exempt military com-manders (*askeri*) from their tax-paying subjects (*reaya* or 'flock'). On falling under the Ottoman banner, newly conquered lands were declared property of the sultan (*miri* lands), and their inhabitants his subjects. *Askeris* – overwhelmingly *sipahis* – were then granted non-hereditary rights to a *dirlik* of varying yields (the most widespread being a *timar* – literally, 'horse-grooming'), conditional upon ren-dering military service to the sultan. Simultaneously, the palace appointed a *sanjak bey*, or district governor, as mili-tary commander of diverse *dirlik* – or fiefholders within a given province. His chief responsibility was to mobilize *sipahis* and other fiefholders for the sultan's military campaigns.

By way of buttressing this military–tributary complex and, in particular, undermining the temptation of distant fiefholders turning into feudal lords independent from the sultan, there emerged a system of cadastral registration which allowed palace officials to monitor at regular intervals the collection and transfer of tax revenues from subjects to rulers. This was gradually codified into a distinct body of Ottoman law – or *kanunname* – which, though drawing heavily on local custom, and despite its uneven application across the empire, did however become the major source of metropolitan authority in the provinces. Such a body of secular law was complemented by Islamic institutions, most notably *sharia* law applied to Muslims by *kadis* or judges, who in many instances also acted on behalf of the palace in secular matters of crime or property.

The net result of these various overlapping layers of fiscal–legal authority, military power and mechanisms of surplus appropriation was a distinctly imperial organization of space. The military extension of the frontier paved the way for a redistribution of lands and peoples along both social and geographical hierarchies: a class of fiefholders (be they *akinji* or local aristocrats) exploited direct producers while state officials appointed by the palace – both secular and religious – administered the provinces and regulated the collection and transfer of revenues to the centre. In most respects, such structures point to the existence from the sixteenth century of a modern, centralized and bureaucratized national state, with its own standardized administrative norms, rationalized taxation, powerful standing armies and an extensive system of record-keeping. Yet in the crucial area of territorial administration the Ottoman state betrayed its imperial character, as even at the very height of its powers the Sublime Porte was not always and everywhere willing or able to exercise absolute control over the full extent of its territories.

The combination of direct and indirect rule, of centralization and devolution, that had guided initial Ottoman expansion in the Balkans was applied to its later acquisitions in the Arab world. Here too the Ottoman authorities adopted a pragmatic posture towards territorial rule. Long-standing administrative or commercial hubs such as Algiers, Tunis, Tripoli, Cairo, Aleppo, Damascus, Baghdad, Mosul and

Basra became the capitals of new provinces or *vilayets* in the course of the sixteenth century. Metropolitan officials, *kadis* and janissary troops were posted to these areas in order to collect revenues and protect Ottoman geopolitical and commercial interests against Iberian and Safavid rivals. On becoming 'Servants of the two Sanctuaries' at Mecca and Medina, and guardians of the holy places of Jerusalem and Hebron, Ottoman governors in the Hijaz and Syria also acquired religious duties. Yet in all these cases imperial rule rarely extended beyond urban centres: the Ottomans relied heavily on allied tribes and rural notables for both the collection of revenue and the protection of trade and pilgrimage routes. Even within these provincial outposts, the power of governors was compromised by alternative sources of local authority emanating from Muslim clerics, Sufi brotherhoods or corsair syndicates, while many developed their own 'creole' ruling classes formed, as in the North African case, by *Mamluk* or *Khouloghli* elites.[40] At the very height of its sixteenth-century zenith, then, the Ottoman empire was, like most other empires, obliged to reconcile its centralizing aspirations to local conditions. The Ottomans plainly extended their rule through powerful and sophisticated administrative structures, but these were neither functionally equivalent nor geographically uniform across the empire. Indeed, as Suraiya Faroqhi has usefully pointed out, the relations between metropole and province fluctuated considerably throughout Ottoman history, with many ostensibly centralized provinces reverting to semi-autonomous rule.[41] Speaking of the Ottoman rule over Arab lands, Albert Hourani neatly summarized such fluctuating arrangements thus: 'In the course of time, after the first conquests, different systems of government grew up, with varying balances between central control and local power.'[42]

Spain's American empire

Six months before his first landing on Caribbean shores in the autumn of 1492, Christopher Columbus reached an agreement (*capitulación*) with the Catholic monarchs of Castile and Aragón. The latter would sponsor the search for a westward sea route to the Indies and in exchange grant Columbus admiralty over the Ocean sea and a hereditary governorship of any lands discovered or conquered in the course of his voyages, as well as a right to a tenth of any riches derived from such an enterprise. The agreement was sealed at the Santa Fe encampment, on the outskirts of a besieged Granada, where only a few months earlier crown representatives had secured another capitulation – that of Boabdil, the last of the Moorish emirs of Iberia. The fall of Granada thus marked the end of a protracted 'reconquest' of Muslim Spain by Christian forces, thereby also signalling the closure of the Islamic–Christian frontier which had shaped the peninsula's history over the previous seven centuries. This was, notoriously, also the year in which Spain's considerable Jewish population was forced to convert or face expulsion from the realm, ostensibly with the purpose of 'cleansing' the new polity at its very birth from any un-Christian pollution.

Santa Fe has since symbolized the continuity between reconquest and conquest: as one frontier was closing in Iberia (or, in fact, relocating southwards and eastwards to African and Ottoman lands), another was soon to be opened in the Americas.[43] But the capitulations of Santa Fe also represent the contradictory logic which informed the whole Columbian enterprise and the imperial conquest which ensued. On the one hand, the capitulations conform to a standard practice which accompanied both the Christian settlement of Iberian lands 'reconquered' from the Moors and previous maritime expeditions along African coasts sponsored by the Castilian crown, most notably the one leading to the Spanish acquisition of the island of Gran Canaria. Subsequent to the fall of Toledo in 1085, the Castilian monarchy adopted a central role in authorizing and coordinating Christian colonization of lands south of the River Duero. Frontier warrior bands gradually formalized into monastic military orders such as those of Calatrava, Santiago and Alcántara were entrusted with the *repartimiento* (distribution) of conquered territories, awarded aristocratic privileges in the taxation and administration of newly established towns and associated estates, and granted rights to booty in cross-frontier raiding.[44] In exchange for this licensing of frontier colonization, the crown not only extended its political reach – both geographically and juridically – but also levied the royal fifth (*el quinto real*) from the spoils of war and, by the thirteenth century, used its advance position to extract tribute from the southernmost Moorish vassal emirates.

Similar arrangements governed the occupation of the Canary Islands in the late fifteenth century. Like his peninsular counterparts, the *adelantado* (frontier commander) was granted administrative privileges and landed titles as *mercedes* (grants or rewards) for the successful campaign of occupation. 'From this', Manuel González Jiménez has suggested, 'we can deduce the fundamental point about the medieval history of Spain: all the frontiers with Islam, even those which were the most lasting, were regarded as being impermanent because of this ideology – frontiers which, at some point, would cease to exist.'[45] Moreover, underlying this ideology was the powerful alliance between Church and state: 'The church provided the moral sanction which elevated a plundering expedition to a crusade, while the state's approval was required to legitimate the acquisition of lordship and land.'[46]

This crusading spirit was plainly present in Columbus's quasi-mystical understanding of his mission to open the westward route to the Indies. It certainly informed the application of a papal bull, the *Inter Caetera* of 1493, in legitimizing the Catholic kings' possession of American lands. Yet the Columbian enterprise, and the colonization that followed in its wake, was also driven by a commercial ambition and supported by a project of incipient absolutism, both of which were alien to the frontier institutions of the Reconquest. Columbus's scheme only made sense in the context of Portuguese and Italian mercantile expansion – its selling point was the opening of new sea routes in the search for commercial gain, not the occupation of foreign lands. Domestically, the Catholic kings were concerned with affirming their public, patrimonial authority over the private interests and power of magnates and orders emerging from the Reconquest. Externally, they were preoccupied with strengthening the geopolitical standing of their new kingdom vis-à-vis continental rivals and the rising Ottoman power. For their part, the first conquistadors of mainland America were driven by lust for gold, not by any proselytizing zeal or by the desire to cultivate the lands of the New World or establish commercial relations with their inhabitants.

The competing motivations for Castilian expansion across the Atlantic – commerce, conversion, plunder and power – were to play themselves out in the Americas for several decades after Columbus's first voyage, as conquering caudillos, crown administrators and missionary clergymen fought, mostly all too literally, to stamp their authority on the New World. Matters were further complicated for the Spanish by the astonishing speed of their conquests. As they first defeated the largely pacific inhabitants of the Antilles and thereafter acquired control over the extensive and densely populated pre-Columbian mainland empires, the Spanish were presented with a perennial problem for colonial rulers: how can a vastly outnumbered foreign minority govern over an indigenous majority?

An initial answer emerged in the fifty years following the discovery, first in the Caribbean stronghold of Hispaniola, and from there to be exported to the American mainland with varied success. It essentially involved the application of Reconquest solutions to New World conditions. First, the subjection of Amerindians had to be secured. The Spanish did so in one of two ways: by cooperation or through force. The former method underwrote the 'pacification' of the two great agrarian empires of pre-Hispanic America. The motley bands of fighters led by Hernán Cortés and Francisco Pizarro conquered the Aztecs and Incas by decapitating their deeply hierarchical structures of rule and reaping the benefits of large-scale collaboration among Indian subjects who had only recently been integrated into these pre-Columbian empires by force, and therefore had little to lose from their disappearance. Thus, the Spanish conquest of the major areas of pre-Hispanic settlement, though ultimately reliant on violence and coercion, resembled a political annexation by default more than a well-orchestrated and systematic military campaign of occupation. Where the conquistadors faced Indian resistance, they justified a resort to war through a ritual adopted from the Iberian frontier: the *requerimiento* (summons or requisition). This document, recited in Spanish to bewildered locals, enjoined them to submit to Catholic (i.e. Spanish) sovereignty or face the following consequences: 'I [the conquistador] will subject you to the yoke and obedience of the Church and His Majesty, and I will take your goods, and I will take your wives and children, and will make them slaves . . .'[47]

That this was no idle threat was to be proven in subsequent centuries. Columbus and his associates had from the beginning resorted to enslavement of native islanders as a source of labour. Influenced by the theological disputes over the status of the Indians (the term was of course generic), Queen Isabel outlawed Indian slavery in 1500, declaring native Americans 'free subjects' of the crown, except in those instances where they were captured in the course of 'just war'.[48] As was to happen time and again with metropolitan legislation, this injunction was unevenly enforced for decades to come. Yet it was soon superseded by the introduction of a different mechanism of native control and exploitation, the *encomienda* or trusteeship. An American variant of the Iberian *repartimiento* mentioned above, the *encomienda* granted designated settlers the lifetime rights to the unpaid labour and tribute of an assignment of Indians. In return, the trustee or *encomendero* was obliged to evangelize his workers and care for them in the Christian way. Insofar as these rights were to the labour of Indians, not their lands, the *encomienda* differed from the *repartimientos* of the Reconquest. It furthermore took on a local inflection by building on pre-Hispanic systems of forced and enslaved labour. But in its missionary zeal, its principle of rewarding private colonization and its insistence that the Kingdom of Castile was sovereign over pacified lands and the Indians its subjects (entrusted to, but not owned by settlers), the *encomienda* bore all the hallmarks of the Iberian frontier.

Notwithstanding its medieval origins, and despite undergoing various reforms (in part resulting from the denunciations of clerics such as the Dominican 'apostle to the Indians', Fray Bartolomé de Las Casas), the *encomienda* and its regional derivations – the Andean *mita*, the Mexican *cuateqitl* or the Colombian *alquiler* – remained a key tool of Spanish rule during the Habsburg period and beyond. This is in many respects surprising since in their original form such exploitative arrangements threatened the reproduction of imperial rule in at least two ways. First, the *encomienda*, and indeed the *requerimiento* which paved its way, led to a drastic decline of native populations in the century and a half after the discovery. Contact with European pathogens, combined with atrocious working conditions of entrusted labour in mines, rivers and fields and the sheer brutality of occupation, reduced the estimated pre-Hispanic populations across Spanish America to a tenth of their original size through disease, overwork and settler violence.[49] Here once again the conflicting interests of crown, Church and conquistadors shaped the political and socio-economic responses to what was obviously a crisis of manpower and, more broadly, of imperial authority. The alliance of Church and state attempted through successive legislation to curb the abuses of *encomenderos* and protect the welfare of the crown's Indian subjects. Yet these objectives – whether driven by ethical or political considerations – raised a second problem for imperial rule: they ran contrary to the principal sources of metropolitan wealth, namely Indian tribute and mineral wealth extracted through the *encomienda* system.

By the mid-sixteenth century a compromise emerged which, in a regionally uneven fashion, survived into the Bourbon period. The *encomienda* was transformed into an exclusively tributary mechanism – now relabelled *repartimiento* – providing head-taxes and draft labour administered by the crown but supplied through the intermediation of indigenous chiefs known as *caciques* in New Spain and *kurakas* in Peru. At one stroke, Madrid recouped monopoly over access to Indian wealth and prevented the much-feared emergence of an independent nobility of American *encomenderos*, while transferring responsibility over the reproduction of Indian labour to native authorities and, on the frontier, to missionary reservations. This system of devolved sovereignty was subsequently reflected in the administrative structures and patterns of settlement in the New World. Administratively, the crown prevailed over the conquistadors by appointing two viceroys – one based in Mexico City, the other in Lima – as direct representatives of the monarch in the Indies. They held responsibility for maintaining law and order among all of Spain's New World subjects and for the economic administration of Spanish America. A network of regional *audiencias*, or courts, staffed by a bureaucracy of metropolitan *letrados*, or legal clerks, assisted the viceroys and governors in both these tasks. The direct extraction of wealth, on the other hand, was to fall into more local hands, both Spanish and Indian.

From the outset, Spanish settlement of the Americas built on the 'municipalism' of the Castilian frontier, where newly founded towns – many of them modelled on the Santa Fe encampment – became the seat of government over a subordinated hinterland. In the American setting, this strategy of colonization through urbanization involved a radical rearrangement of political and economic space, reproducing center–periphery relations on a local scale. Natives were uprooted from their pre-Hispanic settlements and reassembled into self-governing 'Indian republics' headed by Spanish-appointed *caciques*. They were segregated from the urban 'Spanish republics' ruled by corporate oligarchies which tended to dominate the *cabildo* or town council. 'Although the notion of two republics suggests co-equality', Richard Morse reminds us, 'the republic of Indians became a euphemism for the regime of detribalization, regimentation, Christianization, tribute and forced labour.'[50] Thus, imperial mechanisms of exploitation and rule were spatialized along a hierarchical chain: the *caciques* of the smallest *pueblos de indios* collected tribute and organized draft labour for the local *cabildos* or *corregimientos*. These fell under the jurisdiction of regional *audiencias* which, in principle at least, regulated and distributed tributary extraction on behalf of the metropolitan centres of accumulation and administration in Seville and Madrid.

With the gradual commercialization of colonial Spanish America from the seventeenth century, geographical units other than the tributary *cabildos* and *corregimientos* acquired greater political and socio-economic significance. Demographic crisis and the growth of an internal market encouraged the concentration of land in large estates known as *haciendas* or *estancias*, dedicated to provisioning urban centres and manned by wage labourers from the outlying countryside. Large mining towns and commercial ports such as Potosí and Callao in Peru or Zacatecas and Veracruz in Mexico grew on slave, bonded and free labour imported from other American regions and beyond, thereby breaking down the simple Indian–Spanish racial dichotomy into much more complex ethnic gradations. Yet even in these instances, the organization of space was premised on the political, cultural and socio-economic domination of urban centres, disproportionately Spanish and Creole, over rural peripheries inhabited chiefly by Indians, blacks, mulattos, mestizos and their offspring. The latter supplied labour, revenue, foodstuffs and raw materials while the former consumed and administered them. Moreover, although the urban miscegenation among plebeian classes was eventually to prove unstoppable, the Habsburg authorities did their best to reproduce the racialized distribution of space in many inland cities by segregating the various *castas* into distinct and hierarchically organized wards. The consequences of such experiments in urban segregation during the colonial period, Richard Morse suggests, delivered a dispossessed urban population characterized by 'a common sense of disinheritance rather than a sense of common cause'.[51]

Metropolitan blueprints guided the reshaping of New World political and economic geography. Yet such remodelling did not always conform to the designs issued from Madrid, mainly because, like most empires, the Spanish state did not possess sufficient resources to control its colonial dependencies directly. This is especially true of Spanish America's imperial frontiers which, in characteristic fashion, were never finally and exclusively delimited by the Spanish but fluctuated according to varying military, socio-economic, environmental and cultural dynamics.

In his indispensable study of the subject, Alistair Hennessy identifies at least nine types of frontier in Latin America, corresponding roughly to three interrelated objectives of the Spanish conquest: to pacify, proselytize and prosper.[52] The missionary and mining frontier often fused, as Franciscan and later Jesuit missionaries accompanied the prospecting expeditions in Mexico and the Andes, from there penetrating the northern frontier of New Spain and the Amazonian jungle respectively. By the time of independence, hundreds of thousands of Amerindians had been incorporated into the empire through Christian baptism. The frontiers pioneered by the Jesuits, however, contracted after their expulsion from

Spanish America in 1767, once more leaving substantial areas of the Amazonian jungle free from European control. The missions were partly sponsored by the crown, and occasionally played a pacifying and administrative role. But the mining and, later, cattle and agricultural frontiers extended Spanish reach into areas that had been historically hostile to foreign rule.

The so-called Indian Frontier thus developed as Spanish settlers encountered nomadic and hunter-gathering communities such as the Araucanians of southern Chile or the Chichimecs and Apaches of northern Mexico. The skilful adoption of horseback warfare by the Plains Indians allowed them to continue a pre-Columbian history of resistance to sedentary encroachments from outsiders, in some cases right until the end of the nineteenth century. For decades before the 1810 Mexican War of Independence, Apaches and Comanches of the northern Spanish American frontier harnessed their equestrian skills to raiding and extracting tribute from colonizers and subject Amerindians alike. In the southern reaches of the continent only the horsemanship of mestizo gauchos was able to keep the Indian frontier in check, until superior technology and the concerted effort of a modern army eventually exterminated the last remnants of what today would be southern Argentinean Amerindians.[53]

Finally, the crown was to face challenges to its territorial control from within and outside its Spanish American domains in the shape of what Hennessy respectively labels the 'Maroon' and the 'Anglo-Hispanic' frontier. As in the Caribbean, runaway African slaves on the mainland formed their own hideaway communities, known as *palenques* in Spanish America and *qilombos* in Brazil, often in cohabitation with local Amerindians and other mestizos and poor whites. The historical duration and political disposition of these communities varied considerably across different parts of the continent – many selling their loyalty to the highest bidder during the peak of European inter-imperial rivalry in the eighteenth century. But the very existence and indeed spread of such autonomous communities once again undermined the colonial state's monopoly over territory, let alone the means of violence. 'Although in retrospect the maroon problem may seem unimportant', Hennessy indicates, 'it was not so at the time. No colonial society felt safe as long as there was a potential focus for resistance and opposition.'[54] Such insecurity also arrived in the shape of other states, as the Spanish expansion across the Rio Grande confronted not just the unruly Apaches and Comanches, but the expansive designs of Anglo-American settlers and the British, French and Russian empires. Spanish authorities did attempt to demarcate a permanent defensive line of fortresses or *presidios* on the outer reaches of their American dominions, but once more, in reflecting the imperial tendency to an open frontier, such fixed delimitations were neither exclusive – they continued to police a zone, rather than mark a border – nor, in the end, effective.

Imperial legacies: nation and citizenship in a post-colonial world

The imperial conception and administration of political space, this chapter has argued, is characterized by the permanent tension between limitless territorial expansion and the maintenance of a bounded socio-political order; between recurrent assimilation of barbarians and their hierarchical exclusion; and between the fastidious delimitation of lands inside the empire and a studious disregard for the definition of its outer edges. All this has, in practice, delivered multiple, indeterminate and often overlapping expressions of territoriality where imperial rule is delegated to suzerain authorities, where colonies and provinces are granted incommensurable powers, and where citizens and subjects, not territory, define the limits of empire. Such spatial arrangements – in all their historical and geographical variations – are deeply antithetical to the contemporary organization of the world into two hundred or so territorially discrete sovereign states. Whereas empires thrive on fluctuating frontiers, national states can only survive within tightly demarcated borders; where empires rule culturally diverse peoples through separate jurisdictions, sovereign states claim to unify populations culturally under a single, overarching national jurisdiction; while empires mainly seek to control peoples, national states aim to control territories. Indeed, empires can be said to control territories through their command over people – be they colonial settlers or vassal subjects – whereas sovereign states control people through their command over bounded territories.

The transition from imperial hierarchy to international anarchy, from a world dominated by empires to one ruled through a system of sovereign states, has, quite clearly, been neither smooth nor absolute. Imperial legacies persist in the contemporary organization of political space, as in other areas of our social lives. More specifically, the complex inter-action between a post-colonial present and an imperial past has manifested itself in two key expressions of contemporary politics: nationalism and citizenship. These in turn have been essential to the reproduction of sovereign state as the domi-nant form of modern territoriality. In closing this chapter, I briefly consider how the imperial organization of political space still casts a long shadow over the contemporary inter-national system of sovereign states.

The first and most obvious legacy of modern imperialism to the international system is the universalization of state sovereignty itself. The benefit of historical hindsight allows us to see how, paradoxically, the construction of European colonial states across the Americas, Africa and Asia paved the way for an anti-colonial nationalism which, through the principle of *uti possidetis*, accepted the existing colonial boundaries as the borders of newly independent states. With the possible exception of a handful of island states such as Sri Lanka or unusually long-standing political communities such as Korea, few post-colonial states have borders that correspond to pre-colonial boundaries (tellingly, in both these examples sovereignty is currently in dispute). European empires, then, set the geographical limits of most post-colonial states and therefore the territorial organization of the present international system.

This development was not, however, simply imposed from above. Modern imperialism also fostered the kinds of social relations and modes of political contestation which enabled the rise of anti-colonial patriotism: in the Americas initially in the shape of a creole liberalism, and thereafter in Africa, the Middle East and Asia in the form of both elite and mass nationalisms. European empires have certainly divided and ruled over native populations, but they have also (unintentionally no doubt) united and mobilized them against colonial authority. As Benedict Anderson famously suggested, the colonial state and its direct antagonists generated – through the spread of a vernacular literature, the promotion of a public sphere of readers and administrative exercises like the census – an 'imagined community' of fellow-nationals in Africa, Asia and the Americas where it had previously been absent. In particular, as we shall see in the next chapter, the penetration of these continents (not just their coastlines) by the capitalist world market generated social forces and political responses – ranging from trade unions to the mobilization of urban petty traders and lumpenproletarians – which by the interwar period had crystallized into mass nationalist movements responsible for attaining state sovereignty. These in turn, as chapter 4 will illustrate, were inspired and informed by broader international ideological trends, from communism to pan-Islamism, which were often imported from or indeed forged in one metropolitan capital or another. In sum, modern imperialism created its own antithesis in the shape of nationalism by seeking to territorialize colonial rule and exclude locals from full citizenship rights, yet open their everyday lives to the vagaries of the world market and the transnational flow of anti-imperialist ideas.

All these processes seemed irreversibly to lead in the course of the twentieth century towards the modern institutions of a capitalist economy and national sovereignty. In fact, however, they were accompanied by powerful countervailing tendencies which, reflecting various imperial legacies, sought to diffuse, not centralize, power in the colonies, and to rule through the indirect means of customary law or newly forged traditional authorities in the shape of urban notables, rural tribes or local chiefs and elders. One consequence of this has been the reproduction of ill-defined frontiers and the persistence of overlapping, 'heteronomous' sources of territorial authority in many parts of the post-colonial world. The contemporary Middle East has in particular been a notable site of the tension between aspirations to unified and centralized national state and the imperial legacies – both Ottoman and European – of diversified and devolved rule by religious, kinship or ethnic networks. Not only have various Middle East states (e.g. Jordan or Saudi Arabia) been built on the slender social basis of British-appointed dynasties, but many nationalist movements and revolutionary post-colonial regimes have themselves reinvented, manipulated and mobilized diverse subnational or supranational allegiances in the very attempt at reproducing state sovereignty.[55] The dominant expression of political space in the Middle East therefore remains that of a territorially sovereign state, yet its realization is still compromised by other, non-territorial sources of political power. 'The transition period from empires or chiefdoms to modern territorial states', one important study concludes, 'was either too short or too abrupt and uncomfortably fashioned from European models of states formation. Consequently, the new states still reflected certain tribal habits and had to accommodate a certain measure of tribal power.'[56]

This contradictory and generally crisis-ridden predicament has led some to argue that post-colonial borders are therefore artificial, and that they are in consequence a perennial source of conflict in what used to be called the Third World. Both these assertions are correct. Yet, the first statement is true of all modern states, whether colonial or otherwise, while the second is tautologous (post-colonial borders are deemed to be a source of conflict because they are artificial and they are artificial because they are a source of conflict). Post-colonial borders have indeed been a source of conflict within and among states, but they have by and large remained intact, as opposed to the extraordinary territorial mutations among modern European states right up to the 1990s. Moreover, it is not the existence of territorial sovereignty and exclusive borders *per se* that generates conflict but rather the uses (and abuses) to which those borders are put for the purposes of mobilizing, oppressing or exploiting local populations. Modern nationalism and state sovereignty are not by themselves the cause for international conflict, but rather the manifestation of broader social antagonisms, which have indeed been shaped by imperial legacies.

The struggle between two peoples over one land in the former British mandate of Palestine is perhaps the most powerful expression of this in the Middle East. Like other peoples across the world involved in territorial disputes – in Kashmir, Cyprus, Northern Ireland, Kurdistan or Western Sahara – the descendants of one-time imperial subjects in Palestine continue to struggle violently for their own national state. Much of the persistent antagonism between Israelis and Palestinians is the result of military–political and socio-economic developments which are very recent in origin (the occupation of the West Bank and – until recently – Gaza, the rise of Palestinian Islamism, the pauperization of Palestinian refugees). Yet the principal cause behind successive wars between Arabs and Israelis – control over land – has deep roots in the legacy of the Ottoman and British empires for at least two reasons. Firstly, because the very object of dispute, Palestine/Israel, was a product of British administration and nationalist minds. Until the end of the First World War, Palestine had no independent or unified existence. Three incommensurate Ottoman districts – the Sanjak of Jerusalem, with its own status as the third signal Muslim holy place, and two other dependencies falling within the provincial boundaries of Beirut and Syria – were welded together to constitute the British mandate in 1920.[57] It was the fixed borders of this colonial state, and not elusive and indeterminate religious or cultural boundaries of biblical, Koranic or Ottoman geography, which have served as a reference point in the twentieth-century conflict between Jews and Palestinians. In this respect, the Arab–Israeli conflict is best compared to the Indo-Pakistani dispute over Kashmir or the Moroccan–Sahrawi stand-off over the Spanish Sahara as an instance of competitive state-building in the context of a retreating empire.

Secondly, nationalism, as the modern doctrine which claims that culturally distinct peoples have the right to their own state, has been central in fuelling and thereby legitimating the conflict over the lands of mandatory Palestine. Yet, contrary to most nationalist accounts emphasizing continuity, nationalism itself is an historical product of socio-economic and political change. Both Palestinian and, in slightly different fashion, Jewish nationalisms resulted from radical transformations in Europe and the Middle East effected in large measure by modern capitalist empires. The early history of a self-conscious Palestinian nationalism is very closely tied to the rise of a new generation of urban notables affected by the Ottoman incorporation into the world economy and, with it, the wider international political currents, both pan-Arab and Western. Zionists, for their part, though chiefly advocating a nationalist response to European and Russian anti-Semitism, were the product of empire insofar as they became, perversely, the *de facto* European colonizers of Palestine – though without a metropolitan motherland. In both instances, the gradual but irreversible commercialization of the Ottoman Levant, and subsequently the Middle East more generally, brought about changes in property law, land tenure, finance and social relations of production which facilitated the Zionist colonization of Palestine and spurred on the turn to mass, popular politics among Palestinian nationalists.[58] Attention to imperial histories and their legacy, therefore, can offer fresh insights into the changing and often contingent nature of nationalism, as opposed to the way it is generally presented by nationalists – as a perennial and essential expression of their people's identity. This in turn can add a further dimension to the explanation of contemporary international conflict without necessarily reducing the latter to poorly drawn imperial boundaries.

In Latin America, too, the peculiar political and economic geography of the Spanish empire bequeathed a distinctive post-colonial problem of citizenship. Here the fault lines of conflict found expression not so much between states as across and within them. The liberal republicanism which had informed Latin American nation-building in the aftermath of nineteenth-century revolutions sought to undo the imperial distinction between the Indian and Spanish republics and replace it with the universal principle of citizenship. The liberal institutions of state and newly formed conceptions of national identity, explicitly built on the celebration of *mestizaje*, were to buttress this new political order. If the ideological project of liberal state-formation by itself was insufficient to uphold the novel institution of citizenship, the deepening integration of Latin American economies into the circuits of the capitalist world market during the course of the nineteenth century furthered this aspiration by transforming peasants into workers, tribute into profit and communal rights into private, alienable property. This, at least, has been the aspiration of liberal elites – and no few subaltern forces – throughout the better part of post-colonial Latin American history.

As in the Middle East, however, such tidy, unilinear projects in modernization stumbled across the remnants of imperial society in the shape, among other examples, of elite patronage, local trade networks, the defence of communal landholding and the reinvention of indigenous identities. The results were predictably uneven and contradictory, delivering forms of post-colonial citizenship riddled with racism and discrimination yet simultaneously offering the possibility for contestation and redress with reference to the rights and institutions of citizenship proffered by the modern state. Speaking of Andean Latin America during the second half of the nineteenth century, Brooke Larson has suggested that

> [l]iberalism and modernity seemed to unleash a new cycle of territorial and cultural conquest, which set in motion a series of intense conflicts between peasant groups, regional over- lords, and the centralizing modernizing state. At a deeper level, these converging pressures of modernity created an arena of interpretive struggle over indigenous political rights, social memory, location and identity, which reflected the postcolonial predicament of so many native Andean peasants caught between the contradictory legal-political discourses of colonialism, liberalism, and racism.[59]

Underlying many of these modern, post-colonial conflicts was arguably the legacy of imperial conceptions and organi- zation of political space. For the remapping of post-colonial Latin America along the lines of modern, liberal statehood so as to facilitate the reproduction of modern capitalist markets required considerable social upheaval and political antagonism. Geography and territorial ordering, as in the imperial past, became a major battleground in the construc- tion of Latin American republics and its attendant notions of citizenship.

Focusing still upon the Andean region, Benjamin Orlove illustrates how key geographers of post-colonial Peru aimed, in the latter half of the nineteenth century, to reorder the new republic by measuring, delimiting, representing, penetrating, classifying and thereby controlling its territory and population.[60] Whereas colonial geography had relied on textual representations of space, with its attendant classification of peoples and places according to natural characteristics (places were either cold, dry or wet; Indians were peaceful or belligerent; mountains snow-capped, volcanic or 'magnetic'), republican geography on the other hand deployed scientific conceptions of region, altitude and biology to construct the modern Peruvian national state. 'Colonial orderings', according to Orlove, 'emphasized historicized racial differences among persons with relatively balanced and homogenous space, while postcolonial orderings stressed the naturalized regional differences among places with a homogenous, though covertly racialized, population.'[61]

Once again, such republican reorderings were not merely the product of intellectual designs, but the outcome of concrete struggles over the shape of the Peruvian state and economy. The advent of republican geography coincided with Peru's deepening integration into the world market through the prized commodity of bird droppings, or *guano*. The strong international demand for this powerful fertilizer coupled with the advent of the oceanic steamship and continental railway made Peru's capital one of South America's principal commercial and financial hubs during the latter part of the nineteenth century. It also enabled the state to shift revenue-collection from land to trade. Together, these political and socio-economic developments produced an uneven republican geography: 'Peru's booming coastal economy . . . turned ever more seaward for its markets, and imported food, technology, capital and European values. By contrast, the mountainous interior – a land of somnolent Indian villagers, feudal landlords, and unruly caudillos – seemed to lag ever farther behind the coastal engine of growth.'[62]

It is against this backdrop that republican conceptions of political space became allied to liberal projects of nation-building through the extension of citizenship. According to Orlove, Peru came to be divided through policy and discourse into three geographical regions – coast, highland and jungle – each corresponding to 'a story of national progress . . . as the spread of civilization, as the integration of the people and places into the nation-state, or as some combination of the two'.[63] The Indian highlands thus became both a figurative and a literal obstacle in Peruvian state-building as successive liberal administrations sought, through fiscal reform, economic development, highway construction or military conscription, to turn Indians into citizens. 'The spatialization of the Indian', Orlove astutely observes, 'became a way to speak of race in an era of citizenship: the overt topic could be the integration of the highlands into the nation, while the subtext continued to be Peru's Indian problem.'[64]

The results were predictably mixed: highland Peruvians were not merely passive subjects of such experiments in state-formation and capitalist development, nor were liberal elites all-powerful or consistent in engineering such transformations. In the course of the nineteenth century and beyond, Andean communities and liberal elites refashioned colonial forms of indirect rule through the figure of the local magistrate or *alcalde*, while long-standing regional economies such as that of wool in the southern Peruvian highlands were revitalized through their incorporation into the world market. 'As the market unleashed threatening forces of communal divesture and alienation', Larson reminds us, 'it also opened up pathways of economic and cultural mobility for some Andean people, driven or drawn into the modernizing urban sector.'[65] Most importantly, the republican organization of space paradoxically enabled the emergence of a static, primordialist and idealized understanding of Amerindian identities through the various strands of *indigenismo*. Accordingly, colonial distinctions of race were not simply replaced after independence by the post-colonial promise of universal citizenship. Racism in post-colonial Latin America has instead been *displaced* through citizenship from the juridical–political realm onto other, socio-economic and cultural domains of public life, where ethnicity and colour continue to play a signal role – both oppressive and emancipatory. In Mark Thurner's evocative phrase, the shift has been from 'two republics, to one divided',[66] yet both the sources and continuing dynamics of post-colonial racism in Latin America continue to be tied to the spatial organization of Iberian imperialism.

3
Empire as Market

Markets, understood broadly as social mechanisms of exchange between buyers and sellers, have existed for millennia. The exchange of land, labour and goods – be these precious materials, foodstuffs, machinery or livestock – has in different forms shaped the history of humankind and, more often than not, done so under the auspices of one kind of imperial rule or another. Empires have fostered the administrative, communication, legal and military infrastructure necessary for both long-distance trade and local commerce. They have in turn centrally accrued wealth from such commercial transactions via taxation, customs duties, privateering or the creation of state monopolies. The relationship between empires and markets is therefore in many respects mutually reinforcing: the circulation of products, peoples and money within and across imperial frontiers has contributed to the prosperity of most empires. Similarly, the political order issuing from imperial rule – be it in the provision of a common currency or in the policing of those very frontiers – is instrumental in the sustained reproduction of markets. So central has the flow of commodities been to the historical existence of empires that many have defined empire, and its more active cognate 'imperialism', as the extensive control of extraterritorial markets from an imperial centre, or, put differently, as a structure of economic exploitation of a colonial periphery by a metropolitan core.

It is the aim of the present chapter to explore this connection between empires and markets in greater critical detail. For despite (or perhaps because of) the seemingly self-evident association between the economic reproduction of markets and the political authority of empires, it has been only in the past five hundred years or so that the search for profits has driven imperial expansion – first in the shape of commercial empires, later in the form of capitalist imperialism. It was with the globalization of capital under nineteenth-century British hegemony that the world market emerged as a distinctive social domain governed by a specific form of exchange – what the influential social theorist Karl Polanyi called 'the price-making market'. For Polanyi, this latter form of exchange should be distinguished from what he called 'operational exchange', based on goods simply changing hands (roughly corresponding to barter or kin-based reciprocity), and 'decisional exchange', premised on an extra-economically set rate (approximating a redistributive economy governed by a central political authority). In contrast to this, price-making markets operate through the bargaining of rates, which in turn tend to spread this logic of 'integrative exchange' laterally to other domains of social life. 'The rise of the [price-making] market to a ruling force in the economy', Polanyi averred, 'can be traced by noting the extent to which land and food were mobilized through [integrative] exchange, and labor was turned into a commodity free to be purchased in the market.'[1] And this process, as Karl Marx pointed out a century earlier, had only just kicked off in northwest Europe during the seventeenth century with the primitive accumulation of capital through the dispossession of direct producers from their means of subsistence.

As we noted in the preceding chapter, before the advent of early modern European commercial empires, imperialism had in the main been a land-grabbing exercise chiefly concerned with the extraction of tribute and taxes from subject populations, in some instances complemented by the extensive exploitation of slave labour. Operational or decisional exchange in the form of trade and barter or duties and monopolies certainly played an important role in the reproduction of these pre-modern empires, but such transactions were generally embedded within the broader juridico-political, religious and military structures of imperial rule; markets in this instance oiled the wheels of empire rather than driving the whole imperial juggernaut forward. Indeed, the socially inferior, sometimes pariah-like, or simply 'foreign' status of merchants in many of these pre-modern empires testifies to the subordination of commerce to other landed, military or prebendary sources of wealth.

The rise of European seafaring empires from the fifteenth century marked a shift in the relation between political and economic power as expansion became increasingly market-driven. The juridico-political and military power of the nascent merchant states still played a signal role in guaranteeing the accumulation of commercial wealth by, among other things, licensing and regulating the very companies engaged in intercontinental trading, and supporting their operations diplomatically, financially and occasionally militarily. But the European 'discovery of the sea' was, to employ an anachronism, very much a 'public–private partnership' – with most of the burden falling on the latter part of the relationship. The Iberian colonizing enterprises, as we saw in the earlier chapter, received only nominal state support. They constituted, in the apt words of one economic historian, 'merely a vast contracting-out system' where the crown issued the licence and 'Castilian or Genoese bankers, or other private individuals, put up the money.'[2] Their Dutch and English successors developed a more symbiotic relationship with juridical and political authority, but their own trading companies remained joint-stock ventures privately responsible for everything from credit-management to the construction, administration and defence of their overseas commercial outposts. Early modern European imperialism, then, notwithstanding different degrees and forms of state sponsorship, regulation and intervention, was essentially propelled by the private interest of merchants. Moreover, under such mercantilist arrangements, the imperial state no longer expected surplus in land, booty or tribute but sought revenue instead by extracting taxes, duties or loans from commercial enterprises concerned with profits in overseas trade.

In the course of the nineteenth century, this inversion in the historical relation between states and markets became even more pronounced, eventually resolving itself in the form of a distinctively capitalist imperialism. Here, profits were not merely generated in a mercantile fashion by exploiting price differentials between separate markets ('buying cheap and selling dear', as the saying goes). They were now being realized mainly in the process of capitalist production – that is, the competitive exploitation of wage labour for the valorization of capital. Moreover, rather than being exploited directly at the periphery to be accumulated in or redistributed through the metropolitan centre, capital and labour-power were now being exported as commodities from the metropolitan core to the colonial peripheries, and indeed beyond. By the turn of the twentieth century, the early modern commercial empires had either been transformed, as in the British and French cases, into properly capitalist empires or, as in the Spanish and Portuguese cases, been superseded by the newly industrializing German, Japanese or American capitalist imperialism.

The difference made above between properly capitalist (or price-making) markets and early or pre-modern commercial circuits is a subtle one which, as will be discussed in a later section, ultimately hinges on the role of commodified land and labour in the accumulation of wealth. 'What we must be clear about', Eric Wolf suggested in his magisterial account of modern world history, 'is the analytical distinction between the employment of wealth in the pursuit of further wealth, and capitalism as a qualitatively different mode of committing social labour to the transformation of nature.'[3] It is also an important distinction in underlining how the challenging question in this instance is not so much over the relationship between empires and markets in general (that connection is obvious), but rather between particular forms of market and specific expressions of empire. This is exactly the issue which has vexed many theorists, historians and analysts of empire. The early twentieth-century critics of capitalist imperialism were in particular exercised by the question of how and why a mode of production such as capitalism, ostensibly premised on the peaceful, contractual economic exchange by free individuals across states, could take on the violently nationalist, militarist and territorially expansionist character of the 'new' imperialism at the turn of the twentieth century. Why, in short, did the temporal dynamics of the capitalist market adopt the spatial logic of imperialism?

The final part of this chapter is dedicated to surveying, albeit only briefly, the kinds of answers given to this question by Marxist and other, rival theorists of capitalist imperialism. In so doing, we shall also explore the socio-economic and political consequences of this specific type of imperialism. For the globalization of capitalist markets through European and, later, US and Japanese imperialism was not merely an 'economic' process. Capitalist imperialism generated social structures and political forces – ranging from mass nationalism to world communism – which were central to the history of the twentieth century, and arguably continue to shape our world today. As such, the story of capitalist empires is very much, as the closing chapter in the book will argue, the experience of the 'present as history'. Before delving into either the history or the analysis of capitalist imperialism, however, it is necessary to consider at some length the origins and nature of the modern commercial empires which preceded and, in many senses, conditioned this new form of world market.

Trade and empire

If expansion from a territorial centre is one of the essential characteristics of empire, international trade must be seen as a key process in empire-building. Long-distance trade was a feature of successive Muslim empires – from the Ummayads to the Mughals – and it formed an important component of both the Aztec and Incan empires before the Spanish conquest. Recent decades have witnessed the historical retrieval and reassessment of these and other long-standing networks of international trade in and between Asia, Africa and the Americas, bringing to the fore the complex socio-economic and political structures and processes that characterized these civilizations long before European hegemony.[4] Yet, for all this rich and dynamic history of extra-European commercial interaction, long-distance trade has become most closely associated with the rise of European imperialism.

This is so mainly because it was this experience in overseas commercial expansion which, for good or ill, came to dominate subsequent world history.

There was, of course, nothing inevitable or even predictable about such an outcome. Indeed, the riddle of modern world history, in Alan Macfarlane's expression, is not so much why Europeans became globally hegemonic after 1492, but why other contemporaneous centres of economic activity and interaction in Asia, Africa or the Middle East did not get there before. The answers to this type of question are long and complicated, and therefore lie beyond the scope of this short book. But the query itself is relevant to our concerns insofar as it underlines two themes in the history of empire which inform this study, and more specifically the rest of this chapter: firstly, the importance of ruptures over continuities in the development of modern European imperialism, and, secondly, the centrality of 'peripheral' actors in the unfolding of this European expansion.

Towards a world market

The areas of northwest Europe which came to dominate the modern world market from the seventeenth century onwards were relative latecomers to the business of empire. At the time of Columbus's Caribbean landings, England (and certainly Scotland) were backwaters of European, let alone intercontinental, trade. Although England was integrated into the continental markets for wool and later cotton, and the City of London had consolidated itself as a hub of European trade and finance, the extent and density of English economic activity with the outside world was until the start of the seventeenth century dwarfed by that of the Hanseatic League, the Italian republics or the burgeoning Iberian empires.[5] Dutch ports were more closely tied to long-distance commercial networks, particularly through their increasing control of the Baltic carrying trades and their access via inland waterways to the vibrant markets of the Rhine valley and upper Danube. Amsterdam and Rotterdam furthermore benefited from the influx of refugee traders – Jews, Walloons, Huguenots – from Portugal, Spain, France and Flanders, making them cosmopolitan financial and commercial centres. But the Netherlands' subjection to Habsburg domination meant that, until the turn of the sixteenth century, its overseas expansion was curbed and diverted by Spanish military power and economic interests.

European commercial ascendancy is therefore very much a fitful story of Iberian imperial overstretch and decline being exploited by new Protestant polities in the context of deep and prolonged socio-economic upheaval and political–military conflict across Europe. It was certainly not the seamless outcome of some inherently enterprising Western spirit which, armed with superior technology and ideological purpose, delivered the natural expansion of markets through the fabled human tendency to truck and barter. Rather, European commercial expansion, though no doubt infused with some of these driving forces, was essentially the result of military competition over lucrative trade routes. The common denominator in this process was the search for profit in trade, but the way in which this objective was pursued varied considerably among successive European commercial powers. Profit-making and war-making combined in generally complementary fashion, boosting both trade-related industries such as shipbuilding and rope-making, and services such as maritime insurance and finance, as well as swelling state revenues in customs, excises, taxes and levies. In the end, it was the capacity to harness political and military power to the dictates of trade which shaped European overseas expansion during the 'long' sixteenth century: 'While the Iberian powers fell prey to foreign commerce and France eschewed it, the United Provinces of the Netherlands and England adapted to it successfully.'[6] And the key elements to this successful adaptation were, tellingly, the two historical sources of Roman *imperium*: law and war.

At the heart of Dutch and English colonial expansion were their respective East India companies. Much has been made of the innovative business practices and corporate organization of both the Vereenigde Oostindische Compagnie (VOC, or Dutch United East India Company, established in 1602) and 'the Company of Merchants of London trading into the East Indies' (otherwise known as the East India Company,

EIC, chartered in 1600). A clear, concise and exclusive patent to monopolize trade with Asia, the right to export bullion for this purpose, a transparent and efficient operational structure, and, perhaps most importantly, their constitution as joint-stock ventures are generally cited as instances of such innovation.[7] Yet many of these practices were adapted from earlier Genoese and Venetian experiences – certainly that of pooling of risk into long-term or permanent joint-stock companies. What distinguished the early history of the Anglo-Dutch companies from that of their Italian forerunners was the unprecedented combination of the state's public authority with the private resources of merchants. It was the legal mandate to exploit the Eastern trade routes, with all the prerogatives this entailed, and not merely the operational capability to do so, that arguably strengthened the commercial prospects of the two companies. 'The underpinning of this confident outlook', one historian of the English company suggests, 'can be found in the nature of the relationship the Company shared with the state through its royal charter.'[8]

By effectively transferring responsibility over external economic relations to the chartered companies, the state authorities acknowledged their secondary, supporting role in Dutch and English commercial expansion. This, however, was an entirely calculated political decision. It represented a mutually beneficial division of labour among the different factions of the ruling class, and was not tantamount to the state's abdication of its role as ultimate guarantor of law and order – either domestically or internationally. True, the English state initially kept at a safe distance from the EIC, committing fewer resources to the company than its Dutch counterpart and even rescinding the company's charter in 1653 under Cromwell's Commonwealth. Yet the passing of the first Navigation Acts in 1651 establishing an English monopoly over the carrying trade into and out of English ports suggests that this was a tactical – though of course not unimportant – policy decision within a broader mercantilist strategy of supporting national prosperity through overseas trade. The restitution of the EIC's charter in 1657 and the subsequent passing of the second Navigation Act in 1660 under the restored monarchy presaged what was to be a century and a half of profitable partnership between crown and company.[9]

In the Dutch case, the marriage of coercion and commerce had been transparent from the outset of the VOC's foundation. Contrary to the EIC's charter, the VOC was granted regal rights to wage war, make peace, and sign treaties with foreign entities as well as exercising juridico-political sovereignty over its overseas 'factories'. The connections between the company's seventeen-strong governing body (the Heeren-XVII) and the Dutch States General were so tight 'that until Japan's destruction of the Netherlands' imperial rule in the 1940s Compagnie and Holland were one and the same thing to the indigenous peoples of Indonesia.'[10]

Despite fierce competition, and the increasing subversion of their monopolies by smugglers and interlopers, the second half of the seventeenth century saw the two companies controlling the vast bulk of European trade with Asia. The Dutch company was initially far more profitable than its English counterpart, the latter weakened both by a limited mandate and by civil war at home, but by the end of the seventeenth century the EIC was paying spectacular dividends of up to 50 per cent on initial capital.[11] For its part, the VOC delivered an average of 18.7 per cent return on initial investment during the first century of its existence.[12] Public authorities were not oblivious to this wealth and, in exchange for their political sponsorship, levied taxes and duties on traded goods that accounted for a significant percentage of public revenue – in the British case, well over half of the state's total income between 1750 and 1815.[13] When faced with financial difficulties, each state could always turn to its respective company for loans on privileged terms. In England the sums escalated from £15,000 in 1659 to £70,000 in 1667. By 1709, the government could demand that the company's entire capital (£3 million) be mortgaged to the crown.[14] Under the Dutch arrangements this often involved the reversal of conventional roles, with the company itself lending warships to the States General.

In the course of the seventeenth century, then, England and Holland had moved from being the laggards in the process of European overseas expansion to becoming the world's largest and most powerful mercantile empires. They had created Western counterparts to their East India companies, thereby encroaching on Iberian and French interests in the Americas. They had moreover interconnected these colonial outposts into a commercial network which was supremely rich in the range and quantity of products and indeed peoples trafficked, but also in its capacity to direct such circulation of wealth, credit and power from and towards the metropolitan centres. The Dutch in particular were so successful in imposing their commercial supremacy on Asian markets that they effectively usurped age-old trading patterns in the Indian and Pacific oceans by linking their own regional network of fortified entrepôts, along the littorals of the Indian Ocean, the South China Sea, and as far north as Nagasaki, with the Dutch East India capital of Batavia.[15] Whatever the primary driving force behind this extraordinary commercial reach, and notwithstanding the eventual decline of one of its hegemonic powers, the century-long expansion of Anglo-Dutch trading colonies across all five continents resulted in the creation for the first time of an integrated, intercontinental world market in goods, people and money.

As we have already seen, this process was in no sense purely 'economic' or commercial. If the legal–political recognition of private monopoly in overseas trade was the domestic precondition for the successful operation of the Dutch and English companies, their military–diplomatic protection abroad constituted the guarantee of their enduring profitability. No one was more aware of the need, when seeking economic gains, for buttressing commercial acumen with the persuasive power of violence than the governor general of the VOC himself. 'You gentlemen ought to know from experience', he famously wrote to his directors in 1614, 'that trade in Asia should be conducted and maintained under the protection and with the aid of your own weapons, and that those weapons must be wielded with the profits gained by the trade. So trade cannot be maintained without war, nor war without trade.'[16] The interchangeable use of 'protection' and 'war' in this statement is quite revealing, for there was more than a passing resemblance between the VOC's Asian operations and that of modern-day protection rackets. At the height of its power in the mid-seventeenth century, the VOC could interpret its Eastern monopoly as excluding from Asian markets not just other Dutch traders, but any foreign merchant. On several occasions during the latter decades of that century the Dutch deployed their own version of gunboat diplomacy by threatening to enforce, or actually enforcing, their monopoly by bombarding spice towns which dared to trade with competing nations.[17] The Dutch also used forceful population transfers, the violent eradication of competing spice plantations and ruthless policing of indigenous clove production towards this end.[18]

The brunt of the violence, however, was reserved for European rivals. No matter how much they might try to avoid their opponent's spheres of influence, or indeed protest their interest in 'trade, not war', no merchant company could escape the violent competition for trade routes. By the turn of the eighteenth century every major European power had trading companies seeking to penetrate the markets of Asia, Africa and the Americas. In a mercantilist world where existing wealth was deemed to be finite and profit was generated not through productivity gains but by the transfer of goods from one market to another, the onus was on the absolute and exclusive control of trade. And, at the time, the tried and tested way to exercise such control was to defeat the competition in war.

For the better part of the following century Europeans did just this by engaging in protracted international warfare on their own continent and beyond with the primary aim of curbing their rivals' share of this emerging world market. The imperialist character of such competition became apparent if nothing else in the European assumption that their own disputes could be resolved by carving up other people's lands and resources. During the first half of the century, the Dutch wrenched control from the Portuguese of the more significant East Indian sea lanes and forts in a sequence of naval battles. The Anglo-Dutch trade wars of the 1660s and 1670s were, it is true, eventually settled in the peaceful 'business merger' of 1688.[19] But thereafter it was France which posed the biggest threat to the new British state and its emerging global hegemony. During the Seven Years' War of 1756–63 this continental rivalry was fought out in North America, the Caribbean and Asia, drawing in not only the peoples of these regions but also Prussians, Russians, Spaniards, Portuguese and Austrians. It was, one historian of empire has suggested, 'the nearest thing the eighteenth century had to world war . . . at stake was the future of empire itself. The question was simply this: Would the world be French or British?'[20]

We now know the answer was, eventually, the latter. Yet the British domination over the modern world market came at a price. One casualty of the Seven Years' War was Britain's thirteen American colonies, the loss of which unfolded in a complex process of anti-colonial struggle tied famously to the democratic claims for representation in return for largely war-related taxation. The American War of Independence formed part of the broader Atlantic 'Age of Democratic Revolutions' and presaged an era of nationalist resistance to empire across the globe. As it happened, the loss of the thirteen colonies did not diminish British access to American markets, but it did, notwithstanding military defeat, mark a shift towards a territorialized and militarized form of imperial control prompted, in large measure, by such resistance. Whereas Tudor and Stuart England had aimed to create a maritime empire of commerce, emulating the Portuguese and Dutch reliance on coastal entrepôts rather than Spanish inland conquest and settlement, Hanoverian Britain found itself increasingly entangled in campaigns to control and administer foreign lands and their inhabitants. The implications of these interconnected developments became fully apparent only with the 'new' imperialism of the late nineteenth century. But already in the course of the eighteenth century some of the tensions inherent in the imperial rule of a world market were in evidence: the struggle was no longer chiefly over access to trade routes or the monopoly of commercial exchange in prized goods; it now involved wars over the control of inland areas and the administration of subject populations. Peoples and territories, not just luxuries and bullion, were once again becoming the source of imperialist rivalry, and this was to give seemingly peripheral actors of the colonized regions a central role in the construction of empires.

Imperial transformations at the centre and periphery

The discussion of trade and empire has thus far focused on European commercial expansion in Asia. Yet the rise of the modern world market has its origins in the Iberian conquest of the Americas. It is time now, therefore, to pay closer attention to the place of the Western hemisphere in the construction of imperial markets, not least because European imperialism in the West was built on a unique feature – largely absent in its Eastern expansion – which is critical to the relationship between empires and markets, namely large-scale settlement.

The European colonization of the Americas and the Caribbean had two signal consequences for the development of the world market. The first of these was the supply of bullion that fed the early modern European commercial expansion discussed above. Silver and gold plundered from the Americas not only financed the military revolution which underpinned such expansion, it also provided the initial means of exchange in European trade with the East. It furthermore encouraged the establishment of financial, commercial and insurance institutions necessary for the completion of such transactions, as well as creating a substantial market for overseas luxury goods in urban Europe. A second key result of European settlement of the Western hemisphere was the opening of untapped sources of production and consumption in the New World. European colonizers not only extended westwards the circuits of Eurasian commerce, they also integrated indigenous Americans and their natural resources into this nascent Atlantic economy and, crucially, created a new market in African slave labour used to man American and Caribbean sugar, cotton, coffee, indigo and tobacco plantations. By the mid-eighteenth century the New World colonies of settlement were fuelling an economic recovery in Europe following the seventeenth-century crisis, with the infamous triangular trade in African slaves, American stimulants and European firearms contributing towards the incipient industrialization of the first capitalist nation.

Different waves and patterns of European settlement delivered diverse forms of consumption and production. As we saw in the preceding chapter, Spanish settlement was concentrated in urban centres geared primarily towards the administration of tribute and plunder. Agricultural production remained closely tied to the provision of local mining towns and political capitals, and was therefore not initially linked to overseas trade. Portuguese colonization on the other hand was from the outset organized around the cultivation of sugar for export. Here conquest delivered a plantation economy powered by slave labour and directed towards the exclusive supply of agricultural staples to metropolitan markets. A third form of settlement was that pioneered by the English in the first of their Western overseas colonial forays – to Ireland. As opposed to the Spanish lust for silver and gold or the Portuguese desire to profit from the cultivation and export of marketable crops, English colonialism was initially motivated by the more sober ambition of simply 'improving' land.

Behind this seemingly prosaic aspiration, however, lay the foundations of the type of empire which was to triumph in later centuries. This was a form of colonialism driven by what Ellen Meiksins Wood has labelled the 'economic imperatives' of agrarian capitalism, that is, the extraction of profits through the commercialization of land rights and the accompanying commodification of both agricultural labour and its products. By the turn of the seventeenth century, such capitalist imperatives had made significant inroads into the social relations of the English countryside, and so the initial ambition of Tudor expansion was to emulate this new productive system: 'The stated intention [of Tudor colonization of Ireland] was to reproduce the social property relations of south-east England, introducing the landlord–tenant relation that had been establishing itself in the English countryside, with the object of reproducing English commercial agriculture.'[21] At the core of this enterprise was the use of English and Scottish settlers as living agents of capitalist transformation, as purveyors of an economic logic of productivity, differentiated from the prevailing customary rights to land, and premised on the market-led 'improvement' of farmland through the proper, commercial exploitation of enclosed land by tenant farmers and their waged employees. As one contemporary advocate of this new capitalist colonialism eloquently put it:

> [c]ivility cannot possibly be planted among them [the Irish] by this mixed plantation of some of the natives and settling of their possessions in a course of Common Law. ... half their

land doth now lie waste, by reason whereof that which is
habited is not improved to half the value; but when the
undertakers [the settlers] are planted among them . . ., and
that land shall be fully stocked and manured, 500 acres will
be of better value than 5000 are now.[22]

The problem with this kind of scheme was, of course, that
those subject to such colonialism were not generally per-
suaded by the simple logic of economic imperatives. In
Ireland, as elsewhere in the world, this type of plantation
settlement was to encounter opposition among locals, particularly those classes which stood to lose land, freedom or
status by accepting the laws of capitalist productivity. In the
specific context of English colonization of the Americas,
indigenous resistance to the encroachments of the market,
coupled with the peculiar social composition of the colonists
and, not least important, the environmental and demographic
constraints on capitalist agriculture led to the reproduction
of all kinds of economic regimes but those characterized by
capitalist imperatives. Paradoxically, the attempts at forcefully transplanting capitalist social relations across the Atlantic through settlement eventually led to the prevalence of
non-capitalist modes of exploitation in Britain's American
and Caribbean colonies, the most powerful of which became
slavery.

The contradiction of a world market created through
imperial rivalry finds one of its most acute expressions in the
coexistence – some argue, combination[23] – of plantation
slavery in the colonies with capitalist development in the
metropole. At the end of the eighteenth century, Britain was
experiencing the birth pangs of its first industrial revolution.
The mechanization of production, the concentration of wage
workers in urban centres and their employment in factories
or through work regimes dominated by a rationalized division of labour all contributed, by the first decades of the
nineteenth century, to the acceleration of productivity gains
and the deepening of capitalist market relations in both town
and country. Yet Britain's merchant marine had by then also
become the largest transatlantic carriers of African slaves,
and its planters major purchasers of slave labour in the Americas and the Caribbean, second only to the Brazilians. By the

turn of the nineteenth century, West Indian colonies accounted for close to 30 per cent of British imports, while 'the share of exports taken by the plantation-related Atlantic markets [rose] from 43 per cent to 57–59 per cent over the period 1784 to 1806.'[24] At that time, Britain certainly remained the celebrated 'workshop of the world', characterized as it was by an unassailable leadership in the processing and production of primary products and manufactured goods ranging from cotton to cast iron, its domination in the export of these and other commodities, and their domestic consumption by an extensive home market. But such production and consumption was closely tied to the economies of the Atlantic seaboard: the American and Caribbean plantations not only sourced staples of the British coffee houses and breakfast tables and, after 1800, the raw cotton used to manufacture the clothing of many seated at those tables; they also served as key export markets for the more dynamic British industries of the period, including wrought iron and textiles.[25]

Underpinning this intense circulation of commodities was the Atlantic slave trade itself. The Portuguese were the first to import slave labour from West African trading stations to their Atlantic sugar plantations during the late fifteenth century. Thereafter, Dutch, French and English slaving companies fought for this Atlantic market in humans, forcibly transporting an estimated 1,314,000 Africans to America and the West Indies in the course of the seventeenth century. It was the eighteenth century, however, that witnessed the sharpest rise in cross-Atlantic traffic, now dominated by British traders: from 1701 to 1810 an estimated 6 million captive Africans arrived on New World shores – an average ranging from 60,000 to 80,000 a year – overwhelmingly destined for the sugar plantations of British Jamaica and French St Domingue. Despite the British abolition of its Atlantic slave trade in 1807, a further 2 million African slaves had landed on Caribbean shores by 1870.[26] Approximately 1 million – about 15 per cent – of the captives transported during the eighteenth century did not survive the Middle Passage, while one scholar estimated that, 'in order to deliver nine million slaves to the coast in the entire period 1700–1850, some twenty-one million people were probably captured – the gap between the two figures is explained by the death of five million within a year of capture and the reduction of a further seven million to slavery in Africa, helping to sustain the African-based apparatus of capture and commerce.'[27]

Several questions central to our understanding of empire as market emerge from this discussion. The first relates to the economic contribution of the periphery (in this instance the Atlantic colonies) to the industrialization of the metropolitan centre (in this case Britain). As we shall see later in the chapter, many theories of empire and imperialism hinge on the answer to this question, with some claiming that European industrial development required the simultaneous economic underdevelopment of its colonies, while others argue the exact opposite, namely that it was capitalist imperialism which developed the colonies economically. The experience of the 'first' British empire explored above indicates that capitalist markets at home can readily coexist with non-capitalist exchange abroad, thus seemingly backing a view of imperialism as the structurally unequal economic exchange between metropolitan core and colonial periphery. Indeed, in one of the more careful and balanced assessments of the colonial contribution to British industrialization, Robin Blackburn concludes that 'capitalist industrialization in Britain was decisively advanced by its success in creating a regime of extended primitive accumulation and battening upon the super-exploitation of slaves in the Americas.'[28] According to Blackburn, profits realized through the slave trade and the plantation economy were repatriated to the metropole and reinvested in the form of credit, capital and communications infrastructure to account for up to 55 per cent of Britain's gross fixed capital formation on the eve of the industrial revolution in 1770.[29] Moreover, access to the colonial markets of the Atlantic indirectly served to boost metropolitan economic activity in industry (shipbuilding), services (insurance) and revenue-collection (taxes, customs and excise). This does not, it should hastily be added, amount to an argument that colonialism in the Americas begat capitalism in Europe: it is understood that capitalist social and property relations needed to be in place for any colonial remittance to be realized as metropolitan capital. Nor is it to foreclose the argument about the costs and benefits of the British empire *in toto*. The jury is still out on the British empire's profitability, as there exists powerful evidence supporting the free marketeers of the time who claimed that nineteenth-century empire was a drain on British wealth.[30] It is simply to underline the point made long ago by Eric Williams to the effect that 'The profits obtained [through the triangular trade] provided one of the main streams of that accumulation of capital in England which financed the Industrial Revolution.'[31]

The second issue raised by the discussion thus far concerns the role of colonial settlement in the transformation of imperial peripheries. Whatever the socio-economic and political impact of colonialism on the metropole, the white settlement of what one historian has called the 'neo-Europes' of the Americas and, later, Africa and Australasia plainly had a momentous impact on the history of these and indeed other colonial regions and their inhabitants.[32] Among the more obvious consequences were the expropriation of land, the extraction of resources and the violent subjection of the bulk of the autochthonous population to European ways of life, and indeed death. Yet even here there is room for nuance, as neither were all native Americans or Africans passive victims of European commercial expansion, nor were all colonists unreflective instruments of metropolitan domination.

In the course of their mercantile expansion, Europeans encountered societies with their own complex political structures and socio-economic hierarchies, often open to collaboration and accommodation with strangers. This was most painfully apparent in the role of African potentates and merchants in the Atlantic slave trade. Europeans certainly created the demand for chattel slavery in western Africa, and plainly controlled both the trade and exploitation of slaves across the Atlantic. But it was African chiefs, middlemen and slave raiders that supplied this human traffic. West and Central African rulers drew on customary forms of enslavement ranging from pawning, criminal punishment or warbooty to furnish European demand. In exchange they received prestige goods, money and, crucially, firearms and ammunition which played an instrumental role in the political economy and geopolitics of the African regions of supply. At the height of the trade, local middlemen – many of them mulattos – became self-styled 'big men', mustering considerable autonomous coercive, diplomatic and economic resources in their role as brokers between African rulers and their European clients. Even the most violently hierarchical structures of European imperialism such as the Atlantic slave trade were therefore conditioned by the collective and individual agency of non-Europeans: global domination was in this respect very much premised on local collaboration.

The same must be said about the consequences of settlement, either forced or voluntary, on the other side of the Atlantic. Out of American colonization and its attendant population transfers emerged distinctive colonial societies, with their own dynamics of accommodation and resistance and, as we shall see in more detail in the next chapter, with their own creole cultures arising out of both elite and demotic miscegenation. From the very outset of European settlement, dominant and subordinated classes of the New World were entangled in complex processes of socio-economic political struggle and cooperation. Some Amerindian nations became local clients of varying European powers, often drawing on such alliances to defeat competing native American polities and occasionally playing off Europeans against one another. Others, such as the Sioux nation, stereotyped in many a mid-afternoon TV Western, resolutely defied the white man's westward expansion. Similarly, runaway African slaves, free Amerindians and rebellious European sailors and labourers formed independent and much-feared maroon communities which some have portrayed as actually existing democratic utopias that challenged New World oppression.[33] Yet Africans, *petits blancs* and Amerindians (and the offspring of all three) also acted as plantation overseers, bounty-hunters and slave-drivers. Equally, those thousands of subjects of the thirteen colonies loyal to the British crown migrated northwards towards what is now Canada in the course of the American War of Independence. As is often the case, such dissenting groups within the polity often get screened out of nationalist accounts of imperial history.

The eighteenth century witnessed not only a boom in the triangular trade and the consolidation of a distinctive Atlantic market – much of it centred around the economic and social integration of the American mainland and the Caribbean, especially after 1783 – but also the rise of a transnational public sphere which turned the New World into a focal point of political agitation during the two decades either side of the French Revolution. A cross-Atlantic Republic of Letters was forged around the writings and political activities of luminaries of the time such as Tom Paine, Simón Bolívar, Thomas Jefferson or Francisco de Miranda. It would be difficult to understand the Latin American revolutions which followed the Napoleonic Wars without reference to this new creole internationalism. Perhaps the most emblematic event of this period was the slave revolt which, under the leadership of Toussaint L'Ouverture, delivered the Republic of Haiti, formerly the French plantation colony of St Domingue.

The European colonization of the New World was, in sum, the product of a mercantile search for profit which by the end of the eighteenth century had created an Atlantic market under an unequivocally imperial aegis. But such hierarchical commercial expansion and its attendant population transfers did not unfold without political struggle and social upheaval, both at home and abroad. Markets are never just about the economic exchange of commodities but are also, and fundamentally so, about contested and generally antagonistic relations between social classes. The construction of empire, in this instance the 'first' British empire, was therefore as much the product of metropolitan commercial designs as it was the outcome of political accommodation and resistance to such endeavours displayed by colonial subjects.

This last observation points to a third and final issue emerging from a view of imperial markets as relations between core and periphery, this time pertaining to the forms of rule which accompanied European commercial expansion. The modern world market was undoubtedly the product of an imperial – that is, structurally hierarchical – organization of intercontinental trade from and for metropolitan centres. International market exchange was here not the great leveller so beloved of many (neo-)liberal economists, but the exact opposite, namely a mechanism for extracting wealth from subordinate territories and their populations. Yet the fact that European imperial powers were dominant in this process does not mean that they always controlled it. As was mooted earlier, Britain in particular was during the eighteenth century increasingly drawn from coastal trade into inland wars, thereby testing its claim to its having an empire of commerce, not conquest. Insofar as the British state faced this shift reluctantly – at the time it certainly proved militarily and politically unfit for an empire of administration – this drives home the fact that even the most powerful empires are unable to rule under circumstances of their own choosing.

Nowhere was this clearer than in the British experience in India towards the end of the eighteenth century. The British crown had been involved in a costly territorial war over the thirteen American colonies, but only because these were deemed to be settled by its own subjects. In India, however, there were no claims to wasteland needing improvement, no barbarian savages requiring forceful civilization, and therefore no extensive white settlement. The British – following other foreigners before them – had instead made diplomatic and commercial arrangements with long-established and powerful polities. The EIC only operated in India with the license of Mughal authorities, and its business profited considerably from the existing commercial and juridical infrastructure.[34] The company's commercial success during the first century and a half of its existence was in this respect significantly dependent on the fortunes of Mughal rule. Inter-imperial warfare, most notably during the Seven Years' War, coupled with a protracted unravelling of Mughal imperial power across India, eventually led to a general crisis across the subcontinent by mid-century. The response from the company's 'men-on-the-spot' such as Robert Clive and Warren Hastings was to seize the crisis as an opportunity for territorial expansion. In the space of two decades after the end of the Seven Years' War, the three EIC presidencies at Madras, Bombay and Calcutta grabbed administrative, fiscal and military control of their respective hinterlands from Mughal rulers. By 1784, and not without considerable political controversy and turmoil at Westminster and beyond, the EIC was reorganized as a revenue-collecting bureaucracy with a military and diplomatic branch ostensibly directed from the government's Board of Control in London. From then until the company's demise in 1857 its original functions were taken over by other agents: the monopoly over trade was eroded by independent merchants – both local and overseas – while the security and defence of the company's jurisdictions were now managed by the Indian Army. In sum, the division of labour between crown and company set by the original charter had, by the turn of the nineteenth century, been inverted and its principal source of wealth transformed. Instead of profit in trade, the company now collected and administered revenue in tax. For its part, the British state, contrary to its original arm's-length relation to the EIC, now controlled the company and governed over its Indian jurisdictions.

Whatever the sources of this shift towards militarized territorial rule in India – and the evidence points to a haphazard and contingent process on the ground rather than some grand strategy masterminded from London – the results indicate that the British state was ill-prepared for land-based imperial administration in the style of Roman or Spanish empires. Indeed, for the remainder of their presence in India, the British experimented with forms of 'indirect rule' in the subcontinent which had significant implications for the development not only of that part of the world but also the regions of Africa and the Middle East, where a similar template was later adopted. As we shall see in the following section, British imperialism in India after 1857 was characterized by a perverse combination of selective capitalist development and tributary forms of governance. Political authority was delegated to a disparate range of indigenous rulers (some of them granted legitimacy through 'invented traditions') while responsibility for the military was transferred to an Indian Army largely reliant on local soldiers.[35] At the end of the nineteenth century, the vast territory of the British Raj was still administered by approximately 950 European officials and policed by a mere 50,000 (mainly Indian) troops.[36] If even the jewel in the crown of the Great British empire could not be ruled without the assistance of indigenous maharajas, sepoys and zamindars, what hope was there for a metropolitan control over the more marginal regions of empire? How could an empire built on commerce, 'improvement' and industry succumb to the extraction of wealth through tribute, tax and – in its Western reaches – slavery? Was not Britain's rule in India evidence of how the 'empire of liberty' was being corrupted into the vilest form of 'Oriental despotism'?

The consequences of capitalist imperialism

These and other related questions were at the heart of British political debate at the turn of the nineteenth century and indeed spurred on a distinctive British contribution to the history of ideas on imperialism and anti-imperialism thereafter.[37] In the event, British territorial expansion experienced a relative lull for the fifty or so years after Waterloo until the advent of the 'new' imperialism of the 1880s and 1890s. Its rule in India, despite continued territorial aggrandizement in the subcontinent, did not occasion further corruption at the heart of empire, but rather coincided with profound political reform and socio-economic transformation in the metropole, led principally by domestic social forces. But most significant, the Georgian debates over empire and liberty soon became superseded as the contours of a new type of empire began to take shape in the wake of the Napoleonic Wars. This was an empire of capital, driven no longer exclusively, or even mainly, by the search for wealth in trade, but rather increasingly concerned with realizing profit through investment. International exchange continued to play a pivotal role in this new imperialism, but the wealth-creating transaction was now between workers and capitalists, less between merchants and traders. Markets were increasingly geared towards production, not consumption, capitalists more interested in the creation of value through the exploitation of labour, not merely in making commercial gain by circulating commodities from one market to another. Most important of all, the world economy of the nineteenth century did not just include the exchange in luxuries, manufactured goods, raw materials or primary products, but began to entangle more and more of the world's peoples and territories in the laws of the capitalist market. It was the protracted and uneven, but largely irreversible, commodification of land and labour-power that above all characterized this properly capitalist world market. And it was the autonomous logic of this 'price-making' world market, increasingly separated from the political power of states, that gave capitalist imperialism its distinctive features and contradictions.

The transformation of the world market through the globalization of capital was initially a very British affair. The United Kingdom emerged from the Napoleonic Wars not only militarily and diplomatically triumphant, but also as the most powerful capitalist economy in the world. Until the industrialization of its continental rivals in the second half of the nineteenth century, and the consolidation of capitalist social relations in post-Reconstruction USA and Meiji Japan, the world economy was dominated by Britain. In 1840 the UK accounted for the bulk of the world's coal, iron and steel production and unsurprisingly produced 40 per cent of the global economy's value in hardware.[38] During the following three decades world trade increased fivefold, and by 1874 'Britain probably accounted for two-fifths of it, nearly as much as the total of France, Germany and the United States together.'[39] Britain was, until the mid-nineteenth century, by far the largest exporter of capital, investing abroad four times the value of its closest rival, France.[40] Finally, and in large measure resulting from this central role in the world economy, sterling became the currency of international trade and the City of London the capital of global credit and financial services.

Yet only a relatively small fraction of this international economic activity involved Britain's formal empire. Most foreign direct investment until the 1870s went to the USA and Latin America, if it left Europe at all. Similarly, the bulk of Britain's trade throughout the nineteenth century was with markets outside its imperial domains. This lack of correspondence between Britain's colonial territories and its chief economic partners led some historians of empire to speak of 'the imperialism of free trade', where the indirect influence of markets and not the direct administration of territories served as the prevailing mechanisms of imperial expansion. This device, Robinson and Gallagher suggested in their seminal piece on the subject, 'had the advantage of saddling foreign governments with the liability of rule whilst allowing Britons the commercial advantage.'[41]

One important implication of such an argument is that British capital and its attendant financial, commercial and monetary institutions were during the mid-Victorian period creating a world economy with an autonomous logic from that of the military or diplomatic impetus of historical empires. Put differently, empire and imperialism were increasingly being detached from their old geopolitical moorings, and increasingly associated with the newly independent, profit-maximizing dynamics of a market which cut across national borders. Pushed further, the argument might even suggest that, instead of imperial power, Britain was exercising leadership or hegemony in an open, competitive economy, and remained uninterested in controlling and administering foreign lands and peoples in the fashion of previous empires. The expansive flow of the market was, on this reading, trumping the static hierarchies of territorial empires, and the military–diplomatic corollary to this was a 'blue water' policy built around the maritime control of the world's major sea lanes and the off-shore balancing of continental rivals.[42] Many liberal advocates of free trade, most prominently Richard Cobden, argued in the middle decades of the nineteenth century that an open international economy would do away with the waste, corruption and inequality that accompanied empires. Even some of Marx's own writings at the time echoed the liberals in suggesting that the cosmopolitan logic of market exchange would eventually triumph over irrational nationalist parochialism, ethnic bigotry and aristocratic privilege attached to empires. Capitalism in this respect was the gravedigger of empires.

Such understandings of the relationship between markets and empire during the global expansion of industrial capitalism would, however, be both misleading and inaccurate. For a start, any absolute separation between formal and informal imperialism does violence to Gallagher and Robinson's own argument, which was aimed not at replacing the notion of 'imperialism of administration' with that of 'imperialism of free trade', but rather at emphasizing the complementary relation between these two expressions of empire in upholding British paramountcy 'by informal means if possible, or by formal annexations when necessary'.[43] Moreover, the period of 'free trade imperialism' was relatively short-lived:

as we shall shortly see, the outbreak of inter-imperial rivalry and protectionism in the last decades of the nineteenth century, the carve-up of Africa that accompanied it, and the world war to which it led belie the notion that industrial capitalism replaced the archaic and hierarchical structures of empire with a peaceful, cosmopolitan world market. Rather, as Giovanni Arrighi has suggested, two distinct logics of power combined to give imperialism a uniquely capitalist inflection at this time: the one, territorial insofar as it 'conceive[s] of wealth/capital as a means or a by-product of the pursuit of territorial expansion', the other capitalist in that it 'identif[ies] power with the extent of . . . command over scarce resources and consider[s] territorial acquisitions as a means and by-product of the accumulation of capital.'[44] The critical contribution of this distinction is that it highlights the paradox whereby the increased mobility of industrial factors of production in the capitalist world market – including of course wage labour – presented political authorities with the challenge of controlling and regulating such movements. The global reproduction of capitalism and the intensification of empire- and state-building during the late nineteenth and early twentieth centuries are on this account entirely compatible: they simply point to the concrete historical unfolding of the dialectical tension between abstract forms of territorial and capitalist logic.

Accepting this claim, however, still leaves us with a related problem of historical causality associated with the notion of capitalist imperialism. For many critics of the term, speaking of capitalist imperialism suggests that British – and other European – overseas expansion in the nineteenth century had strictly economic causes; that it was industrial capitalism, with its relentless search for fresh markets, that drove the British and other European powers into a violent frenzy of territorial annexation and led Britain, in Roland Robinson's evocative phrase, to 'colour most of the world's map in red'. Yet, such sceptics point out, if economics was the motivation, British nineteenth-century imperialism proved to be one huge mistake, since by the start of the twentieth century, they argue, the empire was burdening the British taxpayer with costs greater than it was delivering in economic benefits. Moreover, as we have just seen, most of capitalist investment during the nineteenth century was outside the circuits of empire. Other critics have, from a slightly different angle, questioned the 'diffusionist' assumptions implicit in the terminology of capitalist imperialism, suggesting that it underplays the role of non-Europeans in the construction of modern empires.[45] Finally, political historians cast doubt on the coherence between economic interests and policy outcomes, or indeed on the existence of any kind of consistent imperialist policy, indicating that European imperial expansion was more the result of contingency and improvisation – generated, *inter alia*, by factional politics, inter-departmental rivalries and the highly mediated chains of command and communication between metropole and periphery – than the consequence of an imperial grand strategy.[46]

Important as they are, none of these factual statements or qualifications strictly precludes using the label 'capitalist imperialism' to describe and explain the renewed processes of European overseas expansion in the nineteenth century. Few scholars would dispute that the unprecedented economic integration of the world market during the course of the nineteenth century was the result of capitalist industrialization in Europe and North America. Marx and Engels were surely right when they claimed that 'The need of a constantly expanding market for its products chases the bourgeoisie over the whole surface of the globe.' The self-valorizing logic of capital and its competition with other capitals has indeed 'given a cosmopolitan character to production and consumption in every country'.[47] It was the enormous advances in communications, transport, technology and finance, all fuelled by industrial capitalism, which facilitated and spurred on the imperial circuits of capital. Regardless of the success or desirability of the outcome, the construction and reproduction of a capitalist world market was necessarily 'diffusionist': the economic imperatives propelling capitalist globalization at the start of the nineteenth century originated in Europe and were at that time absent elsewhere. To that extent, however important the contribution of Asians, Africans and Latin Americans to the construction and reproduction of a capitalist world market, it was always under the aegis of European dominance. Simply emphasizing the 'excentric' sources of European imperialism – whether these were deferential or defiant – only brings us back to the original question of why Europeans might have sought peripheral allies and collaborators in the first place.

That most European empires were by the turn of the twentieth century neither profitable nor directly at the service of the dominant business interests does not diminish the capitalist character of their imperialism. Significant sectors of the European ruling class may not have profited directly from imperial expansion, but enough *bona fide* capitalists organized 'for-themselves' around a *Parti Colonial* or a *Kolonialverein* in order to lobby and promote, generally successfully, the imperialist penetration of other continents. Their business decisions may have occasionally proved disastrous, but they were still guided by the prospects of profit through capitalist investment: bankruptcy does not make a company any more or less capitalist. In any event, even if capital export to the colonies is considered as insignificant for the economic development of the metropole, it was plainly not so for the periphery.

Most important of all, the notion that capitalist imperialism denotes a purely 'economic' process needs to be challenged. From its very origins, the reproduction of the global capitalist market relied on public bodies and coercive institutions capable of guaranteeing private contracts, enforcing property rights, providing communications infrastructure and securing investment in the factors of production. This might explain why, for most of the nineteenth century and beyond, metropolitan capital seeking profit overseas directed investment overwhelmingly to other economies where the process of primitive accumulation was complete and basic public infrastructure was in place. The global circulation of capital during that period was in that respect premised on the earlier phases of European expansion and conquest. Whenever European capital ventured to lands where market dependence and modern sovereignty had not yet been established, it was left to the colonial state and its coercive apparatus to attempt such transformations. Juridico-political and military–diplomatic dimensions of state power have therefore always accompanied capitalist social relations: they adopted an imperialist character, intoxicated with the territorialist logic of power, only where the conditions for the expanded reproduction of a capitalist market society were absent. To that extent, once more, the capitalist imperatives driving European expansion were not merely 'economic' in a narrow, liberal sense but also found expression, albeit in a peculiarly capitalist form, as Europeans extended their military domination and political rule over the peoples of Africa, Asia and the Middle East.

Regardless of whether industrial capitalism is considered a cause of the 'new' imperialism of the late nineteenth century, it certainly became a consequence of imperialism on the periphery. European and, later, American and Japanese colonies were transformed by the forces of industrial capitalism, delivering a new world characterized in large measure by the modern phenomena of wage labour, urbanization, mass politics, territorial sovereignty and total war. Such globalization of capitalism through imperial structures produced very uneven results, both socially and geographically, often, as we shall see in the next chapter, reorganizing and reasserting existing hierarchies of kin, caste and ethnicity or, more frequently, grafting new racial categories onto emerging class divisions. In many instances across Africa, South America and Asia, aspects of industrial capitalism combined in the most invidious ways with pre-capitalist forms of exploitation, including slavery and various forms of bonded labour. But the modern history of colonial and post-colonial societies would be difficult to explain without reference to the attempts at imposing capitalist social relations from the metropole and the social contradictions and transformations this elicited.

The export of railways is a good illustration of how this new logic of capitalist accumulation came to mobilize enormous human and natural resources within and across empires in its quest to realize profits. If the merchant ship concentrated within its hull the various socio-economic and political features of seventeenth- and eighteenth-century mercantilist empires, under nineteenth- and twentieth-century industrial capitalism it was the railway that played this emblematic role. Railroads expressed the acceleration and intensification of industrial activity in their British birthplace: they transported and consumed the coal that powered the second industrial revolution; they were built with the iron and steel and the engineering expertise that gave Britain its technological edge in this and other fields; and they displayed in their operations many of the new characteristics of Victorian capitalism – from the organization and financing of investment to the accelerated communication and deepening integration between regional economic hubs.

Many of these features were to accompany the impressive expansion of railways outside of Europe and North America in the four decades after 1850. Before that date no country in Africa, Asia or Latin America (with the exception of Cuba) possessed a railway; by 1880 there were 9,300 miles of railway in India alone and 2,900 across Africa.[48] Although this still amounted to only 8 per cent of worldwide railway mileage at that time, the effect on the political economy, demography and geography of these regions was to be profound.[49] For a start, railway construction reproduced capitalist social relations in the colonies by creating waged employment for a whole range of indigenous and immigrant workers – navvies, machinists, foremen, clerks and stationmasters – and attracting both local and foreign capital, with its attendant professionals – engineers, surveyors, financiers, prospectors – to these areas. Many of these groups brought with them not just their labour-power and expertise, but also new forms of political mobilization and social organization ranging from trade unions to chambers of commerce. Secondly, as in the metropolitan centre, rail construction on the periphery linked different regions – town and country, inland and littoral, plain and mountain – often for the first time, thus spurring on the development or reconstruction of home markets in both goods and people, and all the possibilities this generated for 'national' forms of socio-economic and political exchange. Railways made such activity relatively fixed and permanent, and so, as in the metropolitan centre, urbanization – and with it disease, prejudice and poverty – followed the rail track as new neighbourhoods, suburbs and even entire towns across Asia and Africa emerged along rail routes. Finally, and by no means least important, the construction, management and operation of these emerging rail networks required the public authority of the state: land titles had to be secured; huge sums of public and private funds needed to be raised and regulated, rail workers and train passengers policed and protected and rail infrastructure maintained and replaced. Although the division of labour between public and private authority and wealth varied considerably across different regions of the periphery, the enforcement of private property rights – be they in railway stock or the land which the tracks ran through – was a requirement for any significant investment in such monumental engineering projects.

The export of capital to the colonies, rather than its mere accumulation in the metropole, was, then, the first novel aspect of capitalist empires. A second feature was the mobilization across the empire of commodified labour-power. As we have already seen, empires have historically been a conduit for colossal population transfers across land and sea through slavery, conquest, commerce and war. This continued into the age of capitalist empires, but now millions of imperial subjects moved across oceans to engage principally in contracted labour. Here again, two important qualifications reflect the contradictions of capitalist imperialism. Firstly, most European workers migrated to centres of accumulation outside their respective empires: labour transfers followed capital flows. Secondly, varying forms of indentured labour replaced slavery as the dominant form of imperial labour-power. In this regard, once more, the capitalist wage relation was distorted in the colonies through the racialized filter of imperial hierarchy. A good concrete illustration of such a phenomenon is the use of 'coolieism' – a term denoting forms of wage labour premised on unfree or unequal contract – in fuelling nineteenth-century imperial economies.[50] 'As the rulers of India', one scholar indicates, 'the English had sole control over the second largest supplier of coolie labour in the world, the first being China. They used this reservoir of labour power first and foremost for their own colonies in America, Asia, Africa and Australia, but from time to time they also permitted the recruitment of workers by other colonial powers.'[51] According to Potts's calculations, at least 5 million Indians left their country between 1834 and 1937 to work as coolies in the European mines and plantations of the Caribbean, east and southern Africa, the Indian and Pacific oceans and Australasia. 'As well as Indian coolies', she estimates, 'there were another 5 or 6 million workers at least from other parts of Asia employed under the coolie system to build infrastructure and to produce goods for the world market.'[52]

European empires of the nineteenth and twentieth century, we have seen, introduced two new commodities to the colonies: capital and wage labour, albeit both laced with peculiar hierarchies of imperial control and domination. The world market in capital and labour was thus channelled towards the reproduction of capitalist empires, even if the latter did not directly correspond to the former. The final major European export to the colonies during this era of capitalist imperialism was the sovereign, territorial state. This particular export was of course not meant for native consumption – the late nineteenth century 'standard of civilization' fashioned by leading international lawyers was after all aimed at justifying European sovereignty *over* colonial peoples, not *for* them.[53] Instead, the closure of the colonial frontier and attempts at establishing territorially exclusive, bureaucratically centralized colonial states emerged during this period as a mechanism of control for indigenous labour. As mobility in the factors of production extended not just to capital and goods but also to labour markets, the colonial state became increasingly preoccupied with harnessing the labour-power of natives to capitalist production, not least before rival imperial powers grabbed land and peoples for themselves. Local populations, however, did not passively accept this instrumental imposition of sovereignty by the colonial power: they began to construct the nationalist ideologies and mass organizations which, in large measure propelled by the social transformations wrought by colonial capitalism, demanded a substantiating of such sovereignty in the form of national independence.

Jeanne-Marie Penvenne has charted the micro-history of such processes in her social history of the Mozambican colonial port of Lourenço Marques (today's Maputo).[54] There she demonstrates how, from the late nineteenth century, the Portuguese authorities developed a complex legal infrastructure aimed at coercing and controlling a resistant indigenous workforce. As labour demand in Mozambique grew on the back of Transvaal mining, the colonial administration launched a system of forced requisition (*shibalo*) in the rural hinterlands. Local authorities and African notables were entrusted with the task of supplying male labour through the primitive mechanism of round-ups. In their attempt at escaping *shibalo*, many of these villagers found themselves seeking work in Lourenço Marques, only to face a more sophisticated legal regime known as the *indigenato*. This system classified the bulk of the city's African population as *indígenas* (natives) and forced them to take up salaried work in the port or face heavy penalties for 'vagrancy'. African workers were expected to purchase a *chapa* (tag), worth roughly a day's wage, and wear it as a confirmation that they were engaged in contracted labour on the waterfront. The subordinate status of African labourers was reinforced by further legislation excluding *indígenas* from rights to unionization, access to apprenticeships and wage negotiations. Thus, through a combination of the *shibalo* and *indigenato*, Portugese imperialism had by the 1920s in Lourenço Marques both produced an African working class and developed the bureaucratic and territorial infrastructure of modern sovereignty in its ambition to regulate labour. Yet the racist ideology which underpinned this process engendered a class structure divided along racial categories. Consequently, class consciousness in Lourenço Marques could not but be accompanied by a sense of ethnic identity which was to deliver corresponding political movements for national liberation.

Mozambicans were of course to wait for another half a century before attaining independence, but in many other African and overseas colonies the combined forces of modern class- and state-formation were in the early decades of the twentieth century paving the way for mass political movements of nationalist, liberal and socialist orientation seeking national liberation. Such demands for independence were accelerated as European latecomers to capitalist industrialization, most prominently Germany, challenged the long period of British imperial dominance, and sought themselves to fashion a 'place in the sun'. Inter-imperial rivalry was accompanied by deepening class antagonism in Europe at the turn of the century, expressed among other things in the unprecedented power of organized labour both inside and outside representative institutions. The combination of 'vertical' social antagonisms at home and 'horizontal' geopolitical rivalries abroad delivered a turn to protectionism, territorial expansion, and military competition among the great capitalist powers which in large measure played itself out in the last of the *terrae nullius* in the European imagination: the African continent. Thus, the second Moroccan (Agadir) crisis of 1911, declared by one eminent historian of the First World War as a 'critical year' in the events leading to the impending conflagration, perfectly illustrates the synchronic interconnections between capitalism, imperialism and war.[55] The dominant capitalist empire (Britain) had entered into diplomatic alliances with its erstwhile mercantile rival (France) in order to meet the challenge of a newly emerging industrial challenger (Germany), which in turn sought to defend the political integrity of a tributary African kingdom (Morocco) against the designs of an early modern imperial power in terminal decline (Spain). Recently hatched geopolitical rivalries certainly combined with historical animosities to produce an especially explosive international situation among these countries in 1911. But underlying this geopolitical and diplomatic crisis was the driving force of capitalist transformation in all four of the European countries and the crumbling of tributary rule in the North African kingdom in the face of external financial and commercial pressures. Thus, the Agadir crisis of 1911 brings to the fore the complex interaction between radical domestic change and violent international conflict associated with capitalist imperialism. On this reading, capitalist imperialism is seen as a dynamic, agent-driven process encompassing all aspects of society – most notably class-formation, mass political mobilizations and the cultural or ideological forms which accompanied them – and not merely as a phenomenon issuing mechanically from changes in the 'productive base' or 'the economy'.

Explaining capitalist imperialism

That the scramble for Africa might ignite war in Europe was a proposition many contemporary analysts of empire and imperialism took very seriously. Both 'colonialism' and 'imperialism', understood as conscious policies of territorial aggrandizement, were relative newcomers to the lexicon of European languages and only acquired wider currency in political debate and analysis towards the second half of the nineteenth century.[56] By the turn of the new century talk of imperialism in Europe and elsewhere became inextricably associated with the reality of war abroad (most notably in southern Africa) and its potential outbreak at home. It was in this context that a new wave of writings on imperialism sought to explain why a seemingly peaceful and contractual system of economic exchange such as capitalism could take on the violent, militarist and racist form of territorial expansion.

John Hobson's *Imperialism: A Study*, first published in 1902, remains to this day, together with Lenin's belated contribution of 1916, the reference point in discussions over the 'new' imperialism of the late nineteenth and early twentieth century. As an economic journalist with first-hand experience of the Boer War, Hobson employed as his starting-point the need to explain why, over the previous decades, '[a] number of European nations, Great Britain being the first and foremost, annexed or otherwise asserted political sway over vast portions of Africa and Asia, and over numerous islands in the Pacific and elsewhere.'[57] His answer was attractively simple: 'the business interests of the nation as a whole are subordinated to those of certain sectional interests that usurp control of the national resources and use them for private gain.'[58] Arms producers, capital exporters and financiers were singled out as the chief beneficiaries of imperialism. Hobson labelled them 'parasites upon patriotism', in that they gained 'business and lucrative employment from the expansion of military operations, the opening up of new tracts of territory and trade with the same, and the provision of new capital which these operations require . . .'[59]

If these were the sectional interests behind the drive for imperialism, the question still remained as to why they had acquired such power at the turn of the twentieth century. Here Hobson presented the concentration of industry into 'trusts' or 'combines' and the attendant 'underconsumption' of commodities by the home market as the 'economic taproot' of the new imperialism. He had in earlier chapters of his study already dismissed commerce and demography as sources of expansionism and instead focused his attention on the production glut which had emerged in the industrial nations as a result of the competitive concentration of capital. Such a crisis of overproduction lay, however, not in industrial capitalism itself, but rather in the speculative investments in 'rents, monopoly profits and other unearned or excessive elements of income'.[60] From all this, Hobson concluded that 'Imperialism is the endeavour of the great controllers of industry to broaden the channel for the flow of their surplus wealth by seeking foreign markets and foreign investments to take off the goods and capital they cannot sell or use at home.'[61]

It is not difficult to see how Hobson's pioneering study came to influence later theories of capitalist imperialism. Aside from its being the first such comprehensive statement on the new imperialism, Hobson highlighted in his book a number of themes and concepts – finance and monopoly capital, overproduction, underconsumption, class fractions, cartelization, the arms industry, militarism – which were to play a central role in subsequent economic theories of imperialism.

Perhaps the most significant of these was a succession of Marxist works which in the years leading up to and during the First World War sought to analyse the relationship between capitalism and imperialism and, crucially, to develop strategies to avert war, or alternatively to harness it to revolutionary transformation. The international socialist movement had by the turn of the century already recognized the violent impact of colonial expansion and inter-imperial rivalry on European politics, both domestically and internationally. The 'colonial question' was placed on the agenda for the first time at the Second International's Stuttgart congress of 1907 and subsequently became a defining political issue within the movement, right up to the dénouement of August 1914, and thereafter in the creation of the Third or Communist International. The classical Marxist debates on imperialism must therefore be interpreted within the context of the protracted social and diplomatic crisis in Europe, and with due attention to all the political urgency associated with respective theoretical statements.

Rather than offer a blow-by-blow account of such complex debates, it may suit our purposes better to identify the political spectrum within which the writings of Marxist theorists of imperialism such as Rudolf Hilferding, Rosa Luxemburg, Nikolai Bukharin, Karl Kautsky and Vladimir Illich Lenin might be placed.[62] In essence, all these authors defined imperialism as the militarized, geopolitical rivalry between European states and, echoing Hobson, explained this phenomenon with reference to the power acquired by finance capital under a new, monopoly stage of capitalism. With the exception of Rosa Luxemburg, none of these theorists considered in any depth the impact of capitalist imperialism on the colonies or its consequences for the uneven development of global capitalism; they remained principally concerned with the impact of colonial expansion on Europe. There existed, therefore, a considerable degree of methodological convergence. Most Marxists at the time accepted the contradictory tendencies of an inherently expansive capital which nonetheless produced national concentration in large companies, and a footloose finance capital which simultaneously unified the world market and manipulated the foreign relations of powerful national states. They furthermore adopted Marx and Engels's view that the apparatus of the state existed to serve ruling class interests. Their principal differences lay, then, in the political conclusions arrived at with this knowledge.

On one end of the spectrum, Lenin's pamphlet *Imperialism: The Highest Stage of Capitalism* effectively summarized the earlier work of Hobson, Hilferding and Bukharin in arguing that imperialism was defined by five features: the concentration of production to such an extent that monopolies 'play a decisive role in economic life'; 'the merging of bank capital with industrial capital' and the subsequent creation of 'finance capital'; 'the export of capital'; 'the formation of international capitalist monopolies which share the world among themselves'; and, finally, 'the territorial division of the whole world among the greatest capitalist powers'.[63] For Lenin, as for Hilferding and Bukharin before him, the shift from competitive to monopoly capitalism and, internationally, from free trade to imperialism was an inevitable structural feature of this latest stage of capitalist development. It was also the principal cause behind war and global inequality. Lenin put the case forthrightly in his 1920 preface to the French and German editions of the pamphlet:

[t]he true class character of the [world] war is naturally to be found not in the diplomatic history of the war but in the analysis of the objective position of the ruling classes in all belligerent countries. . . . capitalism has grown into a world system of colonial oppression and of the financial strangulation of the overwhelming majority of the world by a handful of 'advanced' countries. And this 'booty' is shared between two or three powerful world marauders armed to the teeth (America, Great Britain, Japan) who involve the whole world in *their* war over the sharing of *their* booty.[64]

Lenin's tract was published mid-way through the war, as the international socialist movement splintered into various factions, including the 'Zimmerwald Left' – named after the Swiss village where Lenin and other exiles launched an anti-war 'Two-and-a-Half International'.[65] Lenin's aim in *Imperialism* was thus as much to provide a 'popular outline' as it was to demolish the mainstream Second International views of imperialism as presented by Karl Kautsky. The latter had in the years preceding the outbreak of war presented an account of imperialism which was in most respects analytically consonant with that of Hobson, Hilferding and, by extension, Bukharin and Lenin: imperialism was a phenomenon issuing from the cartelization of capital and the disproportionate influence of finance capital. It was, furthermore, fuelled by the gaps between production and consumption and characterized by violent competition and militarism. It was, however, Kautsky's article *Der Imperialismus*, published in September 1914, which drew the greatest ire from Lenin and Bukharin.[66] For Kautsky not only 'arbitrarily and *inaccurately*' associated imperialism '*only* to industrial capital in the countries which annex other nations', he furthermore 'detaches the politics of imperialism from its economics, speaks of annexations as being a policy "preferred" by finance, and opposes to it another bourgeois policy which, he alleges, is possible on this very basis of finance capital.'[67]

If we cut across the shrill polemical tone, the fundamental difference between Kautsky and Lenin revolved around the degree to which the current phase of monopoly capitalism was irreversible, and therefore whether working-class movements could do anything to avert war. Both of these were essentially tactical questions. 'From a purely economic stand-point', Kautsky had ventured, 'it is not excluded that capitalism may still live through another phase, the transference of the policy of cartelisation to foreign policy, a phase of ultra-imperialism, which of course we must fight against just as energetically as we fought imperialism. Its dangers would lie in a different direction, not in that of the armaments race and the threat to world peace.'[68] For Lenin, such views made Kautsky's position indistinguishable from bourgeois reformism: 'According to his argument', Lenin concluded, 'monopolies in economics are compatible with non-monopolistic, non-violent, non-annexationist methods in politics. . . . The result is slurring-over and blunting the most profound contradictions of the latest stage of capitalism, instead of exposure of their depth.'[69] Lenin and Bukharin thus insisted that imperialist warfare was a structural consequence of monopoly capitalism which could only be superseded through the revolutionary overthrow of capitalism, while Kautsky continued to claim that, since imperialism was a *policy* adopted by a fraction of the ruling class, it could equally be reversed through political agitation and reform within the capitalist system.

One political outcome of such disputes was the creation in 1919 of the Communist International, overtly committed to redressing the 'social-imperialism' of its predecessor by explicitly supporting the national liberation of colonized peoples across the world. Paradoxically, very little of the classical Marxist theorization on imperialism had previously concerned itself with the colonized world: the focus of attention had been inter-imperial rivalry and war in the European metropole. Tragically, the one Marxist leader and intellectual who had dedicated considerable attention to the uneven and violent reproduction of capitalism beyond Europe, Rosa Luxemburg, was assassinated months before the founding of the Third International. Yet it is in Luxemburg's monumental revision of Marx's critique of political economy, *The Accumulation of Capital*, first published in 1913, where we find the most sustained theoretical engagement by a classical Marxist with the problematic of capitalist imperialism.

Luxemburg was concerned in this work with the so-called realization problem: that is, how surplus value latent in the capitalist production of a given commodity is transformed into money through the medium of the capitalist market, and then is in turn spent in acquiring more capital. For Luxemburg, the 'expanded' or 'enlarged' reproduction of capital through the continuous production and consumption of value is unthinkable within the confines of a closed capitalist economy: 'the realisation of surplus value for the purposes of accumulation is an impossible task for a society which consists solely of workers and capitalists.'[70] Instead, Luxemburg proposes that expanded capitalist reproduction relies on the existence of 'such social organisations or strata whose own mode of production is not capitalistic.'[71]

The theoretical premise and execution of Luxemburg's solution to the 'realization problem' is highly controversial, and, for some, plain wrong. But this is not our concern here. What is of interest for our purposes is Luxemburg's insertion of two critical claims for future discussions of imperialism: that capitalism reproduced itself globally in coexistence with, and indeed in requirement of, other non-capitalist modes of production, and that it did so necessarily through violent, militarized and racist means. By shifting the focus from inter-imperialist rivalry in Europe to the forceful 'destruction of the natural economy' abroad, and, furthermore, by highlighting the dialectic of accommodation and resistance to this process in the periphery, Luxemburg reintroduced the historical dynamics of social and cultural antagonism into a predominantly economistic and structuralist conception of imperialism prevailing among Marxist discussions of the subject. She also considered at length the impact of capitalist accumulation on colonial social formations and the persistence of seemingly archaic forms of oppression and domination under global capitalism – both themes which would concern post-colonial and development studies in later decades. In sum, as Anthony Brewer has indicated, Luxemburg's real insight was 'to insist that the mechanisms of primitive accumulation, with their concomitant use of force, fraud and state power, are not simply a regrettable aspect of capitalism's past, but persist throughout the history of capitalism at the margin where capitalist and pre-capitalist economic systems meet.'[72]

For both political and theoretical reasons, Marxism has been the dominant idiom in the analysis of modern imperialism. But its heavy emphasis on political economy left the terrain open for non-Marxists to explore the cultural and sociological dimensions of imperialism. Two towering figures of Central European social theory, Joseph Schumpeter and Hannah Arendt, though separated by a generation, produced the most influential non-Marxist accounts of imperialism after Hobson. Both these authors start from the premise that capitalism and imperialism are driven by different logics and, consequently, that the explanation for the imperialist turn of European capitalism must be found in social forces other than those characteristic of what Schumpeter ideal-typically labelled the 'purely capitalist world'. While not completely discarding the economic dimensions to the new imperialism – Arendt approvingly cites Hobson, Hilferding and even Luxemburg, while Schumpeter recognized the socio-political changes wrought by finance capitalism and cartelization – both authors proffered essentially sociological reasons for this phenomenon.

Schumpeter defined imperialism broadly as 'the objectless disposition on the part of the state to unlimited forcible expansion' in contrast to the pursuit of concrete state interests.[73] Since 'pure capitalism' in his view, based mainly on the English experience, drew no benefits from such objectless expansion, it followed that imperialism surviving under capitalism had to be considered as 'atavistic in character. It falls into that large group of surviving features from earlier ages that play such an important part in every concrete situation. In other words, it is an element that stems from the living conditions, not of the present, but of the past.'[74] Specifically, Schumpeter ascribed imperialism to a peculiar combination of old and new social classes which, without saying so explicitly, he considered unique to late industrializing societies such as Germany and his native Austria: 'The social pyramid of the present age has been formed, not by the substance of and laws of capitalism alone, but by two different social substances, by the laws of two different epochs. . . . Whoever seeks to understand Europe must not overlook that even today its life, its ideology, its politics are greater under the influence of the feudal "substance".'[75] Nationalism, militarism and the autocratic state which embodied them were on this account remnants of a previous chivalric era which attached themselves to the bourgeois age and developed a symbiotic relationship with capitalism. 'Nationalism and militarism', Schumpeter concluded, 'while not creatures of capitalism, become "capitalized" and in the end draw their best energies from capitalism. . . . And they, in turn, affect capitalism, cause it to deviate from the course it might have followed alone, support many of its interests.'[76]

Some thirty years after Schumpeter wrote these lines, Hannah Arendt would echo such themes in her own postwar and post-Holocaust reckoning, *The Origins of Totalitarianism*. In the central essay of the book Arendt distinguished 'imperialism' from 'empire-building' by suggesting that the latter implied some political integration between metropole and colony, while in the former 'national institutions remain separate from the colonial administration although they are allowed to exercise control.'[77] Like Schumpeter, Arendt believed that there was no structural connection between imperialism and capitalism and, following Hobson, that national aggrandizement in the creation of political colonies was entirely different from the 'spectacle of a few capitalists conducting their predatory searches around the globe for new investment possibilities to the profit-motives of the much-too-rich and the gambling instincts of the much-too-poor.'[78] They only became conflated in the last decades of the nineteenth century as a result of socio-political crisis, from the fact '[t]hat all [European] governments knew very well that their countries were secretly disintegrating.'[79] Indeed, for Arendt it was two social forces, rather loosely defined as 'the bourgeoisie' and 'the mob', which, in the context of deep antagonism at home, sought to resolve their differences by expanding abroad under the banner of nationalism. 'The new fact in the imperialist era', Arendt proclaimed,

> is that these two superfluous forces, superfluous capital and superfluous working power, joined hands and left the country. The concept of expansion, the export of government power and annexation of every territory in which nationals had invested either their wealth or their work, seemed the only

alternative to increasing losses of wealth and population. Imperialism and its idea of unlimited expansion seemed to offer a permanent remedy for this permanent evil.[80]

These two non-Marxist accounts, then, drew out the sociological and ideological dimensions of capitalist imperialism by highlighting the role of nationalism, racism and class antagonism in ways which – with the possible exceptions of Kautsky and Luxemburg – had been elided in Marxist political–economic analyses. After the Second World War a new wave of Marxist and radical scholars returned to the theme of imperialism, this time chiefly with reference to the political economy of development and underdevelopment. The conjuncture facing analysts of postwar imperialism was, however, entirely different to that of the early decades: empires were crumbling, not annexing fresh territories; communism and radical nationalism had triumphed across half the world; the dominant capitalist power now exercised global hegemony through states, not over them. Consequently the problematic of imperialism also changed. Uneven development and global socio-economic and political inequality replaced war and Great Power rivalry as the major areas of concern for theorists of imperialism.

As we shall see in the following chapter, the Cold War decades witnessed the rise of a new brand of American revisionist historians keen to associate the exploits of their own country with imperialism. But it was in the field of so-called development economics – itself an expression of the new power relations in a post-colonial world – that a fresh wave of theories of imperialism was to emerge under the label of 'dependency theory'.[81] Most of the dependency theorists stemmed from Latin America, Africa and the Caribbean, and their concern was no longer with geopolitical rivalry in Europe but with the consequences of global capitalism in their own countries and regions. Their inspiration was still Marxist, but their approach married history, sociology and anthropology with political economy. Paradoxically, given earlier Marxist fixations with war and capitalism, the use of the term 'imperialism' during these postwar decades shifted notably from the realm of militarism and violence to denote the economic inequalities inherent in world capitalism.

The diverse body of writings that comes packaged under the neat label of 'dependency theory' in fact encompassed both scholarly investigations into class formation and antagonism in colonial and post-colonial social formations, the integration of extra-European peoples and territories into the world economy, and more polemical interventions into the nature of 'sub-imperialism' in dependent states such as Brazil or the persistence of neo-colonial 'underdevelopment' in a post-colonial world. Notwithstanding these variations, and mindful of the injunction by leading 'dependentista' (and, more recently, president of Brazil) Fernando Henrique Cardoso not to quantify or reify the phenomenon, 'dependency' can be defined thus: 'The relation of interdependence between two or more economies, and between these and world trade, assumes the form of dependence when some countries (the dominant ones) can expand and can be self-sustaining, while other countries (the dependent ones) can do this only as a reflection of that expansion.'[82] Implicit in this definition, and explicit in other writings on dependency, was the assumption that the economic development of the capitalist metropole had required the economic underdevelopment of its colonial periphery.

The intellectual force of such assertions derived in large measure from the political power of Third World nationalism and radicalism. Like preceding debates over imperialism, research into development and underdevelopment carried a strong polemical content. For one trenchant critic of dependency theory, the thesis of underdevelopment was a useful fiction which, 'with its emphasis on parasitism and its pillage of the Third World, was perfectly suited to the psychological needs and political requirements of the Third World nationalists.'[83] The reality and prospects of Third World economic growth on this account were not only highly feasible, but had furthermore been facilitated by the experience of capitalist imperialism in the periphery: 'The overall, net effect of the policy of "imperialist" countries and the general economic relationships of these countries with the underdeveloped countries actually favours the industrialization and general economic development of the latter.'[84] Other, more dispassionate evaluations have broadly concurred with this view, offering substantial statistical evidence in support, while the methodological presuppositions behind dependency theory and its cognate, 'world-systems' theory, have also been subject to devastating critique.[85]

The net result of a century's theorization of capitalist imperialism has in many respects returned us full circle to the problem of violence and force under capitalist social relations. For all their political and theoretical differences, Marxists and their contenders alike have accepted that the capitalist market has a logic and dynamic that is antithetical to imperialism. Yet plainly the militarism, territorialism and racism associated with the latter is not foreign to the former. During periods of relative stability and prosperity for the privileged, such as the 1890s and 1990s, many have assumed that markets and empires are antithetical. Recent developments in world affairs have, however, once more brought the troubled relationship between contract and coercion into sharp focus and, as the final chapter will try to elucidate, occasioned a fresh bout of intellectual and political discussion on the subject of empire today.

4
Empire as Culture

Empires, as we have thus far seen, are built on distinctive structures of political rule buttressed by specific forms of surplus production, distribution and appropriation. They mobilize immense political, military and socio-economic resources across different parts of the world from and for a metropolitan centre. But such monumental endeavours are always undertaken by human agents with their own individual and collective histories, their own memories, customs, languages and beliefs. Colonists, slaves, missionaries, proconsuls and merchants as well as metropolitan administrators, soldiers or workers all adopt distinctive worldviews corresponding to their position in the imperial order, but they are also forced to make sense of their particular lives with reference to each other in the context of a wider imperial universe. To that extent, in addition to political–military and socio-economic entities, empires must be seen as human communities which generate their own expressions of subjectivity, meaning and collective identity – that is, distinctive forms of culture.

This chapter examines the central role of culture, broadly understood, in sustaining and at the same time undermining imperial power. Special attention is paid to the tensions between imperial integration and contestation in the cultural realm; between the various ways in which empires unify peoples by constructing new cosmopolitan identities, while they simultaneously use culture as a tool of oppression, segregation and domination. Following Robert Miles's original formulation, this chapter argues that imperial culture is engendered through the contradictory but concurrent processes of 'civilization' and 'racialization'.[1] From this perspective, the racialization of culture is central to the construction of imperial civilization. Empires and imperialism shape and promote both the demotic and anarchical miscegenation of cultures as well as the most rigidly hierarchical and violent forms of cultural exclusion. The result is a set of cultural practices and institutions, ranging from a common language to shared religious beliefs, which give form to distinctive imperial civilizations. Whatever one thinks of their outcome – and much of contemporary social and political discourse and practice examines precisely such legacies under the banners of 'post-colonialism' or 'multiculturalism' – these interrelated processes are the unique historical product of imperial interactions: empires may not hold a monopoly over cultural domination and hybridity, but they have certainly been the main suppliers of these contradictory phenomena throughout history.

Culture will be employed here in its widest acceptance, including both notions of 'high' culture linked to civilizational achievements in literature, the visual arts or science and everyday expressions of 'popular' culture in music, sport, language, fashion or cooking. Two core propositions guide the discussion. The first, echoing the work of Edward Said and others, is that culture is one of the elementary tools of imperial domination. As we saw in previous chapters, imperial centres and their metropolitan populations have throughout history crafted cosmologies and myths of origin which grant them a preordained mandate to rule over the world. During the past five hundred years or so, the pre-modern imagery and mythology of the 'Other' as a mere stranger – however menacing and uncouth – has been grafted onto modern socio-economic and political institutions which codify the inferiority of 'Others' and organize their subjection to imperial power along racial categories, phenotypical taxonomies and ethnographic classifications. Although the shift was a subtle and protracted one, I will argue in this chapter that racist culture is inherent to modern imperialism in a way that was not the case in previous empires: to borrow a phrase from David Theo Goldberg, modern imperialism, perhaps because of its coincidence with modern state- and nation-building, transforms existing principles of gradation into new doctrines of degradation.[2]

This first section is thus organized around the elucidation of three interconnected strategies of racialization which, despite appearing at different conjunctures in modern history, have to different degrees been combined by imperial authorities when ranking subject populations along a hierarchy that is always topped by those belonging or closest to the metropolitan centre. The first of these strategies naturalizes collective inferiority mainly with reference to perceived habit and behaviour. It is chiefly a product of Christian understandings of barbarism which, though informed by distinctions deriving from contexts as diverse as ancient Greece and medieval Europe, places whole groups in the inferior, primitive and infantilized 'state of nature'. To paraphrase Anthony Pagden's formulation, it is an ethnographic expression of racialization.[3]

Since the advent of modern imperialism, Europeans, and later Americans and Japanese, have justified their domination of foreign peoples through mechanisms of cultural gradation which in the course of the nineteenth century crystallized into legal–institutional forms of racism, legitimized by modern scientific methods. Here biology, not simply behaviour or custom, becomes the touchstone of difference as races are distinguished and ranked according to claimed hereditary features. This is a properly racist strategy of racialization, in that it ties the subordination of colonial peoples to their congenital inferiority, attested through scientific methods and findings which are demonstrably and conclusively false, but whose authority at the time was instrumental to imperial domination.

Finally, imperial projects of racialization have also drawn on so-called indigenous sources of cultural identity, reinforcing and often inventing local 'traditions' such as institutions of chieftancy or the fighting spirit of certain 'martial races' to buttress colonial rule through a strategy of 'nativism'. These instances appear less obviously gradated as specific tribes, ethnic groups or religious entities are granted a legal–

cultural autonomy within the colonial framework which seems to respect customary cultures and institutions. Yet, as we shall see below, such imperial exercises in cultural engineering were premised on fixed and hierarchical notions of the 'Other', and to that extent clearly fall within the dialectic of civilization through racialization. As in the case of antiquity, these various ideological constructs – be it the Aristotelian state of nature, polygenetic racialism or customary nativism – did not merely represent delusions of imperial grandeur or cultural prejudice: they were mobilized and deployed in the process of European expansion as an integral and vital component of imperial conquest and administration.

The second core assumption of the chapter is that such forms of domination are variously contested, usurped, refashioned or appropriated and thereby modified by those individuals and collectivities at whom they are targeted. Such reactions in turn create new cultural patterns manifested chiefly, though by no means exclusively, in the quotidian lives of imperial subjects. Anti-imperialist and anti-racist opposition has, as was briefly mooted in previous chapters, taken many other forms: political, economic and military. But the cultural realm of the everyday is perhaps where imperial schemes of domination through static, orderly and hierarchical cultural frameworks are most immediately disrupted and subverted. This is not to apportion racist culture exclusively to the colonist and imperialist, and its multi-racial counterpart to the downtrodden peoples of colour. The everyday demotic culture of colonial societies, be it culinary, musical or linguistic, was shot through with all the patriarchal, racial and class hierarchies associated with imperial institutions (the main difference being that the latter possessed the socio-economic and political wherewithal to enforce such inequalities). As in other domains of imperial relations, numerous colonial subjects willingly adopted or adapted to the dominant imperial culture because it offered them individual or collective benefits and opportunities. Many mulattos or mestizos internalized and exploited to their advantage the complex racial gradations, or 'pigmentocracies', established by Europeans in the New World. Similarly, white settlers rarely formed homogenous or unified cultures, as the persistent ethnic tensions and class cleavages between, say, Afrikaners and Englishmen or French colonial *grand familles* and other *petits blancs* demonstrate. Only their shared status as a privileged cultural minority ruling over and living among a dominated majority led whites of different nationalities to unite politically in French Algeria, southern Africa or parts of Latin America.[4]

Yet notwithstanding all this, in bringing together diverse peoples, commodities, customs and institutions, empires facilitate the kind of unpredictable cultural cross-fertilization which is inherently resistant to orderly categorization. Imperial subjects combine foodstuffs, languages, rhythms and rituals to produce new, syncretic and generally unruly culinary cultures, dialects, musical forms and belief systems. In the realm of 'high' culture too, imperial connections fostered some of the most striking contributions to universal art and literature. During the first half of the twentieth century in particular colonial artists and intellectuals, perhaps reflecting 'combined and uneven' development of their homelands, fused local idioms with emerging forms of modernism in Europe and America to create powerful expressions of vanguard art and politics.

Above all, however, imperial subjects engaged in the one activity that often accompanies the indulgence in food, drink, music or ritual celebration, and which imperial authorities find hardest to regulate: sex. The miscegenation of races, or the union between distinct ethnic groups under the imperial mantle, produces offspring with hybrid identities and mixed heritages. Many empires – Roman, Ottoman and even Chinese – have accommodated such ethnic diversity into an overarching political and socio-economic imperial hierarchy, often absorbing and thriving on the cultures of conquered populations and their progeny. Modern European empires, however, have displayed greater apprehension about the admixture of imperial subjects, to the extent that, as we shall see below, sexual relations between colonists and natives, even more so between different imperial races, acted as a concrete expression of the perils associated with imperial transgressions. Robert Young has indicated how the socio-cultural dislocations generated by nineteenth-century capitalist imperialism became visible to Europeans in two ways: in the disruption of domestic culture, and the increasing anxiety about racial difference and the racial amalgamation that was apparent as an effect of colonialism and enforced migration. Both these consequences for class and race were clearly undermining the cultural stability of a more traditional, apparently organic, now irretrievably lost, society.[5]

The contradictory dynamics invoked by Young between integration and dislocation, unity and differentiation, or stability and displacement are at the core of the discussion of imperial culture that follows. Accordingly, a second main section of the chapter offers an overview of how cultural forms are imposed by the metropole, combined in the colonies and re-exported back to the centre in ways that are distinctive to the imperial tension between civilization and racialization. Imperial culture, to use Edward Said's celebrated formulation (first employed by the Cuban anthropologist Fernando Ortiz), is considered here contrapuntally, generating identities and subjectivities 'which are involved with one another ... hybrid, heterogeneous, extraordinarily differentiated and unmonolithic.'[6] We shall see in that section how, for every narrative and imperial institution of cultural domination, no matter how powerful, there is an accompanying history and practice of cultural resistance, reinvention and recovery. As in other realms of the imperial experience, colonial subjects are seldom passive victims of empire, but rather active – if structurally subordinated – contributors to imperial civilization.

Such contrapuntal dialectics also characterize our current, post-colonial world: racism and multiculturalism, cultural segregation and hybridity are as much present in our global cities as they were in the metropolitan outposts of modern empires. Much the same could be said about the various cultural and socio-political anxieties over our globalized 'runaway world'. A final section of the chapter therefore briefly considers the question of how far imperial culture and cultural imperialism have outlived the collapse of formal empires, or, put differently, whether there is anything distinctively imperial about imperial culture.

Culture and imperial domination

Like their ancient predecessors, modern Europeans settling among and ruling over foreign populations considered their own civilization to be superior to that of conquered peoples. To acculturate the natives, educate them in the European ways of life, and envelop them within an expanding civilization was one of the primary missions of imperialism and colonization. Unlike the empires of antiquity, however, modern European empires began from the sixteenth century to develop complex mechanisms of social gradation based on colour and physical appearance in order to assist them in ruling over subject populations of Africa, Asia, the Pacific and the Americas. In inventing baroque racial taxonomies, Europeans drew on existing practices of exclusion and subordination, and their accompanying imagery, which had already been deployed in the civilization of savages and barbarians of the old continent. 'The notion of barbarism', Roger Bartra reminds us, 'was applied to non-European peoples as the transposition of a perfectly structured myth with a character that can only be understood within the context of Western cultural evolution.'[7] Such structured myths, however, were to adopt a distinctive inflection as European colonizers encountered and sought to dominate diverse populations at different junctures during their imperial expansion. Notions of 'otherness' and barbarism first forged in Europe to stereotype those who lived on the margins of civilization were superimposed on emerging classifications of non-European peoples. Three such 'moments' in the history of modern European imperialism, each expressing a particular strategy of racialization, will serve to illustrate the particular ways in which metropolitan authorities and their colonial agents created new, racialized social gradations in the course of extending their civilization overseas.

Imperial culture and the end of the state of nature in Spanish America

The first episode in the racialization of imperial rule unfolded in early colonial Spanish America. Here the novel and unique problem for the Iberian settlers was how to classify the Amerindian peoples they had encountered for the first time. For Spanish scholars and theologians in particular, there were two complementary sources of authority to guide them in this endeavour: one was the Christian scriptures, the other was the tradition of natural law which, via the writings of Aquinas, had recovered for the European Renaissance an Aristotelian understanding of human nature. The use of such Old World sources in a New World context was to generate all kinds of contradictions which eventually delivered an entirely novel conception of human difference based on the secular idea of race.

Columbus and his followers had initially justified the enslavement of Caribbean aborigines chiefly with reference to their barbarous behaviour. Their nakedness, sexual licentiousness, illiteracy, rusticity and above all idolatry meant, on this view, that the Arawaks, Tainos and Caribs of the Antilles were by nature cast as savages. Some, like the 'generous and good-hearted' Tainos of Columbus's description, might certainly be 'noble' savages, still living in a golden age uncorrupted by the ways of civil society, but their customs remained patently barbarian and thereby naturally subject to domination by civilized Spaniards. As Anthony Pagden has masterfully documented, such straightforward justifications of natural slavery on the basis of native unreason were soon challenged on two interrelated fronts: the one political, the other theological.[8] The political problem was that Indians had, as we saw in chapter 3, already been declared vassals of the Castilian crown in 1500 and their enslavement other than in the context of warfare thereby outlawed: to enslave one's own subjects was plainly illogical and indeed illegitimate. Moreover, the justifications for natural slavery based on the absence of cultural markers such as clothing, towns and cities, written language or codified social structures were refuted empirically once Spaniards encountered the high civilizations of the Mexicas and Incas. Spanish subjection of native Americans would therefore have to be legitimated through arguments other than the classic Aristotelian justification for slavery on the basis of a natural division of labour.

The associated theological difficulty concerned the spiritual status of Amerindians: since they had been ignorant of

Christian teachings, Indians could not – like Muslims or Jews of the Old World – be chastised for rejecting the ways of Christ. It followed that the souls of pagan savages could after all be rescued and welcomed into the realm of Christian civilization. Together, these two propositions raised the thorny question of Spain's titles over the Americas and its native inhabitants. For embedded in the issue of whether Indians were humans and, if so, what then explained their barbarous condition, was also an interrogation as to what could possibly justify Spain's appropriation of what by the early sixteenth century was conclusively recognized as being a part of the world previously unknown to Europeans.

The first half of the sixteenth century witnessed a succession of intense philosophical and legal debates among scholars and theologians in Spain and the Americas over precisely these issues. Such controversies were in turn part of a wider political struggle among different factions of the crown, the Church and colonists over the nature of Spanish rule in America, and indeed the character of the monarchy itself. In essence, they produced two broad responses to the interrelated questions of the nature of Amerindians and Spanish sovereignty over them, perhaps best represented in the famous disputation held in 1550 at Valladolid between Fray Bartolomé de Las Casas and Juan Ginés de Sepúlveda. For many Spanish commentators, the barbarous character of the Indians could be demonstrated empirically with reference to their customs and behaviour. Human sacrifice, cannibalism, polygamy and idolatry were, among other vices, cited as evidence of the fact that Indians lived irredeemably beyond the pale of civilization. The distance from Christian conceptions of the good life was so insurmountable, men such as Sepúlveda insisted, that only the threat of violence and the subsequent domination as natural slaves could deliver the conversion of Indians. On this account, clearly, the Spanish crown had conducted its Christian duty not only in bringing the Gospel to pagan barbarians, but also in imposing it upon them.

At the opposite spectrum of the debate stood the Dominican friar Las Casas. While not disputing all of the empirical claims regarding Indian customs, Las Casas insisted that there was nothing peculiarly Indian to many of these practices (Abraham had after all acceded to sacrificing his own son), nor did they necessarily preclude peaceful conversion. Indeed, Las Casas argued forcefully in favour of the Indian predisposition towards salvation: 'They are of such gentleness and decency', he said of the Indians, 'that they are, more than the other nations of the entire world, supremely fitted and prepared to abandon the worship of idols and to accept . . . the word of God.'[9] A modified version of this approach, expressed philosophically in the works of Francisco de Vitoria and his Salamanca School followers, conceived of the native American as a proper human with fully rational properties who, by virtue of his isolation from Christian civilization, had simply been unable to realize such potential. For Vitoria, Indians constituted an infantile, backward type of human being in need of Christian cultivation by civilized Spaniards. Despite the complexity of their societies, they remained at a prior, natural stage of development. Aristotelian pleas for the natural slavery of Indians were thus rejected, as were the more outlandish claims about the latter belonging to a third species between man and monkey. Instead, Indians were cast in patriarchal terms as children, requiring pastoral guidance and instruction from the more advanced Christian civilization. Spanish titles over the Americas were correspondingly justified in purely temporal terms, as a form of a trusteeship which the Spanish crown had acquired over a backward people. Spaniards on this account had no dominion over native Americans but were entitled, by virtue of the natural rights to travel, settle and communicate in foreign lands, to rule over Amerindians if they rejected the righteous path of Christ.[10]

These various debates, which generally fall under the common label of 'controversy over the Indies', have since been identified with a range of modern political doctrines and social sciences: the law of peoples and nations, universal human rights, cultural relativism, comparative ethnography and even the discipline of International Relations. For our purposes, the key feature of these early modern disputes lies in their convergence, regardless of political or philosophical outlook, on the notion that a generic 'Indian' could be defined by a series of innate cultural attributes, to be distinguished from those of Europeans. Moreover, the common assumption in these interventions was that the Indian needed to be redeemed from his pagan ways. Whether salvation occurred through peaceful conversion, as envisaged by Las Casas and other missionaries, or through violent subjugation, as Sepúlveda had contended, the objective remained the same: to instruct ignorant pagans in the superior Christian culture. Thus was created the contradictory dynamic of an expansive civilizing mission which at the same time constructed a phenotypical hierarchy between Spaniard and Indian.

The extent to which the ideological debates surrounding the nature of the Indians impacted directly upon the actual structures of rule in the Americas is a matter of dispute. A number of American institutions certainly coincide quite neatly with some of the doctrinal positions defended by scholars and theologians of the time. Vitoria's notion of the Indian as a child requiring Christian instruction and Sepúlveda's more conventional understanding of Amerindians as barbarians found expression in the *encomienda* as a mechanism of both trusteeship and natural slavery. The spatial distribution among Indian and Spanish republics explored in chapter 2 and the distinction between acculturated 'Indians of Reason' and the unpacified 'savage Indians' also fits the mould of the dominant views on the ontological status of Indians.

One overarching material feature of the Spanish conquest, however, fundamentally conditioned the processes of civilization and racialization in the Americas: the fact that the colonizers were overwhelmingly men. This absolute gender imbalance among settlers, coupled with the enduring assumption among frontier societies that women were legitimate booty of war, meant that the sharp and static dichotomy between Indian and European was undermined through the sexual encounter between Spanish men and native women. 'In a way', Magnus Mörner has suggested without ironic intention, 'the Spanish Conquest of the Americas was a conquest of women.'[11] Be they the product of rape, concubinage or marriage, the mestizo children born out of such intercourse plainly challenged the rigid racial distinction between colonizers and natives. The reality of *mestizaje* thus inaugurated one of the enduring anxieties of modern imperialism, namely how to uphold a social order based on racial hierarchies in a world where the constant intermixture of races was blurring these very distinctions.

The Spanish colonial authorities at first met this challenge by simply allocating mestizos to one of the two categories of 'Spanish' or 'Indian'. Both crown and Church initially encouraged colonizers to marry native women, especially those of noble lineage, in the mistaken belief that dynastic unions of the old continent could be straightforwardly reproduced in the New World. Mestizo children born from legitimate unions could thus be granted full Christian rights, and were indeed during the first decades of conquest enthusiastically recruited as soldiers, settlers and administrators in the Spanish campaigns of pacification. The bulk of mestizos, however, were born out of wedlock, generally unrecognized by their fathers, and soon became the source of moral, social and political alarm for the authorities. The Church was principally concerned with mestizos because they incarnated the deleterious moral consequences of concubinage and what was effectively polygamy among Spanish colonizers. State authorities for their part grew increasingly wary about the social and political status of those illegitimate mestizos who belonged neither to the Spanish nor to the Indian republic, straddling the ground, both literally and figuratively, between these two distinct social and geographical domains. By the turn of the seventeenth century, illegitimate children born out of Spanish and Indian intercourse were perceived by the authorities as dangerous, footloose vagrants and were thus denied rights to property and office, forbidden from living among Indian communities, and stigmatized as unruly and treacherous 'mixed-bloods'.

Some commentators have suggested that the antagonism towards mestizos was due more to their illegitimate status than to their colour or racial make-up – in other words, that their discrimination was the product of moral–legal misgivings which applied to 'pure' Spanish foundlings too, rather than a peculiar prejudice against peoples of colour.[12] Yet this is belied by the fact that, as Jonathan Israel has pointed out with reference to seventeenth-century New Spain, mestizos were as a matter of course lumped together with mulattos and blacks as a third, discordant racial grouping or 'caste' of the New World:

The rise of the 'mestizo' as a sub-section of the third community, distinct from Spaniards and the Indians, did not improve the mestizo's position in Mexican society or enhance his reputation. The epithet 'sons of Spaniards' is used progressively less while the association of mestizos with Negroes in the Spaniard's eye becomes closer. Although in theory still rated as *gente de razon* (rational folk), equivalent in potential intellect to white people, the mestizo was identified increasingly in the Spanish mind with the *gente vil* (base folk), the categorization reserved for those non-Indians, mainly blacks, who were not permitted to wear European costume or hold royal, municipal or ecclesiastical office.[13]

The simple dichotomy between Spaniards and Indians was thus undermined soon after conquest not only by *mestizaje*, but also by the arrival on American shores of Africans and Asians drawn into the New World through the imperial circuits of slavery and commerce. African slaves had from the outset accompanied Spanish conquistadors as domestic servants and auxiliary soldiers. They were subsequently imported to labour in mines, plantations and docks, often forming the largest ethnic grouping, together with their mulatto offspring, in urban centres of Spanish colonial America such as Mexico, Veracruz or Lima. Filipinos, Chinese, Spanish-Filipinos or combinations of all three also arrived at the Pacific ports of Acapulco and Callao as either slaves or freemen and women, thence to settle in urban centres across the Americas.

The amalgamation of peoples and cultures which resulted from these imperial population transfers – whether forced or voluntary – were both necessary and dangerous for the continued reproduction of colonial Spanish America. If Spaniards and their creole descendants were to maintain their superior status in the Americas, Indians and the various non-Indian '*castas*' (the term increasingly used to describe peoples of mixed African, Indian or mestizo ancestry) would have to work for them. Yet, in bringing such diverse peoples together to service Spanish and creole supremacy, the latter were increasingly becoming an isolated minority among a sea of mixed-bloods. In an attempt to uphold the tripartite gradation of Spanish, Indian and the residual *castas*, Spanish authorities tried desperately, well into the late eighteenth century, to segregate and regulate the different ethnic groups which were forging new, specifically Latin American cultural identities. Both Church and state continued to nurture the idea of Indians as 'noble savages' and sought to shelter them from the perils of miscegenation by concentrating Amerindians in missionary *reducciones* (reserves) or Indian republics sealed from contact with other ethnic groups – especially *castas*. The latter were in turn subject to laws controlling their movement, outlawing their ownership of weapons, limiting their access to the status of master craftsmen in various guilds, and even enforcing dress codes 'forbidding Negresses and mulattas to adorn themselves with silks, jewellery, and low-cut dresses'.[14] They were also precluded from joining various religious orders – most notably the Jesuits – and private associations ranging from the more prestigious and lucrative silversmith guilds to popular religious *cofradías* or lodges. In many parts of Spanish America, free blacks and mulattos were expected to receive communion in their own churches, attend to public authority in segregated waiting rooms and, should they gain access to schooling, not learn to read and write like their white counterparts, but instead be instructed exclusively in the catechism of the Church.[15]

Such institutionalized discrimination found expression in – some argue, was itself reflective of – broader social prejudices against blacks, mulattos and mestizos in the everyday life of colonial Spanish America. Spaniards and creoles used the stigma of slavery and illegitimacy to typecast peoples of colour as lascivious, deceitful, lawless, indolent and violent. The fear of black and mulatto revolt in particular exercised the minds of the Spanish and creole ruling minorities in the early seventeenth century, leading to collective round-ups, torture and imprisonment of peoples of colour on trumped-up charges and in response to unsubstantiated conspiracies. Such victimization was complemented with racialized stereotypes surrounding the physical strength and exaggerated libidinousness of Africans: black and mulatto men were employed as overseers and foremen in mines and haciendas, enforcing the extraction of Indian tribute or regulating Indian markets on behalf of their Spanish masters, and were also customarily recruited to form emergency militias in times of social unrest. Their sisters on the other hand were prized as courtesans and mistresses by European merchants, officials and, no doubt, the odd clergyman. Both these uses of colour as an organizer of social relations indicated the contradictions, indeed hypocrisy, of societies structurally built on segregation yet constantly interconnecting peoples of varying colour.

The Spanish colonial fixation with an America divided into two neat racial categories of Spaniard and Indian therefore became undone through the very impulses of greed and domination which had brought Iberians to American shores in the first place. By the eighteenth century the racial heritage of most South Americans was so intermixed that it became increasingly difficult to classify society rigidly according to the three official categories. Doing so, a Mexican official of the period complained, '[w]ould imply the gathering of odious information and, if rigorously done, very dark strains already erased in time would be uncovered in well-accepted families.'[16] This did not of course mean that colonial Spanish America was unselfconscious of colour and race. Quite the contrary, as implied by our official's concern to hide 'dark pasts', a 'pigmentocracy' which placed the pale-skinned at the top of the social scale and the dark-skinned at the bottom permeated all aspects of Latin American social life – and continues to do so today.[17] It simply meant that the straightforward scholastic distinction between Spanish and Indian, Christian and pagan, or civilized and barbarian which had informed early colonial notions of cultural differentiation had, three centuries later, been transformed into a secularized conception of culture based on race, which, for all its cruel hierarchies, was more prone to being undermined by miscegenation and by the forces of modern class antagonism and state-formation.

Colonial racism and the perils of miscegenation

If the experience of early colonial Spanish America represents a first 'moment' in the dialectics of civilization and racialization where race and colour begin to trump religion and custom as dominant cultural indicators, the racist culture of 'plantation America', encompassing both the Caribbean and the slave states of the mainland, engendered a second expression of this dialectic.[18] Here the subjugation of men and women of colour was from the outset inscribed in their very status as slaves, former slaves or descendants of slaves. Race and class were welded together from the start, and colonial institutions were consequently geared towards sustaining this biracial hierarchy. Slaveholders found in skin colour the perfect, indelible marker of their human property, and so even legal emancipation brought limited improvement of status for the black and brown populations of plantation America. The plantation societies of the Caribbean and the American South were built on the legal bondage of Africans and their descendants, who despite their varying physical appearance and diverse cultures of origin were pronounced 'socially dead' in the Middle Passage and then branded in the New World with the uniform racial identity of 'negro'.

Scholars of New World slavery have documented at length and in detail how such European claims over the congenital inferiority of Africans combined with the socio-economic benefits derived from bonded labour to produce racist cultures characterized by the brutal and systematic dehumanization of blacks. Every possible expression of African culture – from language to music, ritual and dress – was demeaned and repressed by colonial authorities and slave-owners, not simply out of spite or prejudice but as part of a premeditated and omnipresent calculation that only such violent suppression could secure the myth of innate white supremacy and reproduce modern slavery from one generation to the next. As Robin Blackburn has remarked, claims surrounding the infra-humanity of Africans were contradicted daily by the complex cooperation and coordination involved in plantation labour and by the relentless sexual interest of whites in their black or mulatto slaves: 'The most disturbing thing about slaves from the slaveholder's point of view was not cultural difference but the basic similarity between himself and his property. Africans could procreate with Europeans, and occupied the same ecological niche. As Benjamin Franklin was to observe, slaves, unlike sheep, could rise in rebellion.'[19]

It was precisely these two interlinked preoccupations – racial intermixture and rebellion – which fostered the self-consciously racist culture that accompanied nineteenth- and twentieth-century imperialism. In her pathbreaking work on the emergence of scientific racism in Britain at the turn of the nineteenth century, Nancy Leys Stepan argued that the two most important factors in such a development 'were the existence of black slavery in the colonies of Europe in the New World, and the emergence of the modern, biological human sciences.'[20] Although the two were not structurally related – Stepan is at pains to underline the autonomous dynamics of race science at that time – biological taxonomies of race were first formulated in response to abolitionist arguments and revolutionary upheavals of the late nineteenth century against slavery and in favour of the universality of human rights. Thereafter they came to inform and legitimate the racial hierarchies employed by Europeans in their administration of colonial peoples across the world.

Forged in the crucible of New World slave plantations, this new, biological racism began to emerge at the very moment when colonial slavery was in retreat and the Atlantic slave trade in the process of being abolished. Stepan addresses this paradoxical coincidence by noting the shift from a social or political definition of race towards a biological understanding of colour gradation. The Age of Democratic Revolutions across both shores of the Atlantic produced different degrees of social and political emancipation for American and Caribbean peoples of colour and, with the important exceptions of Brazil and Cuba, had by the mid-nineteenth century dealt a death blow to the natural connection between race and slavery. White supremacism, however, did not disappear, and, ironically, it was the abolitionist turn to physiological arguments for our common humanity that opened up the possibility of renaturalizing racism, thereby stripping it of the very socio-economic or political content which had fuelled anti-slavery campaigns and rebellions in the first place. 'Increasingly', Stepan suggests, of the period between 1775 and 1833,

> the moral claim of the black and other so-called 'inferior' races, slave and free, to equality of treatment was taken to be a matter not of ethical theory but of anatomy. If all races

were found to be anatomically and physiologically alike, then the rights and privileges enjoyed by the European would be guaranteed for all peoples. The appeal to nature in deciding what was in reality a moral issue was fatal, but one made by the anti-abolitionists and eventually abolitionists alike. Nature was now the arbiter of morality.[21]

As with the controversy over the Indies, the status of colonial peoples of colour was the subject of intense theoretical debate and political agitation during the nineteenth century, both in Europe and in the Americas. This time, however, the dialectic of civilization and racialization was played out in the language of modern science and through rational–bureaucratic institutions of social control. In the metropolitan centres, the naturalization and depoliticization of racism took the form of scientific disputes between, broadly, those who defended the prevailing monogenetic accounts of human origins from a common descent and those who adopted polygenetic arguments suggesting that there existed various species of human beings defined by race or 'type'. On this latter account, developed among others by the Scottish anatomist Robert Knox, human beings were not only divided biologically into different species – as in the distinction between humans and primates – but were also organized in a hierarchical fashion, with Aryans topping a scale which descended to the negro as the lowest human type before apes. These expressions of scientific racialism secularized the traditional cosmological notion of 'the Great Chain of Being', which in its various historical incarnations had ordered earthly life-forms along a natural scale which eventually led to an other-worldly Creator. Most important for our purposes, however, is the way such racialist doctrines used miscegenation and its consequences as a scientific litmus test of their theories. For according to polygenists the amalgamation of different races, like the cross between different species, produced infertile offspring. 'If hybrids were fertile through several generations', Robert Young points out, 'then this would undermine the polygenetic argument that the different races were fixed into permanent types for all time.'[22]

The debates between monogenists and polygenists petered out in the latter half of the nineteenth century, but they undoubtedly contributed to the racialization of imperial civilization. Both camps had drawn from existing racist stereotypes – particularly as applied to African-Americans – and popularized notions of biological hierarchies between races in ways which reinforced their legitimacy. The idea, for instance, that the product of white and black unions was barren (and treacherous, effete or surly with it) had been widespread among European colonists since the sixteenth century (as suggested by the etymological derivation of mulatto from '*mula*', or mule). This myth was rendered in scientific form two hundred years later by racialists such as Knox when he proclaimed, among other reasons, 'that, the races of men differ from each other, and have done so from the earliest historic period is proved . . . by the infertility of the hybrid product, originating in the intermingling of two races.'[23] Even when the opposite view was expressed, as in the case of those mid-Victorian authors who saw racial cross-fertilization as delivering an improved 'breed', fusing the best characteristics of both 'stocks', the use of racial categories was both absolute and hierarchical. Following the naturalistic logic that racial properties, like those of species, were the result of acclimatization to different environments, one advocate of racial amalgamation in the Caribbean put it thus: 'Providence has sent white men and black men to these regions in order that from them may spring a race fitted by intellect for civilization; and fitted by physical organization for tropical labour.'[24]

While arguments over the infertility and degeneration or otherwise of mixed-bloods raged among scientists and intellectuals of the metropole, authorities in the colonies had to administer the realities of racial intermixture. Throughout the course of the nineteenth and early twentieth century, and across different imperial outposts, sexual relations between Europeans and natives became the subject of significant social control and political regulation, as did their hybrid 'fruits of passion', whose status was periodically revised in light of imperial requirements of racial hierarchy. In his study *Race, Sex and Class under the Raj*, Kenneth Ballhatchet vividly illustrates the dilemmas faced by the authorities in India, which sought both to uphold the 'social distance' between the British 'ruling race' and the natives and at the same time to deal pragmatically with the socio-cultural and political consequences arising from physical proximity among different races.[25]

One manifestation of this contradiction was the complex infrastructure of so-called Lal bazaars and lock hospitals, the first being red-light districts which serviced the cantonments of the Indian Army, the second clinics specializing in the prevention and treatment of venereal diseases. Although much of the rationale and logistics for the organization of such sexual industry and its attendant public health infrastructure stemmed from European experience, the debates over the relative merits of these two colonial institutions betrayed an assumption that any sexual intercourse between white men and native women, especially among Britons of the lowest social orders, had to take the depersonalized, commercial form of prostitution. British soldiers were on the one hand forbidden from marrying local women, but on the other hand recognized as having 'physiological natural instincts' which required attention in ways other than the abhorrent practices of masturbation or homosexuality.[26] Lal bazaars and lock hospitals, though subject to considerable controversy and local censure, thus reflected an institutional solution to the colonial quandary of keeping a social distance between races while recognizing the need of young British men, especially those of lowly status, to satisfy their basic instincts with local women. Put bluntly, British soldiers could have sex with Indians, so long as they were whores.

Such racialized conceptions of the sexual relations between colonist and native were applied to their offspring too. Clearly there are considerable variations in time and place, but the experience of one Franco-Vietnamese youngster in late nineteenth-century Indochina, recounted in detail by Ann Laura Stoler, is in many respects paradigmatic of the anxiety modern empires have demonstrated about cultural hybridity.[27] This particular story revolves around a nineteen-year-old boy, Nguyen van Thinh, also known as Lucien, the son of a French citizen and his unnamed Vietnamese concubine, who was in 1898 sentenced to six months in prison by a colonial tribunal for assaulting a German naval employee. Van Thinh/Lucien's father appealed this sentence, claiming it was excessively harsh, but the ruling was upheld by the governor-general. Stoler draws our attention to the assumptions underlying the exchanges between the boy's father and the authorities, which reveal a colonial state highly sensitive to any attempt at raising van Thinh/Lucien's status to that of a French citizen purely on account of his father's nationality. (The account, incidentally, also reveals the father's own casual racism and xenophobia.) On this occasion, the appeal was rejected because the child was deemed to act, look and have behaved in a manner that could only make him the 'alleged son' of a Frenchman. It was furthermore implied that the relations between van Thinh/Lucien and his 'alleged father' were of an immoral (for which read homosexual) character. All this echoes many of those experiences of miscegenation mentioned above, with its combined emphasis on appearance, behaviour, parentage and social milieu as cultural markers. 'But', Stoler insists,

> what was more unsettling in this case was another unspeakable element in this story: namely, that Icard [the boy's father] felt such a powerful sentiment between himself and his son and that he not only recognized his Eurasian son but went so far as to plead the case of a boy who had virtually none of the exterior qualities (skin tone, language or cultural literacy), and therefore could have none of the interior attributes, of being French at all.[28]

What seemed to exercise the colonial authorities most, therefore, was the very possibility of recognizing a mixed-race boy as an equal to a 'pure' Frenchman, the idea that a European may express straightforward fatherly love towards his mixed-race son without attention to racial hierarchy. Such a reaction, once again, cannot simply be attributed to misguided prejudice or ignorant bigotry, but rather to the very material requirement for upholding an imperial order built on European racial supremacy. As Stoler demonstrates in her comparison of French Indochina with the Dutch East Indies, the recognition of mixed-race unions and their offspring could have momentous – generally disruptive – legal, socio-economic and cultural implications for imperial rule, and so colonial officials from both metropolitan centres were keen to exchange notes on their common predicament. At the turn of the twentieth century several reforms, reports and campaigns sought to address the condition and status of the *métis* population, generally by upholding a patriarchal understanding of the head of family as the conduit of nationality. This ideal of assimilation through filial recognition of mixed-race children, however, was – as in India – undermined, according to colonial officials, by untidy sexual habits and dishonest practices of poor whites. They alleged that unscrupulous European soldiers and civilians were exploiting the racial differential in labour and penal codes by recognizing native children for a fee. This not only constituted criminal behaviour, but more seriously put into question the racial distinctions which buttressed imperial administration. 'The issue of fraudulent recognition', Stoler argues, with reference to both the East Indies and Indochina, 'like concubinage, hinged on the fear that children were being raised in cultural fashions that blurred the distinctions between ruler and ruled and on the fear that uneducated native young men were acquiring access to Dutch and French nationality by channels, such as false filiation, that circumvented state control.'[29]

Nativism and the invention of tradition in Africa

The tensions between civilization and racialization thus found expression in nineteenth- and twentieth-century European imperialism primarily through the distinctively modern institutions of racial science and the legal–bureaucratic colonial state. The ideal of an imperial order guided by European cultural canons and strict racial hierarchies was constantly contradicted by the realities of an unstoppable and disorderly admixture of imperial peoples. The most consistent manifestation of this imperial predicament became the 'problem of the hybrid': how to define, classify and control those increasing numbers of colonial subjects who fell outside the categories of white and native. But there was a third and final form of the civilization/racialization dialectic, built not so much on scholastic notions of barbarism or on the scientific racism explored above, but rather on a strategy of 'nativism'. This expression of imperial culture, constructed in part on myths of the 'noble savage' and essentialist notions of cultural authenticity, in other respects out of sheer administrative pragmatism, is best represented in the institutions of indigenous rule and native authority which accompanied the imperial penetration of the African continent from the latter part of the nineteenth century.

This strategy of racialization essentially involved two interrelated processes: on the one hand the cultural *differentiation* between natives and non-natives, and among indigenous peoples themselves, and, on the other hand, the subordinate *devolution* of political rule by the colonial state onto groups of differentiated natives. The first process was built on cultural categories which accompanied conquest, be it through military force, Christian proselytizing or the organization of labour markets; the latter found expression in institutions of indirect rule – first tested in India before 1858 – which granted local tribal chiefs, religious notables or regional strongmen the right to exercise authority over locals *on behalf of* the colonial state. The concrete shape adopted and the results achieved by such a strategy varied considerably across different parts of Africa at diverse junctures during the extended European presence in that continent. But it would be fair to say that in all instances the aim was to sustain minority rule by Europeans while recognizing the need to accommodate, and indeed exercise, political authority through various 'indigenous' institutions of rule.

Such bifurcation of power along 'vertical' lines of racial domination and 'horizontal' axes of ethnic differentiation is what Mahmood Mamdani memorably defined as 'decentralized despotism': an attempt 'to create a dependent but autonomous system of rule, one that combined accountability to superiors with a flexible response to the subject population, a capacity to implement central directives with one to absorb local shocks.'[30] As we shall see in a moment, the 'local shocks' Mamdani refers to ranged from military insurgency through to labour shortages or insubordination. But they were all addressed through a highly racialized conception of culture which, despite adopting the guise of ethnic, customary or traditional 'identity', always assumed white superiority. Indeed, as Mamdani indicates in another context, notions of identity built on seemingly neutral categories of ethnicity, custom or kinship did not trump racist culture: '*Culturally,* races were said to be a civilizing influence and ethnicities in dire need of being civilized. Whereas race claimed mainly to reflect a *civilizational hierarchy*, ethnicity was said primarily to be about *cultural diversity*. Neither claim excluded the other.'[31] Let us briefly consider three moments in the process of empire-building – pacification, administration and exploitation – where this nativist strategy of racialization played itself out.

The first is the imperialist domain par excellence, namely that of military conquest. Echoing the experience of past imperial campaigns, particularly that of Napoleon in Egypt, the French pacification of the Maghreb after the invasion of Algeria in 1830 serves as a paradigmatic example of how culture and conquest became deeply intertwined in the process of colonial occupation. Patricia Lorcin notes how, in Algeria, 'Warfare was the circumstance in which the initial contact between the French and the indigenous population was consummated and, because the French in question were military men . . . the images of the indigenous population formulated during warfare persisted and were absorbed into the received wisdom about the Kabyles and the Arabs.'[32] Military men on the spot, such as one commanding officer, Edouard Lapène, became ethnographic authorities on the peoples of the region and were instrumental in crafting the enduring myth of the Berber Kabyles as a 'martial race' descended from Germanic tribes and, like them, characterized by a strong sense of property, a pronounced work ethic and non-aristocratic, consultative forms of decision-making. In the following decades, again in the context of combat, a cultural distinction crystallized in French minds between the virtuous, sedentary mountain-dwelling Kabyles and the treacherous, nomadic Arabs of the plains. This dichotomy subsequently took on various forms, including ascribing to Kabyles and other berberophone peoples of the Maghreb (principally in Morocco) qualities which, in contrast to Arabs, made them naturally inclined to Christian conversion, commercial interaction and diplomatic relations with Europeans. While Berbers were seen as industrious, honest and independently minded, Arabs were deemed by European observers to be indolent, perfidious and submissive.

Much of the power of these stereotypes derived from military encounters between French and local forces. After successful pacification in the middle decades of the nineteenth century, the focus in Algeria, and later in Tunisia and Morocco, shifted towards administration and colonization. This second moment of empire-building in turn compromised simplistic dichotomies between Arabs and Berbers as other, religious and customary, sources of authority were enlisted into the business of colonial rule. In Tunisia and Morocco, imperial conquest left the existing beylik and sultanate intact, allowing the French to use the authority and infrastructure of these two pre-colonial dynasties in buttressing their rule. Similarly, local *qadis* (judges), tribal sheikhs and sufi notables were mobilized for campaigns of both pacification and administration. France's first resident-general in Morocco, Marshal Louis-Hubert Lyautey, applied principles of indirect rule in that protectorate, gleaned from the British experience in India and Nigeria, thus becoming a Gallic version of Lord Lugard.[33] Even in Algeria, where formal annexation to the French *hexagone* in 1848 of the country as three new *départements* delivered more centralized and racialized forms of administration and law, local *qadis* and religious elders were to play a distinctive role as formal representatives of the Muslim 'communities' in the colonial institutions.[34]

It was, however, in the rest of Africa where 'traditional' sources of power and authority were most radically recast to fit the mould of colonial domination, in this instance articulated through the political economy of capitalist imperialism. As Mahmood Mamdani demonstrates in his classic study, the European colonial state 'bifurcated' political authority in Africa by separating the domain of a largely urban civil society, inhabited overwhelmingly by whites and ruled through modern civil law, from that of the rural terrain where natives lived under 'traditional' customary law. Both these realms were artificially constructed on the basis of what Eric Hobsbawm and Terence Ranger have called the 'invention of tradition' in Europe and its colonies alike, during the two or three decades either side of the First World War. Elastic, changing and often indeterminate notions of kinship and custom existing before European conquest were refashioned under colonialism into static institutions of native authority with their accompanying symbols and rituals of power. 'In this colonial middle period', Ranger writes, 'African "paramounts" strove to gain the title of king, to obtain invitations to British coronations, to dramatize their internal authority with crowns and thrones, British-style coronations and jubilees.'[35] Such exercises in cultural engineering were, however, always directed from, or at least authorized by, the colonial power; they were, in other words, expressions of a subordinated or, at best, supervised legal and cultural autonomy.

Among the principal driving forces behind this machinery of collaboration were the peculiar requirements of the colonial economy. As European imperialism moved inland in the late nineteenth century from its trading stations on the African littoral towards the continent's rural hinterlands, the colonial state came into its own as the preferred agent of capitalist development. The stated aim of imperial powers at that time was to civilize African societies by valorizing their natural and human resources, making land and labour productive – or, in the French rendition, facilitating the *mise en valeur* (exploitation) of its colonies. In order to do so, however, the military–juridical power of the colonial state would have to be deployed in breaking the back of the 'natural economy' and inducing a capitalist market for land and labour, as well as building the necessary transport and communications infrastructure for the expanded reproduction of capital to take root. The actual outcome across most of Africa under European control during successive decades was in fact to be very different. The colonial state found it increasingly difficult to reconcile its mandated task of legitimation and accumulation: upholding law and order (as understood by colonial elites) while simultaneously promoting the generation of value through the proletarianization of African peasants, the commercialization of their lands and crops, and the commodification of the continent's natural resources. Time and again during the fifty years before the Second World War, across different parts of the continent, European rulers resolved the multiple contradictions between profit-maximization and policy-making, capitalist development and colonial control, by fostering social relations of production and institutions of government – from forced labour to slavery, from native authorities to military administration – which departed significantly from the metropolitan ideal of a modern capitalist society governed through the neutral, rational–bureaucratic authority of the state. As Anne Phillips suggested in her classic study on British rule in West Africa, 'Colonial rule could be sustained only through a complex of shifting alliances within which local rulers and colonial officials were acutely aware of the limitations of their control. Colonialism was necessarily makeshift. Its history was one of adjustment to conditions it could not dictate, and the abruptness of decolonization gave open expression to a lack of control which had existed all along.'[36]

At the root of this colonial predicament was the African resistance to the commodification of land and labour, combined with demographic and environmental obstacles to extensive and accelerated capitalist development as envisaged by European interests. The absence of an indigenous labour market, coupled with relatively free access to land for the local population, led the colonial state to create a labour force through directly coercive forms of exploitation such as convict or conscript labour, or through the indirect mechanisms of taxation (most notably the 'hut tax') or vagrancy laws.[37] With regard to land too, the initial aim of converting existing patterns of land tenure into a regime of private property stumbled across both local opposition and political discrepancies among and within metropolitan and colonial administrations, thus resulting in a succession of stalled land reforms which in the end reinforced 'customary' uses of land. But the critical obstacle to capitalist development of land lay in the authority over the provision and control of labour the colonial state had invested in African chiefs. For so long as the latter remained responsible for the recruitment and administration of local populations, customary law became entrenched as the dominant source of access to and exploitation of land. This structural contradiction generated an insurmountable barrier to the expanded reproduction of capitalism in colonial Africa, a situation which is once more neatly summarized by Phillips:

> The [colonial] state was forced into an alliance with local chiefs as the only reliable guarantors of labour, which in turn

dictated the terms on which colonialism operated. The recurrent problems of land and labour revolved around this alliance with chiefs. Free access to land precluded the formation of a landless proletariat, and was ensured by relations of communal land tenure which installed the chiefs as agents of political order. The coercive powers of these chiefs provided the colonial state with the means to recruit labour, but to sustain these powers the right to alienate land had to be curtailed. There was no way out of this circle. The proletarianization which could in principle have broken through it was well beyond the capacity of the colonial states.[38]

The category of the 'native' thus played a signal role in each of the three 'moments' of European empire-building in Africa just discussed – pacification, administration and exploitation. Far from 'modernizing' the African continent by forging a pristine culture of capitalism where class trumps ethnicity, the public is neatly divided from the private, and the state acts as a neutral arbiter between the competing interests of civil society. European imperialism delivered a contradictory combination of new and old social forces, capitalist and non-capitalist institutions, which in the event came to reproduce (and sometimes even invent) static and essentialist uses of cultural identity. Such operationalization of the 'native' as an instrument of colonial rule and exploitation was not simply a premeditated metropolitan strategy of control or a mere consequence of local resistance to capitalist encroachment. Rather it emerged, in diverse permutations and at different tempos across Africa, as a pragmatic response to the pressures faced by the colonial state in both sustaining a sociopolitical order and facilitating the capitalist development of Africa on behalf of European interests.

Culture and the subversion of empire

Most of this chapter has thus far been dedicated to outlining the uses of culture generally, and racist culture in particular, in upholding modern imperial rule. Such sustained attention to the role of culture as a tool of imperial domination is warranted because cultural traffic under modern empires has principally been hierarchical and one-directional. The interrelated spheres of language, law and religion are perhaps the most obvious and enduring manifestations of this unequal cultural exchange. It is unsurprising, for instance, that the world's three largest languages today in terms of native speakers – Chinese, English and Spanish – are also the languages of three modern empires, and that the eight successive languages on the list, spoken by close to half of the globe's population, are also connected to the modern world's other powerful empires.[39] Some of this may of course be due to population growth and the policies of linguistic homogenization pursued by national states, but the worldwide spread of Indo-European languages during the past five hundred years, at the expense of existing forms of communication, alone attests to the linguistic power of empire.

Language is obviously a medium of imperial authority, essential to the administration of colonial authority and the conversion to the dominant religion.[40] Here again, metropolitan legal forms and religious practices accompanied imperial expansion, displacing existing expressions of law and belief at best to a subordinate position (as in the case of Jews and Christians under the Ottomans), and at worst to the margins of colonial society (as occurred through the extension of Roman law or, more radically, the Christian conversion of the Americas, Africa and significant parts of Asia and the Pacific). In any event – and notwithstanding all the protracted and uneven unfolding of such changes depending on each concrete experience – empires have in the main been quite successful in imposing their own language, law and religion on colonial populations. In these spheres at least, imperial culture lives up to its claims to omnipotent universality.

Yet an account which focuses exclusively on these real and powerful manifestations of cultural domination risks overlooking the rich, pervasive and often equally powerful expressions of cultural subversion which accompanied imperial expansion. Edward Said has, among other cultural theorists, drawn our attention to the need for a contrapuntal reading of imperial culture whereby narrative – historical, fictional or (auto)biographical – itself becomes a battleground among proponents and opponents of empire. Writing of modern imperialism, Said suggests that, 'to ignore or otherwise discount the overlapping experience of Westerners and Orientals, the interdependence of cultural terrains in which colonizer and colonized co-existed and battled each other through projections as well as rival geographies, narratives and histories, is to miss what is essential about the world in the past century.'[41] Among other things, Said is here highlighting three features of imperial culture which are germane to our discussion.

The first is the recognition that colonial peoples and territories are an integral and vital component of metropolitan culture. Continuing the task he first set out in *Orientalism*, Said dedicated large chunks of his later study *Culture and Imperialism* to uncovering the presence, both literal and figurative, of the colonies in the metropolitan imagination.[42] Through a close reading of canonical texts of nineteenth- and twentieth-century French, British and US culture – ranging from Jane Austen's *Mansfield Park* to Verdi's *Aida* – Said demonstrates how these works inscribe the possibility and actuality of empire, how the imaginary landscape of their narratives is nourished by – and indeed itself nourishes – the reality of imperial expansion. The claim here is not simply that colonial peoples have long been represented – generally in a negative, passive or subservient fashion – in Western cultural forms: that much is evident to any casual observer of Western art. Rather, the argument is that much of this colonial presence is hidden, sublimated or devalued by a dominant narrative. Accordingly, Said is concerned with adding a spatial dimension to predominantly temporal readings of Western culture. 'We should try to discern', Said suggests, in this instance speaking of Austen and Coleridge, 'a counterpoint between overt patterns in British writing about Britain and representations of the world beyond the British isles. The inherent mode for this counterpoint is not temporal but spatial.'[43]

This spatialization of the metropolitan imaginary was of course not limited to the domain of 'high' culture. In the sphere of 'popular' culture too representations of colonial 'Others', primarily, though not exclusively, peoples of colour, also played a signal role. Blacks, Asians, Irishmen and – in a different way – Jews were variously stereotyped in jokes, comics, advertising, adventure stories, children's books, exhibitions and, later, cinema.[44] Their humanity and agency was stripped to one of several essential attributes – aggressiveness, stupidity, childishness, slothfulness, licentiousness, greed and dishonesty – depending on the context, but always by way of highlighting white or, with the rise of jingoism, national superiority over colonial peoples and imperial rivals.

Plainly, this is not to suggest that all Western popular culture was racist or indeed necessarily referred to empire. Nor, more importantly, do colonial peoples appear in Western popular culture for purely instrumental reasons of mobilizing the metropolitan masses behind empire. Instead, the suggestion is that significant expressions of metropolitan popular culture – ranging from Tintin to tartan – were simply unthinkable without empire. As Anne McClintock has demonstrated in her impressive study on the interconnections between race, gender and sexuality in the 'colonial contest', the ideological constructs associated with empire found concrete cultural expression in very quotidian, seemingly innocent forms, like for instance body soap. Taking the Unilever Company slogan 'Soap is Civilization' at face value, McClintock demonstrates how empire was deeply implicated in branding and advertising the humble soap-bar as cleanliness became associated not just to godliness, but to the values, habits and institutions that brought greatness to the British empire.[45] Once again, this was no mere ideological exuberance on the part of jingoistic marketing departments. The new commodity congealed all the constitutive elements of capitalist imperialism: it was made from vegetable oils extracted in colonial plantations, produced by one of ten large conglomerates, marketed with racist and patriarchal imagery which fetishized the purity and domesticity of imperial order, and then sold to both metropolitan slum-dwellers and uncivilized natives as a marker of progress: 'The emerging middle class values – monogamy ("clean" sex, which has value), industrial capital ("clean" money which has value), Christianity ("being washed in the blood of the lamb"), class control ("cleansing the great unwashed") and the imperial civilizing mission ("washing and clothing the savage") – could all be embodied in a single household commodity.'[46]

In the same way that the colonies were replicated in metropolitan culture so, more obviously and overtly, was the metropole involved in the culture of the colonies. Here Said is no less insistent upon the need to read the modern histories of colonial cultures contrapuntally, avoiding what he calls the 'Defensive, reactive, paranoid [anti-colonial] nationalism [which] alas, is frequently woven into the very fabric of education, where children as well as older students are taught to venerate their tradition (usually and invidiously at the expense of others).'[47] Indeed, without erasing the hierarchical and structurally unequal features of cultural traffic under imperial rule, it is nonetheless impossible to understand the modern cultural history of colonial and post-colonial societies without reference to terms such as 'hybridity', 'syncretism' or 'transculturation'. Colonial societies have, even in the most hostile environments, created cultural forms that are the unique product of imperial flows and which cannot be authenticated with exclusive reference to this particular tradition or that specific ethnic group.

Consider for instance language and religion which, as was just indicated, were key instruments of empire. There are currently over fifty pidgin and creole languages – ranging from Réunionais to Macanese – spoken by millions of people across five continents. Both these linguistic forms are the product of European (and to some degree Arab, African and Chinese) commercial expansion; one derivation of 'pidgin' is the Cantonese '*bei chin*', meaning 'give money' or 'pay'.[48] From the *lingua francae* of trade, pidgin languages became Creoles spoken by diverse peoples concentrated by empires in specific colonies, in some cases, such as Mauritian or Papiamentu in Curaçao, even becoming standardized national languages. This process of linguistic creation was clearly hierarchical: it was premised on what Louis-Jean Calvet labelled 'glottophagie'[49] (the gobbling up of other languages by a dominant one) and in many cases reproduced in language the inequality between colonizer and colonized. (In the Philippine island of Zambionga, for instance, the local Chavacano Creole uses Spanish-derived words for positive adjectives and words of Philippine origin for their antonyms – big is '*gránde*' while small is '*dyútay*', smooth is '*líso*' and rough is '*makasap*', and so forth.)[50] Yet Creoles have also been appropriated as 'cultural carriers' – as mechanisms of self-assertion by those exploited and oppressed by imperial power, using them as mediums of communication outside the official channels of rule and therefore turning them into expressions of autonomy and possible weapons of subversion.

Something similar could be said of dominant religions. In the American experience, for instance, Christian conversion produced new, syncretic forms of belief and spirituality which combined elements of European doctrine, liturgy and custom with indigenous practices or imported 'carryovers' from Africa and Asia. African slaves, for example, reconstituted Yoruba worship rituals in the New World and superimposed them upon expressions of Iberian Catholicism to produce belief systems such as the Afro-Cuban *Lucumí* (or *Santería*) and its Haitian and Brazilian cousins *Vodou* and *Candomblé*.[51] Similarly, the Mexican celebration of All Saints' Day, or *Día de los Muertos*, on the first two days of November is also a living expression of how popular Catholicism in the Americas blends and reinvents Iberian and pre-Columbian rituals and imagery.[52] Here, too, ritual offerings, conceptions of death and afterlife, and their representation in artefacts shaped as skulls and skeletons that formed an integral part of Mesoamerican culture before Spanish conquest survived into the post-Columbian period and were reworked within the dominant European idiom.

There is considerable debate surrounding the degree to which these diverse cultural expressions constitute an actual fusion of European and African or Mesoamerican belief systems, or whether they in fact represent deeper continuities in African and Amerindian practices which are simply hidden under a veneer of popular Catholicism.[53] What seems indisputable, however, is that such cultural expressions were unique to the New World insofar as the reconstitution of meaning – be it spiritual or otherwise – had to adapt to, and was necessarily influenced by, the cultural cross-currents produced by imperialism. Thus, for instance, *Lucumí* iconography was not only inspired by Spanish baroque styles but, with the arrival of Chinese coolies in Cuba in the late nineteenth century, also incorporated aspects of Chinese numerology. By the nineteenth century *Santería* was further modified through the import of a peculiar form of Spiritism, invented by the French engineer Allan Kardec, and through the interaction between different African traditions in the

Americas. Similarly, the iconography and rituals of the Mexican Day of the Dead incorporate the distinctive features of diverse pre-Columbian cultures, and have more recently adopted forms derived from French and North American influences. New World popular cultures are thus not merely the amalgamation of reified 'traditions' – be they African, European or Mesoamerican – fused together by imperial fiat, but rather the ever-changing product of multiple and contradictory interactions between custom and innovation, appropriation and rejection, the local and the foreign.

The final, and perhaps most important, element of Said's contrapuntal injunction is that of opposition and resistance. For struggle, dissent and outright antagonism have always accompanied the experiences of cultural interdependence and superimposition surveyed above. No matter how rigidly enforced or violently imposed, imperial cultures have always been contested through both everyday forms of resistance and momentous revolutionary upheavals. In the realm of the everyday, apparently trivial expressions of colonial culture become a field of struggle between the oppressor and the oppressed. In his celebrated autobiographical account of a life dedicated, among other pursuits, to cricket, the Trinidadian Marxist C. L. R. James paints a vivid portrait of West Indian cricket under colonial rule.[54] In the opening chapters of *Beyond a Boundary*, he dissects the organization of his island's cricket club membership along lines of class, colour, education and religion. The top club, Queen's Park Oval, was 'for the most part white and often wealthy. There were a few coloured men among them, chiefly members of the old well-established mulatto families.' The Shamrock, next in terms of prestige, was 'the Club of the old Catholic families'. Other clubs were reserved either for black plebeians, white inspectors, black lower-middle class or, as in the case of the Maple Club, for 'the brown-skinned middle class', who had 'founded themselves on the principle that they didn't want any dark people in their club'.[55] This picture in many respects epitomizes the dynamics of imperial culture: the grafting of a metropolitan game, itself imbued with the class division between landlord and farmhand, onto the distinctively colonial social cleavages, and the appropriation of the game by colonial peoples as a conduit for the assertion of cultural

identity and social status. Yet what is perhaps most interesting for our purposes in James's account of West Indian
cricket is his emphasis on culture as a battleground. For
James, 'in those years social and political passions, denied
the normal outlets, expressed themselves so fiercely in cricket
(and other games) precisely because they were games.' Class
and racial rivalries, he continues, 'were too intense. They
could be fought out without violence or much lost except
pride and honour. Thus the cricket field was a stage on which
selected individuals played representative roles which were
charged with social significance.'[56]

Such social significance stretched to sartorial matters too.
Imperial culture produced social gradations which explicitly
or implicitly mandated what everyone was to wear, and
thereby also solicited expressions of fashion which deliber-
ately or surreptitiously challenged the strictures of imperial
culture. We saw earlier in the chapter how Spanish authorities in Mexico sought to regulate the attire of some urban
blacks and mulatto women, claiming that they dressed too
exuberantly and provocatively. Similarly, in nineteenth-
century Havana, dress and lifestyle became a zone of contestation, as some free Afro-Cubans took to dressing in a
flamboyant style, filing their teeth, growing dreadlocks and
developing an argot incomprehensible to others, all of which
merited the new epithet '*negros curros*', literally 'the black
show-offs' (allegedly inspired by the Goyaesque lowlife
'*curros*' or '*manolos*' of Andalusian ports). As David H.
Brown, building on the work of Fernando Ortiz, has indicated, '[t]he *curros* presented themselves in a manner that
defied easy ethnic or socio-institutional placement within the
colonial society. They were neither members of determinate
African nations, nor the free classes of trades-people. Indeed, their nineteenth-century denomination, *curro*, was not
grounded in empirical social categories, but based precisely
on their manner of cultural performance – their expressive
and subversive "showiness".'[57]

During roughly the same period, this time in India, clothing also became a matter of colonial contestation. Dress (and
undress), next to physiognomy and arguably before language,
has been an elementary marker of colonial distinction, and
nineteenth-century India was no exception. The difficulty for

the British in India, as for other colonists elsewhere, was how to strike a balance between the need for a social distance from the indigenous populations while at the same time bringing them closer to civilization through clothing. Equally, for many Indians, the decision of what to wear and when to wear it was of considerable social and personal import, as it could radically alter the terms of engagement with Europeans, fellow caste members, co-religionists, relatives or regional acquaintances. Moreover, as Emma Tarlo has indicated, clothing is a domain of everyday life where matters of political economy, cultural identity and political affiliation combine in especially perverse ways.[58]

Under colonial rule, colonizers and colonized adopted different strategies accordingly. By the nineteenth century, the British increasingly accentuated the European origin of their dress and behaviour – even if this created difficulties in conducting everyday business in a different climate. This was partly in response to the adoption of Western clothing among increasing numbers of the urban Indian elite. Yet most Indians seemed to have chosen intermediary options between absolute Westernization and 'traditional' local dress: those living in bustling commercial centres might use foreign fabrics in Indian styles; many rural notables in Ceylon combined European and local garments, wearing trousers under their sarongs by way of distinguishing themselves from other villagers; while those Indians who worked in close contact with Europeans might sport Western clothes at their place of employment and change into Indian dress at home. Whatever Indians chose to wear, Tarlo concludes, 'The clothing dilemmas for the Indian élite in the late nineteenth and early twentieth centuries were but one expression of a more general growing discomfort with colonialism. They revealed the impossibility of respectability or neutrality in an environment in which all sartorial options were loaded with negative implications of one kind or another.'[59]

Negative or otherwise, we have seen, the dynamics of imperial culture cannot be reduced to the imposition of metropolitan languages, institutions, tastes and beliefs upon colonial peoples. This is obviously a major part of the story, but it is worth continually introducing the analytical and narrative counterpoint of synthesis and struggle over the form and meaning of imperial culture, both in its vanguard and in its popular expressions. This not only allows us to grasp the full complexity and richness of colonial and post-colonial cultures, but crucially also points to the power of opposition and resistance – once again, in both its everyday and world-historical forms – in shaping and transforming imperial cultures. Indeed, as the concluding section of this chapter suggests, the success of many struggles for an anti-imperialist culture today throws up the question of whether a new constellation of transnational cultural expressions – a global culture, to use the accepted term – has now replaced imperial culture.

Cultural imperialism or global culture?

One way to approach the question of change and continuity in the cultures of imperialism is to consider briefly the life and work of Wilfredo Lam, a signal figure in twentieth-century painting. Born in Cuba in 1902, Lam was the child of a Chinese immigrant father and a Cuban mother of mixed European and African ancestry. He was raised as a Roman Catholic and, like many other Cubans, simultaneously initiated by his godmother into *Santería*. After a spell at a Havana academy, where he studied European academic realism, Lam left Cuba in 1923 for Spain. There he married a local woman, Eva Piriz, and settled for the next fourteen years until the fall of the Spanish Republic. As a staunch supporter of the Republican cause, he was exiled to Paris in 1938. He made the acquaintance of fellow avant-garde artists Pablo Picasso, Max Ernst, Oscar Dominguez and André Breton, among others. With the fall of Paris to the Nazis, Lam began a seven-month trip back to Cuba via Martinique, where he struck up a lifetime's friendship with Aimé Césaire, the leading intellectual behind the *Négritude* movement. Once resettled in Cuba, Lam developed his most significant works, combining *Lucumí* motifs with surrealist techniques and drawing on the flora, fauna and folklore of his Caribbean birthplace to produce distinct post-Cubist expressions of tropical art. 'The result of his ambitious undertaking', one art historian notes, 'might have been no more than an awkward hybrid, but instead it resulted in a vigorous, original art. By asserting the importance of the African cultural diaspora yet assimilating it to the internationally prominent aesthetics of Europe, he also succeeded in declaring the reality of culture in the New World.'[60]

Like many of his contemporaries born into a colonial culture, Lam also personifies the key moment of transition to a post-colonial world in the two decades either side of the Second World War. He physically embodied the creolization of the New World and his transatlantic crossing retraced the movements not just of conquerors and slaves, but also of the ideas and politics of the revolutionary Atlantic forged around figures such as Bolívar, Equiano, L'Ouverture or Paine. Lam's art was the very picture of vibrant syncretism, his politics resolutely democratic and internationalist, and his personal life marked by mixed-race marriages among equals which must be considered as pioneering in interwar Europe, certainly in a Spanish context. Lam's life and work also exemplify the continuing power of racism, the abiding presence of Africa in America, and the persistent struggle for national liberation not just in the political and economic realms but in the cultural one too. In short, Lam's trajectory, his aesthetics and the times he lived through seem both familiar and remote in today's allegedly postmodern, globalized, multicultural and hybridized world. I would therefore like to close this chapter by using Lam as a reference point in assessing how far a global culture has today replaced a bygone imperial culture.

In his lucid appraisal of the term 'cultural imperialism', John Tomlinson identifies four ways of employing this composite notion: as media imperialism, as a discourse of nationality, as a critique of global capitalism and as a critique of modernity.[61] All four are pertinent to our discussion in that they refer in one way or another to the imposition, through direct or indirect means, of a homogenizing, dominant culture by an imperial metropole onto subordinated cultures. Yet it is perhaps the first two that are of most salient relevance in that they attach to the transnational power of Western culture the capacity to undermine and even erase national or local forms of cultural practice. In contrast to this, some cultural theorists have called for a shift away from national or local conceptions of culture towards a notion of global culture or, more recently, a global modernity characterized by transnational flows in media, finance, ethnic identity and technology, which create different, decentred yet often overlapping global spaces of cultural expression.[62]

The first thing to note in looking at the dynamics of modern imperial culture is that such dichotomies between national and international, local and foreign, indigenous and exogenous appear as historically suspect. As this chapter has endeavoured to demonstrate, the cultural hybridity, fusion and disjunction associated with postmodern globalization have long been features of modern imperial culture. There is therefore far greater substantive continuity in the imperial and post-colonial expressions of culture than advocates of a global modernity would allow for. Recognizing this is important not only for the purposes of periodization but also, crucially, in distinguishing between flows, syncretism and exchange under conditions of imperial rule from those that characterize our post-colonial world. Put differently, while we have arguably witnessed the continuity in the *processes* of cultural hybridity associated with empires, the *structural forms* adopted by such processes have radically altered. Specifically, the cultural flows are no longer one-directional – indeed the very locations of hybridity have been displaced from the colonies to the erstwhile metropole, while the processes of cultural fusion are no longer premised on a structural correspondence between the dominant culture and imperial authority. The anti-racist slogan chanted by British blacks and Asians in the 1970s 'We are here because you were there' neatly encapsulates this structural shift: the colonial realities which remained hidden or unstated in the high culture of the imperial metropole have, since the postwar migration of Africans, Asians, Caribbeans and Latin Americans to Europe, become part of everyday popular culture in the former metropolitan centres. The cultural inequalities and antagonisms produced through imperial gradations of race, colour, language or religion have today been relocated to urban Europe, Japan and the USA and have to be reproduced and challenged in the context of political equality, urban multiculturalism and a market economy fully attuned to the benefits of formal 'diversity' (the 'United Colors of Benetton' slogan on this account simply means that Benetton will exploit peoples of all colours equally). The unequal ethnic distribution across urban geography, moreover, continues in many so-called global cities (even more so in their provincial hinterlands) to replicate the racialization of the more institutionalized imperial segregation. Yet here again, the distinction between informal and formal means of separating and subordinating ethnic groups is sufficiently stark to warrant speaking of a racism that is post-imperial insofar as it is increasingly reproduced through the more private, surreptitious mechanisms of the housing or labour markets: racial segregation and degradation are no longer imposed through imperial fiat, but through the differential access to property, education, qualifications or communications chiefly mediated through money (or lack thereof). These expressions of racism are no less troublesome or aggressive – the legacies of imperial culture clearly live on in the former metropoles, they simply manifest themselves in radically different forms to those which guided historic empires.

If the advocates of global culture are therefore right in stressing the displacement of cultural hierarchies in ways that make talk of cultural imperialism as a discourse of nationality appear increasingly irrelevant, those cultural critics who emphasize the power of transnational media as an expression of cultural domination stand on stronger ground. The concentration of the world's audiovisual and printed media production and distribution into a handful of Western-owned conglomerates is evidence for some critics of the continued cultural domination of the world by ex-imperial powers. Dress codes, dominant languages and musical forms, means of communication, or values and beliefs are no longer imposed directly by colonial authorities, but they insinuate themselves through media outlets in such pervasive and surreptitious ways that we can usefully speak, so advocates of media imperialism insist, of a cultural homogenization and domination via satellite. There can be little doubt that such Western media conglomerates do indeed control vast sectors of the world's cultural market. Yet at least three important facts limit the cultural power of such conglomerates in ways that, once more, make talk of imperialism in this context very problematic.

First and most important, unlike the Christian conversion of Amerindians or the exclusive use of European languages in colonial administration, we all have the option of turning off the TV, switching channels or avoiding the Murdoch press. The choice is a restricted one, to be sure, and it often requires considerable extra effort (and resources) to find alternative outlets of information, communication or recreation. But the very existence of a degree of consumer sovereignty which a commodified culture offers must obviously be distinguished from the forceful and institutional consumption of official culture by most colonial peoples. Second, and related, any meaningful usage of media imperialism as a tool of cultural domination would have to account for the prodigious cultural production in many post-colonial societies, most notably India, Hong Kong, South Korea, Mexico or Brazil. It would be disingenuous to ignore the fact that, say, much of Bollywood cinema is for domestic consumption, or that Mexican media outlets are tied to US or European capital. Yet the idea that post-colonial audiences are passive consumers of foreign media, or that powerful post-colonial states do not have the wherewithal to develop local cultural industries which can give shape to distinctive cultural contributions, is itself entirely unrealistic and bordering on the patronizing. Unlike the continent which Lam left for Europe, much of today's Latin America is in a position to exercise a cultural autonomy which was entirely unthinkable in the context of colonial rule.[63] Finally, it should be noted that global cultural trends and patterns of the last decades, ranging from world music to so-called magical realism, point again to the inversion of cultural flows. The royalties and profits from world music collaborations are no doubt still pocketed predominantly by metropolitan performers and recording companies. It is also possible to interpret some of the most commercially successful collaborations between Northern and Southern artists – Paul Simon's *Graceland* is generally cited as an example – as exploitative appropriations of local idioms and, worse still, exercises in essentializing non-Western musics. Yet here again talk of cultural imperialism seems misplaced, as there is no semblance of structural domination of one culture by another. Paul Simon, and other Western artists that have dabbled with 'world music', such as David Byrne, Peter Gabriel or Sting, may be accused of naïve politics, ethnocentric lyrics or artistic self-indulgence, but positing a relation of cultural imperialism in such cases of contingent inequalities devalues the power of the term.[64]

In line with the rest of the book, then, I have argued in this chapter that there have been substantial changes in the vectors of global power since decolonization. The structural forms of cultural domination which underpinned modern imperialism cannot be equated with contemporary inequalities in the global production and distribution of cultural power. Put bluntly, racism no longer operates as an overt and inherent mechanism of rule over foreign peoples and domination of their culture in the way that it did at the height of European, Japanese and American imperialism. Similarly, the cultural cross-fertilization which accompanied European imperial expansion over the past five hundred years is today much more multi-directional and open to egalitarian and democratic intervention, both within and between states and nations. (It is, because of this, also far less subversive.) The legacies of imperialism plainly live on, and the global asymmetries of power clearly persist, but they are organized and manifested in radically different forms to those which obtained under historical empires. Indeed, seen through the prism of Wilfredo Lam's own life and works, it might be argued that the aesthetic syncretism and cultural hybridity which he extolled have very much triumphed over the hierarchies of imperial culture. Only the democratic internationalism which characterized his politics seems today more elusive than it was during his own lifetime.

5
After Empire

The study of empire is above all a study of specific expressions of power. One need not fall into linguistic reductionism when recognizing that the etymological association of empire with 'command' and 'rulership' reveals an essential meaning of this concept. Previous chapters will hopefully have illustrated how the notion of empire has retained some categorical identity across time and place in describing a particular way of enforcing a political order – of exercising power – through a geographically expansive and socially hierarchical combination of political, economic and cultural institutions. Empire, on this account, is about domination: an expression of power which can, and indeed should, be usefully distinguished from other, related concepts such as hegemony, global governance or primacy. For unless 'empire' is to be used as a catch-all phrase to describe any asymmetrical projection of extraterritorial power (in which case, Spain's economic reliance on earnings from Northern European tourists and pensioners might qualify as an 'imperial' relationship) it becomes imperative to distinguish between different manifestations of global geopolitical and socio-economic inequality, and identify the specificity of the social structures which sustain them.

One aim of this concluding chapter is to explore such a proposition in greater detail, with specific reference to recent studies that have also considered the nature of power in international relations more generally, and empire as a particular organization of power. Because of its extraordinary (for many, undeserved) impact on the contemporary debates surrounding empire, the eponymous book by Michael Hardt and Antonio Negri occupies a significant part of the discussion that follows. Whatever one's view on the substance of Hardt and Negri's thesis, their work has the virtue of drawing together a number of historical and conceptual strands to the study of empire which help to focus debate on the contemporary usefulness of the category. To this extent, Hardt and Negri's volume, and the range of concepts and challenges it throws up, will serve as a key reference point in outlining diverse contemporary approaches to empire and other formulations of global power.

A term such as empire, however, is not made and unmade by blockbusters alone. Discussion of empire has become a pressing political issue, and has occupied many of the best contemporary minds across the world, chiefly as a result of American power. The invasion and occupation of Afghanistan and Iraq by US-led coalitions, which followed the terrorist attacks of September 11, 2001, are the main proximate causes for the revival of this term in mainstream debate. Both proponents and opponents of US global power use the notion of empire to signal, variously, the dangers, responsibilities or irrationalities attached to recent US foreign policy. A second principal aim of this chapter is therefore to consider the value of a concept such as empire in explaining the current international conjuncture. Here attention will centre not only upon the different explanations for the 'imperial turn' in US foreign policy, but also on the ongoing – and, for many, related – experiments in international governance of so-called failed states. The last decade has witnessed the emergence of 'new trusteeships' in the form of UN-mandated administrations in the Balkans and elsewhere which raise the question as to whether we are experiencing a return to protectoral or mandatory forms of sovereignty for those states and peoples unable or unwilling to rule themselves according to the new standard of civilization.[1] Here once again the terms 'empire' and 'imperialism' are deployed in different senses, with some making a direct analogy between classical imperialism and the post-Cold War 'imperialism of human rights', while others associate the new interventionism and the ensuing international administrations with a new, more elusive form of empire built on liberal governance and reproduced through the Foucauldian notion of 'bipower'.

The discussion that follows starts with a section dedicated to the uniqueness of the postwar American empire. US ascendancy in the course of the Second World War occurred under a very peculiar world-historical circumstance: one where formal empires were crumbling and national sovereignty was extending itself as a universal norm. This was a world organized politically not through the hierarchy of imperial domination but in an anarchical 'pluriverse' of formally equal sovereign states. Under such conditions, the USA extended its global reach – its empire if one wishes – by promoting capitalist markets and sovereign states or, to use two catch-phrases from American historiography, by opening doors and closing frontiers. This reality forced commentators on postwar US foreign policy to consider the nature of imperialism in a post-colonial world, developing new theories and insights into how and why the USA can exercise global supremacy without formally controlling overseas territories (the Puerto Rican case aside). More recently, in the light of the US military incursions and occupations of foreign lands, a flurry of essays by critical and mainstream scholars have pondered on the breaks and continuities in US external relations after the Cold War, and what can account for this 'imperial turn' under the Bush II presidencies. The section will outline the major contours of these debates, including a range of Marxist and neo-Weberian takes on the character of contemporary US power.

This overview will hopefully set up the historical backdrop and theoretical context for a second section dedicated to a sustained exposition and evaluation of Hardt and Negri's novel and highly influential understanding of empire. According to these authors, power under empire is decentred; that is, it does not issue from any single place or location, but rather is omnipresent in a 'flexible network of microconflicts'. Imperialism of the old, territorial form, they argue, has disappeared and been replaced (so to speak) by a new form of global rule – an Empire – which is boundless and universal in its real subsumption of all the world's population to the power of capital.[2] This is an understanding of empire which chimes with postmodern writings on international relations, insofar as the latter emphasize the annihilation of space by time under conditions of globalization. Yet it also retains a view of empire as control over people, not territories – just like pre-modern and early modern variants. Such eclectic uses of empire, it will be argued, deliver a view of the present international conjuncture which, bizarrely, bears greater resemblance to the neo-liberal utopia of a smooth, unstriated space of market exchange than it does to the world of class, racial and gender hierarchies underpinning the reproduction of global capitalism. Above all, however, Hardt and Negri's view of Empire grossly overstates the demise or transformation of territorial forms of politics in the contemporary world, thereby missing what is arguably one of the defining features of contemporary empire: the use of extraterritorial force to reconstitute state sovereignty.

A penultimate section of the chapter, before the book's closing remarks, considers the shortcomings of such conceptions of empire when addressing the issue of the 'new trusteeships' and the associated notion of the 'new interventionism' as forms of liberal imperialism built on the enforcement of universal human rights. For the post-Cold War humanitarian interventions have been about shoring up state sovereignty and securing the reproduction of liberal norms within states, not suppressing and denying them to local populations as much of classical imperialism did. Recent experiments in state-building and the emerging norm of the responsibility to protect populations threatened by grave violations of human rights are best seen as part of an attempt at enforcing a global liberal order, *but always through the mediation of legitimate state authority*. Insofar as this order is upheld through the use of force beyond the USA and the territories of its allies, it may be deemed imperial. But it is an historically unprecedented kind of imperialism that actively seeks to foster viable national states and prosperous economies rather than violently undermine and militarily defeat rival centres of political power and economic accumulation. Moreover, such 'promotion of polyarchy', to use Bill Robinson's phrase, has found willing takers among local social forces keen to uphold private property relations, free markets and

– here there is a key difference from classical imperialism –
the civil liberties and electoral democracy that are meant to
accompany the liberal package.[3] The global reproduction of
capitalism generates not only impersonal networks of market
exchange, but also forms of social and political subjectivity
which often invoke and mobilize in favour of liberal norms
– even if these are to be imposed from the outside. The particularity of American empire, once again, is that it increasingly relies on this social base of transnational liberalism in
legitimating its own global supremacy.

American empire

On the eve of the Second World War, Stephen Ambrose has
noted, the USA was a hemispheric power with no network
of diplomatic alliances, no troops garrisoned abroad and,
given its size, a modest army and military budget. 'A half a
century later', he continues,

> [t]he United States had a huge standing Army, Air Force and
> Navy. The budget of the Department of Defence was over
> $300 billion [compared to the $500 million in 1939]. The
> United States had military alliances with fifty nations, over
> a million soldiers, airmen and sailors stationed in more than
> 100 countries, and an offensive capability sufficient to destroy
> the world many times over. It had used military force to
> intervene in Indochina, Lebanon, the Dominican Republic,
> Grenada, Central America, and the Persian Gulf, supported
> the invasion of Cuba, distributed enormous quantities of
> arms to friendly governments around the world and fought
> costly wars in Korea and Vietnam.[4]

With the end of the Cold War, such global power projection
has hardly diminished: the USA spends more on defence than
the next twenty-four states put together; it patrols all major
seaways with its five active fleets, has extended further its
international complex of military bases into the Middle East,
Central Asia and East and Central Europe, and dominates
global surveillance networks. It has furthermore activated
this lethal force abroad on at least a dozen occasions since

1991, ranging from the first Gulf War and the Balkan conflicts to the more recent interventions in the greater Middle East. The USA continues to produce 30 per cent of the world's economic output, while the US dollar remains the dominant currency of global exchange. What word other than 'empire' could possibly convey the scale and scope of dominance attached to such an inventory of power?

For most commentators on the left, the answer is plainly: 'none'. Indeed, in the postwar years, a whole school of lazily called 'revisionist' American historians systematically investigated the imperial past and present of the USA, mainly arguing that American overseas expansionism – both formal and informal – could be explained with reference to domestic economic and political factors in much the same way that classical theorists of imperialism had done with Europe at the time of the First World War. Inspired by the radical historian Charles Beard, successive generations of scholars of American diplomacy such as William Appleman Williams, Walter LaFeber, Marilyn Young, Carl Parrini and Gabriel Kolko gave the lie to the idea of American exceptionalism, demonstrating that the USA had from its inception been engaged in empire-building.[5] According to the leading revisionist Walter LaFeber, Washington had annexed Hawaii and acquired the Philippines and Cuba from Spain in 1898 as a result of 'the industrial revolution . . . and, most important, *because of the implications for foreign policy which policy makers and businessmen believed to be logical corollaries of this economic change, the new empire reached its climax in the 1890s.*'[6] His mentor, William Appleman Williams, had earlier argued that the USA built its empire on the basis of the principles of an 'open market for the commerce of the world', enunciated in Secretary of State John Hay's 1898 'Open Door' notes regarding European and Russian trade in China. Significantly, the notes also highlighted 'the administrative reforms so urgently needed for strengthening the [Chinese] Imperial Government and maintaining the integrity of China in which the whole western world is alike concerned.' For Williams, the genius of the US empire (and the tragedy of its diplomacy) lay in its power projection overseas through an 'imperial anti-colonialism': the promotion of free markets and strong states enshrined in the Open Door policy. The latter, Williams insisted, 'is neither a military strategy nor a traditional balance-of-power policy. *It was conceived to win victories without wars*', and instead assumed that 'America's overwhelming economic power could cast the economy and politics of the poor, weaker, and underdeveloped countries in a pro-American mold.'[7] This capability, Williams insisted, is what made the USA an empire.

Such an emphasis on imperialism of free trade, however, begged the question of why, if the Open Door policy was about accruing profit without making wars, the USA became embroiled in various large and small wars, deploying its military forces abroad more than two hundred times during the Cold War. The answer for most revisionist historians seemed to lie in the same drive for markets and the manipulation of a domestic constituency that had characterized earlier imperial adventures. To this they added the emboldened resistance to US imperialism by revolutionary groups who sought to cash in the promise of national sovereignty in a currency different to that of American liberalism and market capitalism. The gap between an American understanding of democracy and freedom and other people's conception of these values, so the revisionists argued, is what accounted for Cold War antagonisms.

Although rich in historical detail and bold in its core thesis surrounding the historical continuities in American imperialism, the revisionist notion of empire as the use of extraterritorial power remained entirely empiricist: there is precious little in these writings about the properties or structural characteristics of imperial power. The causes behind US imperialism are moreover heavily focused on the American metropole: the possibility that peripheral social forces or other geopolitical powers may condition or constrain US grand strategy is heavily muted in the revisionist accounts of the American empire as an essentially proactive phenomenon – and almost always successfully so.

Yet some of the key turning points in US postwar foreign policy – National Security Council memorandum 68, the normalization of relations with China, Reagan's rollback doctrine – were reactions to transformations forged far away from Washington, DC – in China, Vietnam, Nicaragua,

Angola or Iran. Moreover, as Geir Lundestad famously suggested with reference to postwar Europe, the American empire was in large measure fashioned 'by invitation'.[8] Across the various fault lines of the Cold War, local social forces – both elite and popular – eagerly sought military and socio-economic cover from communist and revolutionary threats under the umbrella of US global power. This, some scholars have suggested, is best understood as a form of hegemonic rather than imperial power in that it rests on consent and cooperation, not exclusively on force and domination.[9] More importantly, world hegemony is on this account a form of global power that relies on the coordination of autonomous states and social forces in sustaining a particular order. Unlike empire, hegemony has no final instance, no decisive location or moment of authority, but is reproduced instead through a sequence of coordinated and generally consensual actions by a multiplicity of actors, albeit orchestrated by a leading state and rooted within determinate social relations of production. This notion of world hegemony spawned its own 'neo-Gramscian' school of international relations, and its leading exponent defined the term thus:

> To become hegemonic, a state would have to found and protect a world order which was universal in conception, i.e. not an order in which one state directly exploits others but an order which most other states . . . could find compatible with their interests. Such an order . . . would most likely give prominence to opportunities for the forces of civil society to operate on the world scale. . . . The hegemonic concept of world order is founded not only upon the regulation of inter-state conflict but also upon a globally conceived civil society, i.e. a mode of production of global extent which brings about links among social classes of the countries encompassed by it.[10]

Subsequent neo-Gramscian IR theories have substantiated these claims by considering various historical and contemporary instances of world or regional hegemony with reference to the Trilateral Commission, the European Roundtable of Industrialists, transatlantic relations or US foreign policy more generally.[11] Mainstream scholars such as Joseph Nye or John Ikenberry have also employed cognate terms such as 'soft power' or 'unipolarity' to emphasize that American hegemony is sustained through cultural and institutional sources of authority – ranging from computer software packages and business schools through to international regimes and financial rating agencies – that rely on peaceful, consensual exchange among private parties rather than the public, coercive power of the state.[12]

Plainly, the difference is in part one of emphasis and intensity: both empire and hegemony combine coercion and consent in different measure, although hegemony veers towards the latter and empire towards the former. The Greek origins of hegemony evoke a benign, commercial and voluntary league of states led, as in ancient Hellas, by a selfless democratic republic. It is an image much beloved by defenders of American primacy, and is thus generally preferred to the violent, militarist and territorialist expansionism associated with the Roman *imperium*. The principal distinction between these two terms, however, is a structural one, relating to the kinds of socio-economic and political instruments of power which ruling classes can muster at different historical junctures. The structural power of the capitalist market, for instance, is more conducive to a hegemonic form of rule by virtue of its inherent and necessary reliance on the private domain of economic exchange. We saw in previous chapters how, before the emergence and global spread of capitalist social relations, the world market was deeply embedded in, indeed directed by, military and political institutions of authority. The state and civil society were not structurally separated as they are under capitalism, and consequently power could be and, as in the case of Spanish and Ottoman revenue collection, *needed* to be exercised through the directly coercive, violent and therefore imperial authority of the state and its officeholders. Similarly, the political division of the world into hundreds of territorially discrete national states presents a structural impediment to the imperial organization of political space characterized, as it has been historically, by the constantly shifting and expanding frontier. There no longer exist frontiers to be conquered, only borders to be transgressed. And this, contemporary ruling classes have found, is best done through the world capitalist market and its accompanying regimes of inter-state coordination: that is, through hegemony, not empire.

Such an understanding of American power bears considerable resemblance to the postwar arrangements between major capitalist powers where trilateral cooperation and integration among Americans, Europeans and East Asians on the diplomatic, military and socio-economic fronts replaced the militarized inter-imperial rivalry of earlier decades. But it clearly fails to account for the repeated military incursions of the USA (and indeed imperial and post-imperial European powers) into the regions outside the trilateral zone during and after the Cold War. The war on terrorism and the accompanying wars in Afghanistan and Iraq, together with the enunciation of a new doctrine of globalized pre-emption, have further challenged the view of American hegemony as a principally consensual expression of global power. In the light of these developments, a whole raft of studies have reassessed the issue of American power in our times, generally with reference to the notion of empire. Much as in the early decades of the twentieth century, the central question today is why the world's foremost liberal polity and leading capitalist economy has turned to war and occupation as a means of projecting its power internationally. Linked to this is also the issue of how far the Bush II administrations have marked a break in postwar US grand strategy.

For Marxist scholars, the principal causes behind contemporary US imperialism remain the same as those which animated the classical European imperialism of the early twentieth century, even if the conditions and outcomes are different.[13] As keeper of the world's leading economy, the US state is above all else concerned with making the world safe for capitalism: that is, securing through a combination of multilateral regimes and its own phenomenal military power an international order of stable, sovereign but pliant states that are open to the world economy. Wherever this order is challenged or undermined, the USA has replaced the hidden hand of the market with the iron fist of its military. As in classical Marxist theories of imperialism, the underlying assumptions here are that capitalism's limitless search for surplus value – albeit driven less by 'underconsumption' and more by crises of over-accumulation – constantly transgresses territorial boundaries, and that the state, as a conduit for capitalists' interests, tends to employ its juridical and military resources to this end. Unlike classical theories, contemporary Marxist analyses do not consider that inter-imperial rivalry will inevitably lead to war among capitalist powers, nor do they now associate imperialism exclusively with territorial conquest. But they do insist, in different ways, that the reproduction of global capitalism is structurally uneven and skewed towards US interests in ways that can only be described as imperialist.

On some accounts, under conditions of US unipolarity, the asymmetrical distribution of global power is actually orchestrated and policed from Washington, DC, in such ways as to merit the term 'super-imperialism' or 'primacy'. Peter Gowan has formulated a compelling version of this argument, suggesting that '9/11 offered an opportunity for American class and state leaders to . . . reconfigure the relations between the American state and its external and internal environment in ways that will assure a world order in which American capitalism can flourish as a socio-economic, political and ideological phenomenon.'[14] By encroaching militarily on the rimlands of its main Eurasian rivals (China and Russia), polarizing world politics along the lines of a new Cold War (this time against global terrorism) and unilaterally reconfiguring existing multilateral regimes, Gowan contends, the Bush II strategy of primacy has pulled '[t]he state elites of the main international powers . . . into a new structure of dependence on the services of the American state'.[15] Similar accounts of the Bush II turn in foreign policy have been presented by David Harvey, Ellen Meiksins Wood and Alex Callinicos, although they place different emphasis, respectively, on the demonstrative effect of the Iraqi invasion on possible geostrategic contenders, the control over world energy markets, and the inherent violence in 'accumulation through dispossession' as sources of the new American imperialism.[16]

From another, ideologically sympathetic, perspective, the shift from multilateralism to militarism under the Bush II administrations is explained by 'the increasing difficulties of managing a truly global informal empire'.[17] For Leo Panitch and Sam Gindin, the American empire has since the end of the Second World War operated best under conditions of deep political, military and economic interpenetration between various capitalist social formations. Such conditions were facilitated by the politics of postwar reconstruction and Cold War bipolarity, but under the current 'unipolar moment' the USA faces the challenge of unilaterally and peacefully transforming the world into its own image. 'Since the American empire can only rule through other states', Panitch and Gindin indicate, 'the greatest danger to it is that the states within its orbit will be rendered illegitimate by virtue of their articulation with the imperium.'[18] The critical contradiction within such a state of affairs, they conclude, is that 'an American imperialism that is so blatantly imperialistic risks losing the very appearance of not being imperialistic – that appearance which historically made it plausible and attractive.'[19]

For Marxists, then, contemporary American imperialism forms part of a broader pattern of postwar hegemony built on the USA's role as leading capitalist power. Global markets require political and military regulation by the most powerful states, and, with the collapse of the communist alternative, US elites have seized the opportunity unilaterally to reorder the world's energy markets, political structures and strategic balance in favour of American interests, through peaceful means where possible, with violence if necessary. Marxists disagree on the actual combination of coercion and consent implicit in such a programme; they also differ on which of these objectives – Middle Eastern oil, democratization, deepening commodification, military emasculation of rivals – plays a leading role in such a strategy. But they are agreed that, whatever the aims and means, the outcomes are likely to be contradictory and painful for the USA and the world at large.

Many liberal commentators concur with this assessment, and indeed take the argument further, suggesting that the American empire either is too incoherent to deliver on claims to omnipotence, or actually finds itself in terminal decline. Although he understands power differently as stemming from four distinct sources rather than as a totality with manifold expressions, Michael Mann has echoed much of the Marxist analysis when highlighting the vulnerability of an empire built on the structural foundation of a capitalist market and an international system of states.[20] For his part, the French demographer and economist Emmanuel Todd has offered a quantitative analysis of US power which concludes that 'the declining economic, military, and ideological power of the United States does not allow the country to master effectively a world that has become too vast, too populous, too literate and too democratic.'[21] Capitalist markets are notoriously difficult to control or regulate politically at the best of times, and at present the US economy's current account and fiscal deficits have made it increasingly dependent on investment and credit from its allies and competitors alike. Politically too, the USA cannot cajole and intimidate other large states and their peoples in the way that previous empires did: '[n]ineteenth-century client rulers were much less troublesome than today's. They could not refuse or bargain with the British or French, or even Belgian imperialists. The Europeans overthrew them if they tried.'[22] Contemporary US hegemony on the other hand has been obliged to manage clients with far greater political autonomy and socioeconomic and military resources than erstwhile colonial peoples. It is thus unable, as its European predecessors did, simply to deploy overwhelming financial and industrial clout in dominating markets through informal means. The USA undoubtedly stands alone as a military superpower. But the current American fixation on military supremacy, Michael Mann contends, misses the point that empires must also dominate politically, economically and ideologically if they are to prevail. While the USA may be able to defeat minor military adversaries with relative ease and at little human cost on its side, it finds it much harder to pacify and administer occupied territories in the way that previous empires did. This is not due simply to incompetence, hubris or stupidity (although these always play a part in history) but results instead from the structural limits to the exercise of extraterritorial power in a world of nation-states. For Mann, like Todd, Washington's turn to militarized unilateralism actually betrays the weakness of US hegemony rather than its imperial prowess. 'The American Empire', Mann concludes, 'will turn out to be a military giant, a back-seat economic driver, a political schizophrenic and an ideological phantom. The result is a disturbed misshapen monster stumbling clumsily across the world. It means well. It intends to spread order and benevolence, but instead creates more disorder and violence.'[23]

Postmodern empire

The debates over the relative decline or otherwise of American power are likely to rage on. In the meantime, no matter how incoherent or vulnerable, the USA remains able to wield formidable military force, political authority and economic influence in ways which international actors ignore at their peril. These expressions of power may stop short of imperial domination, but their impact is not lost on Iraqis, Palestinians, Iranians or indeed Europeans, Asians and Latin Americans. Washington, DC, and New York City – and now increasingly Seattle, Atlanta or the San Francisco Bay area – concentrate institutions of power that still have a disproportionate bearing on the socio-economic and geopolitical affairs of the world, while their geographical location remains indicative of the interests they serve.

It is in this context that the most influential account of empire in recent times, released by an Ivy League university publisher, advanced the controversial claim that '*The United States does not, and indeed no nation-state can today, form the center of an imperialist project.* Imperialism is over. No nation will be the world leader in the way modern European nations were.'[24] Throughout their book, Hardt and Negri, contrast the notion of imperialism ('an extension of the European nation-states beyond their own boundaries') which obtained during previous centuries with that of a twenty-first-century postmodern Empire: 'In contrast to imperialism, Empire establishes no territorial center of power and does not rely on fixed boundaries or barriers. It is a *decentered* and *deterritorializing* apparatus of rule that progressively incorporates the entire global realm within its open, expanding frontiers.'[25] Underlying this seemingly straightforward proposition – and the book has a tendency to simplify for polemical purposes[26] – are a host of more complex arguments relating to the forms of rule, production and resistance which permeate the brave new world of Empire. I shall shortly consider the core elements of Hardt and Negri's thesis under these successive headings. Before doing so, however, two important features of *Empire* should be underlined when considering its claims. Firstly, the authors insist that their approach to empire is neither metaphorical nor analytical but rather strictly conceptual: their aim is to offer 'a general theoretical framework and a toolbox of concepts for theorizing and acting in and against Empire'.[27] Purely empirical refutations of their arguments would therefore appear to miss the thrust of their enterprise, which is to identify the dominant tendencies in the constitution of power under Empire and develop new concepts which might capture such transformation in the dominant forms of power. Secondly, and following on from this, although Hardt and Negri's volume is self-consciously eclectic in its use of historical and philosophical sources, it is consistently informed by a peculiar kind of Marxism which blends elements of industrial sociology associated with Italian 'autonomist' or 'workerist' thinking with concepts of biopower, control, de/territorialization and governmentality first employed by the French social theorists Michel Foucault, Gilles Deleuze and Félix Guattari. The result is an often hermetic and self-referential text, the full meaning of which requires reference to 1970s Franco-Italian Marxist politics and theory.[28]

Indeed, it is that decade of crisis and upheaval across the world which, for Hardt and Negri, signalled the passage from the modern world of imperialism to the postmodern world of Empire. The book opens with the constitution of a new world order built on supranational, post-imperialist 'figures of power' which are in turn inscribed in a properly 'imperial notion of right'. Such reconfigurations of juridical power are expressed in the shift from national to supranational authority in the shape of the United Nations; the supplanting of domestic law by universal law; the development – in a Schmittian vein – of a permanent state of global exception; and the concomitant transition from the postwar norm of absolute sovereignty to the post-Cold War right of intervention. This novel constitution of world power is furthermore premised on the accumulation of consensual interventions in the name of universal rights. It does not issue from any specific location, nor does it serve particular national interests. 'Empire', Hardt and Negri insist, 'is formed and its intervention become juridically legitimate only when it is already inserted into the chain of international consensus aimed at existing conflicts. . . . The first task of Empire then, is to enlarge the realm of the consensus that support[s] its power.'[29]

Accompanying this supranational codification of Empire is a reconstitution of territory. Hardt and Negri ascribe to capitalist globalization the tendency to 'flatten' space, and with it the hierarchies attached to modern structures of state and nation. These are, in the authors' view, the product of a transcendental, constitutional conception of *potere* or *pouvoir*, associated with a Hobbesian civil society which in the course of the seventeenth century imposed itself upon, and thereby stifled, another, Spinozian, understanding of power as an immanent, constituent *potentia* or *puissance*. In doing so, the prevailing, national form of modern state sovereignty is always exclusionary, constantly reproducing an 'inside' and an 'outside' – the private and the public, the domestic and the international, the compatriot and the foreigner, the civilized and the barbarian. Modern sovereignty delivered an imperialism characterized by racism, territorial expansion, militarism and fantasies of national exceptionalism and superiority. The move to Empire cuts across these hierarchies and separations to the extent that, as one of the subheadings of the book has it, 'There is No More Outside'. Even social cleavages of race, gender and sexuality have become more fluid and indeterminate under Empire, no longer expressive of a modern strategy of exclusion to a specific space (the ghetto, the household or 'the closet') but now rather defined through 'differential inclusion'.[30] Hardt and Negri write: 'The striated space of modernity constructed *places* that were continually engaged in and founded on a dialectical play with their outside. The space of imperial sovereignty, in contrast, is smooth . . . there is no place of power – it is both everywhere and nowhere. Empire is an *ou-topia*, or really a *non-place*.'[31]

The reconstruction of political space under Empire is buttressed by a parallel reorganization of production. True to their Marxist heritage, Hardt and Negri wish to emphasize the interconnections between the manifold transformations in our socio-economic, political and cultural lives. Capitalist globalization has not just changed the relationship between states and markets, it has also revolutionized our collective metabolism with nature. For Hardt and Negri the real – not just formal – subsumption of the world's population to the capitalist world market has been facilitated, and has itself been accelerated by, the increasing use of information and communication technologies, flexible production chains ('Toyotism') and the 'tertiarization' of the economy in the exploitation of labour. Such networked organization of production and its accompanying empowerment of deterritorialized financial markets, service industries and multinational corporations has in turn put a premium on the 'immaterial' labour derived from affective or communicative capabilities embodied in phrases such as 'customer care' or 'knowledge economy'. Here Hardt and Negri marry notions of 'informatization' and 'post-Fordism' to Foucault's concept of biopower, arguing that under Empire production is increasingly geared towards the direct control of human nature and the reproduction of social life generally: 'In the biopolitical sphere, life is made to work for production and production is made to work for life. It is a great hive in which the queen bee continuously oversees production and reproduction. The deeper the analysis goes, the more it finds at increasing levels of intensity the interlinking assemblages of interactive relationships.'[32]

This emphasis on the biopolitical dimensions of capital leads to a third key component of *Empire*, namely 'the multitude'. Hardt and Negri once again retrieve from autonomist Marxism a vitalist, generative understanding of labour's relation to capital. On this view, the capital relation constantly produces not just commodities, but new subjectivities which themselves bear the potential for shaping and indeed transcending capitalism. Thus, the very networks of immaterial labour and deterritorialized forms of rule that constitute Empire carry within them the latent possibility of immanent power. On the one hand, the strength of Empire resides in its capacity to penetrate ever more dimensions of our lives through the mechanisms of biopower. On the other hand, this very requirement of capital constantly to colonize greater areas of our life world, to impose itself 'throughout unbounded global spaces to the depths of the biopolitical world', generates networks of communicative, linguistic and cooperative interactivity which, in one of their more exuberant moments, Hardt and Negri consider to prefigure 'a kind of spontaneous and elementary communism'.[33]

Postmodern globalization, then, delivers an Empire not just regulated through a supranational constitution and reproduced by networks of capital increasingly valorized by immaterial labour, it also, and crucially, conjures up a new global subject consonant with the immanent and decentred forms of imperial power. The 'multitude' has replaced 'the People' and indeed the 'working class' as the agent of global democracy. While the first is an indeterminate, expansive and constituent plethora of movements, the latter two are, respectively, the product of mediated, representative power institutionalized in the modern sovereign state and the Taylorist, industrial regimes of labour. Struggles against capital built around nostalgic notions of national liberation, the seizure of state power or the mobilization of peasants and workers in trade unions or political parties are, for Hardt and Negri, self-defeating under the rule of Empire. Because power is everywhere and nowhere, since imperial biopolitics permeates the very core of our human existence, it follows that only an equally immediate, ubiquitous and antagonistic political subjectivity of the 'multitude' can challenge imperial rule. Such a counter-Empire cannot be organized around a coherent strategy and led by any named movement; it is instead the constituent outcome of a relentless, unmediated, transversal and rhizomatic militancy.

Hardt and Negri's rendition of Empire is unquestionably the most original and challenging reformulation of the concept since the classical Marxist debates. It binds together in an often inchoate and elusive manner various strands of thinking on globalization, post-modernity, post-colonialism, capitalism, power and resistance in ways that have plainly chimed with the current Zeitgeist (certainly of the northern part of the globe). The book and its core thesis have been subject to both withering critiques (focusing principally on the absence of a rigorous political economy of the world economy) and more sympathetic appraisals which nonetheless note the internal inconsistencies and the conflation of tendencies with realities.[34]

This is not the place to evaluate all these various critiques, but, with the backdrop of previous chapters, one core claim of *Empire* stands out as being especially incongruous at the current global conjuncture. And that is the book's insistence on the constitution of Empire through supranational authority. As the next section will indicate, there is a strong argument to suggest that the dominant concern among international elites revolves around state reconstruction and the shoring up of state sovereignty among so-called failed, collapsed or precarious states. The constitution of a new world order on this view is not about flattening or smoothing the striations of the international system, or indeed about superseding sovereignty with postmodern forms of territoriality. It is rather about bolstering the very modern territorial sovereignty in ways that might allow legitimate states and capitalist markets to secure the expanded reproduction of a liberal world order.

Liberal empire

In substantiating this latter claim, we could do worse than start with one of the dominant anxieties among planners and strategists at the centres of global power. 'State-building', a prominent organic intellectual of the new world order suggests, 'is one of the most important issues for the world community because weak or failed states are the source of many of the world's most serious problems.'[35] In an often-cited statement, another Washington adviser brings Hardt and Negri to the Pentagon, though, tellingly, insisting on the interconnections between globalization and 'stable government':

> I will propose a new map of the world . . . that shows you which regions are *functioning* within globalization's expanding web of connectivity and which remain fundamentally *disconnected* from the process. It will show you that where globalization has spread, there you will find stable governments that neither require our periodic interventions nor warrant our consideration as threats. But look beyond globalization's frontier, and there you will find the failed states

that command our attention, the rogue states that demand our vigilance, and the endemic conflicts that fuel the terror we now recognize as the dominant threat not just to America's future security but to globalization's continued advance.[36]

It is not just intellectuals, however, that are concerned with state-building. In 1994 the US Central Intelligence Agency set up a State Failure Task Force 'to identify factors associated with serious internal political crises'.[37] The task force considered the role of distinct 'variables' – religion, ethnic tensions, economic development and conflict in neighbouring states – when explaining state failure. But the question of 'free trade' plays an especially prominent role in the study. The authors reproduce much of the liberal orthodoxy to the effect that open markets deliver more stable and legitimate states, yet they also note that states must 'secure protection of property and enforcement of contracts, both of which are prerequisites for truly open trade.'[38] The conjugation of open markets and stable states therefore appears as a special preoccupation of the US foreign policy establishment.

From an historical perspective, this emphasis on a strategy of open doors and closed frontiers is unsurprising: it is entirely consistent with the objectives and, more importantly, the resources available to postwar American power briefly discussed above. Indeed, this programme can be traced back to the Wilsonian dream of a post-colonial world made up of independent states and free markets. Like Woodrow Wilson, successive US presidents (and some of their European counterparts) have in the wake of the Cold War sought to produce a new world order organized around liberal internationalist norms and principles. The rest of this section considers, with reference to the phenomenon of 'humanitarian intervention' and the attendant 'new trusteeships' (or, more precisely, 'international transitional administrations'), whether these expressions of liberal internationalism can in any meaningful way be considered 'imperial' or 'imperialist'. The short answer offered here is that they do indeed represent a new form of 'liberal empire' premised on the forceful extension of free markets, electoral democracies and human rights. A longer response, however, would suggest that this is, once more, a very different kind of empire: unlike its predecessors, it actively seeks to promote self-government, civil liberties and territorial integrity. As the conclusion to this chapter will indicate, this does not amount to saying that the aims of liberal empire are either immediately feasible or inherently desirable. It is simply to insist that a liberal world order revolves around a different set of values and a distinct range of power resources to those of other empires.

Previous chapters will hopefully have demonstrated how empires tend to justify their supremacy with reference to lofty principles of peace, order and civilization. The Iberians conquered Americans to save pagan souls; the British acquired large parts of Africa because they sought to rescue Africans from the predations of slavery. In 1999, at the height of the Kosovo War, British Prime Minister Tony Blair declared the air assault on Serbia to be 'a just war, based not on any territorial ambitions but on values'.[39] Cold War bipolarity, he continued, had been replaced by a globalized and interdependent world: 'Now our actions are guided by a more subtle blend of mutual self-interest and moral purpose in defending the values we cherish. . . . If we can establish and spread the values of liberty, the rule of law, human rights and an open society then that is in our national interests too. The spread of our values makes us safer.'[40]

Critics of humanitarian intervention have dismissed these and other similar statements by Western leaders as self-serving rhetoric. The selective pursuit of 'liberty, the rule of law, human rights', depending on the diplomatic alignment of different regimes, they argue, belies the implicit claims to universality. The violent enforcement of such cherished values – spreading human rights through aerial bombardment – they moreover claim, reveals the moral bankruptcy and political duplicity of 'forward-leaning' liberal internationalists such as Tony Blair, Bill Clinton and, more recently, George W. Bush. 'The main concerns of the United States in the [Kosovan] war', one prominent British leftist argued at the time, 'had very little to do with the suffering of Kosovar Albanians. . . . The need to protect the Kosovars served as a pretext for NATO's bombardment, but its real aim was to secure its control of this strategic region and to fortify an extensive NATO bridgehead in the heart of the Balkans.'[41]

Such straightforward reduction of humanitarian interventionism to the Realpolitik of geostrategic aggrandizement raises at least two serious analytical questions. The first is why interventionists use human rights violations as a pretext in the first place; the second is why interventions like those in the Balkans, and more recently in Afghanistan, were succeeded by multilateral experiments in state-building and not permanent occupations.

The notion that the Western intervention in the Balkan wars of the 1990s merely reflected Washington's quest for a geostrategic and/or socio-economic sphere of influence fails to take seriously both the liberal internationalist underpinnings of the new world order and the historical realities of the region. The 'Partnership for Peace' initiative had already softened up Eastern and Central Europe for entry into the Atlantic Alliance long before the Kosovo War, and, as for its Southern European counterparts, NATO membership for former communist states was tied to accession to EU membership. With the collapse of the Soviet bloc, the West plainly sought to extend its sphere of influence eastwards, but did not need war to achieve this aim. The Balkan wars and Saddam's invasion of Kuwait did in fact threaten the post-Cold War liberal order not simply because they undermined the sovereignty of Western allies, but also because they upset a new world order built on the principle of universal human rights. That the latter have not been consistently upheld does not by itself negate the role of values in forging foreign policy – liberalism, perhaps more than any political programme, is riven by the contradiction between its principled aspirations and the realities it produces on the ground. Indeed, the inconsistency in Western interventionism over the past decade might be explained precisely with reference to such contradictions: liberal states are constantly unable to reconcile interests with values, and hence only activate 'humanitarian interventions' when the two transparently coincide. On this reading, Tony Blair's blend of 'mutual self-interest and moral purpose' quoted above must, together with similar statements (ranging from Bush Senior's own declaration on the new world order to Bush Junior's National Security Strategy document), be taken as serious, strategic manifestations of intent. They express a liberal internationalist programme which – with all its aporias – has arguably been consistent with the actual experience of the new interventionism.

Even if we assume the proclamations of humanitarian intent are mere window-dressing, hiding more sinister motivations, the pretext of human rights violations was not one invented by the West. In the case of the Balkan wars, territorial aggression and ethnic violence were premeditated and orchestrated by local nationalists, most notably Slobodan Milošević and Franco Tudjman. Kosovar Albanians had for decades been subject to systematic discrimination by Belgrade and vilification by Serbian settlers transferred to Kosovo by Milošević. Similarly, the victimization and outright murder of Bosnian civilians by Belgrade- and Zagreb-sponsored paramilitaries was, once again, part of a consistent strategy of pan-nationalist expansionism. In Iraq, the situation after 1991 was not substantively different. No sooner had the eight-year war with Iran ended, costing a million lives on both sides, than Saddam Hussein launched his second war in a decade by invading Kuwait. During the course of those two decades the Baathist regime not only persecuted, tortured and assassinated political opponents but also collectively punished whole populations – principally Kurds and southern Shi'ites. It is in this context of sub-imperialist violence and oppression that Balkan and Iraqi political groups unsurprisingly sought allies abroad. Irrespective of the programme of such groupings and the sources or legitimacy of their grievances, it is undeniable that in both these parts of the world gross violations of human rights and naked territorial aggression had been taking place long before Western intervention. To reduce such history to mere 'pretext' is not just politically disingenuous, it is also, and more important for our purposes, analytically disabling when explaining liberal empire. For in both the Balkans and Iraq liberal values did coincide with Western interests and thus gave liberal internationalism a new sense of purpose.

It is the outcomes rather than the motivations behind humanitarian interventions, however, which best reflect the liberal character of the new world order. In an important study on post-conflict 'peace building' during the 1990s, Roland Paris neatly summarizes the Wilsonian underpinnings of such experiments in world ordering:

Peace building missions in the 1990s were guided by a generally unstated but widely accepted theory of conflict management: the notion that promoting 'liberalization' in countries
that had recently experienced civil war would help to create
the conditions for stable and lasting peace. In the political
realm, liberalization means democratization in the exercise
of governmental power, and respect for basic civil liberties,
including freedom of speech, assembly, and conscience. In
the economic realm, liberalization means marketization, or
movement toward a market-oriented economic model . . .[42]

Paris is right to note the 'unstated' nature of this liberal
internationalism, as the major peace-building operations
after the Cold War (he counts fourteen from 1989 to 1999)
have indeed differed considerably in the type of mandate,
resources, and terrain under which they operated. The variet-
ies of rule encompassed under the seemingly neutral (and
generally inaccurate) terms 'peace-building' or 'post-conflict
reconstruction' have furthermore been challenged by the
wars in Kosovo, Afghanistan and Iraq where the peace-
builders have also been the war-makers, and where the UN
has been sidelined by other alliances or agencies in the process
of reconstruction. Yet underlying these various experiments
in post-conflict reconstruction is the idea that sovereign
statehood characterized by liberal governance and a market
economy should be the outcome of such interventions. In
particular, the creation of what Richard Caplan and Simon
Chesterman have called 'international administrations' in
Bosnia and Herzegovina, East Timor, Kosovo, and, more
recently, Afghanistan and Iraq raises the issue of whether we
are witnessing the re-emergence of colonial protectorates,
mandates or trusteeships under a different guise.[43]

There are at first glance some undeniable similarities
between the old mandates and the new trusteeships. Both
systems grant the 'international community' tutelage over
peoples who, for a variety of reasons, are unable or unwilling
to exercise democratic sovereignty of their own accord. Like
the League of Nations Mandates, the post-Cold War international administrations are meant to prepare such recalci-
trant states for full membership of international society,
inducing democratic behaviour and market institutions from
their populations. The interwar language of 'sacred trust of

civilization' has been replaced by its contemporary cognates 'global civil society' or 'humanitarianism', but the broad principles enunciated in Article 22 of the League's Covenant regarding the obligations of mandatory power are consonant with those, say, referring to the mandate of the High Representative for Bosnia and Herzegovina (BiH) set out in Annex 10 of the Dayton and Paris peace agreements. Contemporary analysts have noted that, unlike the League's Mandates (especially those falling under categories 'B' and 'C'), the contemporary international administrations do not hold an indefinite mandate, and, moreover, that they directly involve interested parties in the state-building process in ways that preclude speaking of neo-colonialism.[44] It is furthermore argued that, unlike the empires of yesteryear, contemporary international administrations do not seek to exploit or plunder the peoples and resources of their entrusted polities. Yet, of the half a dozen or so international administrations established since the end of the Cold War, only those in Eastern Slavonia and East Timor have successfully completed their mandates – BiH is still under international rule ten years after the signing of the Dayton peace accords, while the UN Interim Administration Mission for Kosovo continues into its seventh year without a clear prospect of finalizing the status of that Balkan province. With regard to local 'ownership' of the state-building process, the League Mandates – and indeed protectorates before them – allowed for domestic government by locally elected political forces, albeit 'advised' by the mandatory power. This is in most respects no different to the arrangements obtaining in BiH, where the High Representative has the authority to sack uncooperative elected officials. Finally, the assumption that there is no, or little, socio-economic motivation behind the creation of new trusteeships is belied by the explicit mandate to develop market economies in most of these territories, and by the preponderance of Western interests among foreign investors. It may well be the case that Western states no longer seek to invade and occupy other territories exclusively to exploit their human and natural resources (although, as previous chapters have shown, this was never the sole driving force of historical empires), but state-building today is, as during the interwar years, ultimately about fostering the institutional conditions that will allow capitalist economies to thrive in supervised territories, and to that extent the politics and ethics of humanitarianism cannot be divorced from the political economy of liberal empire.

There is therefore considerable mileage in drawing parallels between current experiments in state-building and the interwar mandate system, save for in one crucial respect: the contemporary experience is marked by the reconstitution of *existing* political communities. Previous systems – protectorates, mandates and trusteeships alike – were ordained with the task of constructing state sovereignty from scratch with the final aim of self-government. The postwar experiments in state-building have on the other hand chiefly been about restoring, enforcing or protecting the self-government of actually existing political communities. Many of these – most notably in East Timor – did not possess juridical sovereignty but clearly had a state infrastructure in waiting, ready for the *de facto* assumption of sovereignty from exile. Other political communities – for instance, Albanian Kosovars, Sahrawis or Palestinians – have not yet acquired formal sovereignty, but, once again, possess requisite political institutions able and willing to take on this task. At Versailles in 1919, even more so during the previous decades, only a handful of nationalist movements under colonial rule could claim to mobilize the necessary social and political power to realize self-determination. In sum, the power of nationalism and its attendant norm of self-determination has become universalized today in ways that were unthinkable a century ago. This, in turn, has made the liberal internationalist mission of building viable states and market economies all the more dependent on local acquiescence and cooperation – a form of empire, in short, which is uniquely vulnerable to the vagaries of national and regional politics.

The invasion and occupation of Afghanistan and Iraq have underlined this new imperial predicament as the USA and its allies have found it especially challenging to enforce state sovereignty in these 'collapsed' or 'rogue' states. Without a powerful local social and political base supporting occupation – as was arguably the case in both postwar Germany and Japan – imposing state-building and legitimacy from the outside is likely to end in the same way that the British mandate did in Iraq: with a socially unstable and politically weak state. As Toby Dodge has persuasively argued with reference to Iraq, 'exogenous state-building' along liberal-democratic lines is a highly precarious exercise in societies like those of Iraq, Afghanistan or indeed Haiti, Somalia and the Balkans, ravaged by decades of socio-economic and political crisis. In the absence of a functioning civil society in Iraq, 'external state building is bound to be "top down", driven by dynamics, personnel and ideologies that have their origins completely outside the society they are operating in.'[45] It is this structural contradiction, then, between the Wilsonian aspiration to legitimate states and free markets on the one hand, and the external imposition of sovereignty and its undermining by market forces on the other, which best characterizes liberal empire. It is an empire built on the constantly unkept promise of universal sovereignty and generalized prosperity.

The end of empire?

The contemporary distinction between American, postmodern and liberal manifestations of empire is in many respects a heuristic device. There is no need to fall into a blithe eclecticism when recognizing that the international distribution and activation of power falls disproportionally within US institutions, that these expressions of American power often take the 'postmodern' form of global flows, but that they are above all buttressed and promoted by liberal conceptions of world order. Any sophisticated account of the world today is likely to look at the interactions between these various expressions of global power, weighing up their concrete articulation and relative force, rather than positing a radical contrast between them. The question that has shaped the discussion in the preceding pages is therefore not so much which conception of empire is most suitable, but rather whether the term 'empire' is of any use at all in analysing and evaluating such forms of global power. An affirmative answer will hopefully have come across loud and clear throughout this book, though not necessarily by way of endorsing its use to describe our contemporary world. In fact, the preceding chapters have intimated that the term can be useful in several ways, three of which will be broached in this concluding section of the book.

The term empire is useful to social scientists, firstly, because it forces us to think conceptually about different expressions of power. If empire is to mean simply the projection of unequal extraterritorial power by a named polity, then it becomes indistinguishable from notions such as 'hegemony', 'primacy', 'governance' or indeed 'dominance'. Likewise, if the term is reduced to a purely positivist definition as a system of formal control over diverse peoples and territories by a dominant polity, then much of its contemporary relevance is struck out by definitional fiat. The more interesting approach to the notion of empire, I have argued, considers instead the distinctive features of imperial power as revealed through history. On this account, the concept of empire becomes attached to expansive, coercive and hierarchical forms of power best summarized in the term 'domination'. Empire involves an expression of power that aspires to – if it does not always achieve – control over outcomes. As opposed to hegemony or global governance, empire is a form of power that assumes the possibility of imposing a desired political or socio-economic effect, in the last instance through force. There is little point in being an imperial power, as ideologues of empire from Gattinara to Chamberlain have pointed out, unless desired outcomes can be enforced. Exercising empire does not simply amount to leading or coordinating other polities and economies, it involves controlling and regulating them. It is a form of power premised on final and decisive action in favour of the ruling authority, not on deliberation and consultation among equal parties.

The conceptual distinctiveness of empire, however, can only be meaningfully captured by investigating the actual historical experience of imperial social formations. Attention to empire is thus useful in a second, historical sense in that it allows us to understand modern international relations better: it identifies both the uniqueness of the contemporary international system of states and the continuing presence of imperial forms of power in the world today. With regard to the first proposition, we have seen throughout this study that one facet of empire involves its distinctive organization of political space. The absence of permanently fixed and contiguous territorial borders allied to the aspiration of constant expansion have marked empires out from other forms of political organization, most notably the nation-state. Viewed through the *longue durée*, the disappearance of formal empires in the course of the short twentieth century and their replacement by a system of states is an historically spectacular development. This shift from hierarchy to anarchy, or from large, expansive, multinational polities to territorially contained national states, must surely count as one of the principal historical puzzles for contemporary social science. Yet it is only by investigating the very dynamics of empire-building and the reproductory logic attached to specific imperial formations that this question of transition and change in the globally dominant forms of political organization can be addressed. More specifically, the spatial organization of empires must be connected, as this book has tried to do, with their socio-economic and cultural bases of power. Thus, the territorial organization of the Roman or Han empires was associated in chapter 2 with their reliance on tax and tribute as sources of wealth and with unique creationist cosmologies. Similarly, the early modern Ottoman and Spanish empires were presented as lying at the interstices of an Old World defined by the frontier institutions of horseback raiding, suzerainty and vassalage and the modern world of territorially centralized bureaucratic rule, deepening market dependence and the beginnings of racist discourse and practice.

Plainly, the interactions between these diverse facets of empire have been changing and contradictory, but they issued by the late nineteenth century into a form of empire increasingly defined by capitalist social relations and the accompanying modern form of state sovereignty. Such a transformation was also protracted and uneven, and in large measure propelled by mass mobilizations in support of national self-determination, socio-economic emancipation and cultural liberation which had been largely absent under previous forms of imperial rule. In the aftermath of the Second World War these struggles delivered a world where formal empire was deemed to be variously unworkable, uneconomic or illegitimate. Obvious as it may seem, the fact that today we live in a post-colonial world in itself merits some explanation, and an historical account of the socio-economic and political forces responsible for the rise and fall of empires is a very good starting-point in this endeavour. Indeed, the chief aim of this short book has been to identify the possible conceptual and historical avenues to this end, without thereby prescribing a single or exact route.

A post-colonial world need not, however, be post-imperial. Another thread running across previous chapters in this study has been the legacy – some might argue, persistence – of imperialism in today's world. The enduring socio-economic inequalities within and across different regions of the world economy perhaps best express the continuity of imperialism in a post-colonial world. Certainly, the systematic unevenness of exchange and asymmetries in investment flows between many post-colonial economies in Latin America, Asia and Africa and their former metropoles point to relations of structural dependence characteristic of classical imperialism. But even in this economic realm, where the gross disparities in life chances generated by global capitalism often appear in the starkest light, there is scope for distinguishing between asymmetries produced by political manipulation of markets (imperialism) and the autonomous tendency of markets towards uneven accumulation (capitalism). One of the consequences of political independence has after all been the pursuit of state-directed strategies of accumulation and industrialization which have made post-colonial economies such as those of Korea, India or Brazil some of the most powerful in the world. Political independence has also facilitated the nationalization of lucrative energy reserves among many post-colonial oil and gas producers, while the deeper extension of the world market has opened up possibilities for greater transversal economic interaction among former Third World states.

In the political and cultural realms, too, the post-colonial era has generated campaigns and mobilizations, ranging from the UN-sponsored assaults on racism and apartheid through to the more recent diplomatic initiatives among the Group of 77 states of the global South, which underscore the impact, if not always the success, of national independence.

The abiding cultural and political legacies of empire were addressed in previous chapters, and it was shown there how much of contemporary racism, inter-ethnic conflict, political crisis and cultural production and consumption must be explained with reference to the experience and inheritance of modern imperialism. Yet, here again, the trick is to also account for the profound changes in the forms that ethnic, religious, racial or national conflict and identity have adopted since the collapse of empires. The Arab–Israeli conflict has deep roots in the post-colonial predicament bequeathed by the Ottoman and British empires, but it is unfathomable without reference to the very local and recent developments in both Arab and Israeli politics. On an entirely different plane, the reappearance of sex tourism in Cuba plainly resonates with the island's history as a playground for metropolitan men (and no few women), but it is once more inexplicable outside the historical consequences of Soviet collapse. In sum, in the same way that modern empires gave hierarchies of class, race, nationality and gender a specific inflection, harnessing them to the structures of metropolitan rule, the disappearance of empires and their replacement by a modern system of national states has also reconfigured these social cleavages. Exploitation, oppression and discrimination have obviously not disappeared or been flattened out by capitalist globalization, but have rather been reconstituted along the more indeterminate social axes organized around states and markets, thus making reference to empire and imperialism increasingly imprecise.

Semantic or historical disputes over the meaning of empire or imperialism are not purely of academic interest. The final, and perhaps most important, reason why analysing empire matters today is that it focuses attention on the possibilities of transforming the existing world order. Viable alternatives to the undemocratic aspects of American empire, liberal hegemony or global capitalism will depend greatly on how such power is conceptualized. The core of this book's argument has been that empire is by itself a politically indeterminate term. Although empires have historically been associated with militarized, exploitative and racist forms of rule, there is nothing inherent or transhistorical about such connections. As we have seen, many ancient empires survived without the complex racial gradations of their more recent counterparts, while a number of modern empires have relied for their growth and success more on private commerce than on large military infrastructures. Similarly, different emphases on the American, postmodern or liberal dimensions of world order – whether one assumes it is imperial or not – produce different political strategies in challenging such an order.

Some, stressing the Western and liberal sources of world order, identify reactionary movements such as al-Qaeda and its affiliates, including insurgent forces in Iraq, as the vanguard of contemporary anti-imperialism. This is clearly not an attractive alternative to democrats, nor has it proved to be for most Islamists across the world. With the possible exception of Pakistan's northwest territories, and now Iraq and its neighbouring countries, the kind of politics advocated by Osama bin Laden's base has found no mass support in any part of the world. Independently of the attraction of their political programme and tactics, one curious feature of al-Qaeda and its progeny – especially if they are somehow to be compared with classical anti-imperialists – is the absence of any analytical or theoretical engagement with notions of empire, imperialism or indeed revolution. Osama bin Laden's declarations instead draw on a heady mix of classical Salafi invocations of the infidel '*yahiliyya*' (state of ignorance/godless polytheism), the Prophet's Hegira to Medina and the Islamic *umma*, with references to historical and contemporary events ranging from the Crusades to the alleged impoverishment of Arabian business classes or the American 'military occupation' of Saudi Arabia. Rather than an alternative to American empire, it appears that al-Qaeda represents a complement to it: through its nihilistic, aesthetic and mystical conception of resistance as the 'propaganda of the act', al-Qaeda thrives on its opposite in the shape of an unlimited, ubiquitous and Manichean 'war on terrorism'.

A second contemporary type of challenge to world order emphasizes the American roots of empire, and might reasonably be summarized under the label 'populist nationalism'. This kind of perspective tends to focus exclusively on Washington, DC (and, to a lesser extent, Manhattan), as the main source of the world's problems, and seems closest to a classical understanding of the USA as an imperialist power. For US national-populists such as Pat Buchanan, it is Beltway politics combined with East Coast transnational elites which are undermining US power and hitting the American 'little man'. Others, such as Jean-Pierre Chevènement in France, present the whole of the USA as a homogenous socio-political entity which is intent on world domination. The only viable response to these ambitions, it seems, is an insistence on national autonomy – in the French case, a return to the Gaullist conceptions of an 'eternal France' capable of acting independently from 'Anglo-Saxon' states, and in particular the USA. Perhaps the most sophisticated and certainly less stridently nationalist perspective to fall under this label is that offered by Walden Bello, a leading voice of the 'alterglobalization' movement. Bello envisages a strategy of 'deglobalization' involving a double-movement of deconstructing, or at least stalling, existing multilateral mechanisms of global trade, credit and financial management as represented by the WTO, IMF and World Bank, and then '[r]e-orienting economies from the emphasis on production for export to production for the local market'.[46]

A final, and no less ambitious, alternative to contemporary world order underlines the capitalist sources of world order and therefore takes the shape of what may loosely be called an anti-capitalist internationalism. It is an alternative most closely associated with some of the political forces gathered around the successive global and regional social fora, and is informed by the tenets of a more classical socialist internationalism. This alternative builds on a conception of US power as deriving specifically from its position as the most powerful *capitalist* state and therefore emphasizes the dynamics of social reproduction over a purely geopolitical logic of imperialism. It underlines the centrality of radical social transformation *within* states as a necessary condition of challenging US global dominance. Moreover, though explicitly internationalist – that is, cognizant of the requirement that radical, anti-capitalist transformation be articulated and realized on a global plane – such a strategy also recognizes the potential of the democratic sovereign state and its resources in effecting such transformations. In other words, such an alternative to American-led global capitalism acknowledges the progressive potential of radical social forces attaining office – be it regionally, nationally or internationally – and using the resources of the state in effecting democratic changes to international relations in ways not unlike those proposed by Bello. Finally, it follows from the above that the greatest challenge to American hegemony must come from *within the USA itself*. For without the radical transformation of US society and polity, it is unlikely that alternatives to US power will be sustained elsewhere. The tallest order, then, for anti-capitalist internationalism is persuading Americans and non-Americans alike that the democratization of international affairs very much depends on the democratization of the USA. And an analysis of the past and present of empire, both as a concept and as a practice of power, as this book has tried to show, is key to meeting that challenge.

Notes

Chapter 1 Empires in History

1 *The Guardian*, 27 November 2003.
2 E. Hobsbawm, *The Age of Empire, 1875–1914*, p. 57.
3 For J. S. Richardson the 'secular activity' of Republican Rome 'may be summarised in two words: war and law'; '*Imperium Romanum*: Empire and the Language of Power', p. 1.
4 R. Koebner, *Empire*, ch. 1.
5 Ibid., p. 11.
6 See, respectively, Greg Woolf, 'Inventing Empire in Ancient Rome', p. 317; H. Kamen, *Imperio: La forja de España como potencia mundial*, p. 73; and D. Armitage, *The Ideological Origins of the British Empire*, ch. 4.
7 For instance, Brian Porter, in his *The Absent-Minded Imperialists: Empire, Society and Culture in Britain*.
8 Quoted in A. Pagden, *Lords of All the World: Ideologies of Empire in Spain, Britain and France c.1500–c.1800*, p. 126.
9 A. J. Motyl, *Revolutions, Nations and Empires: Conceptual Limits and Theoretical Possibilities*, p. 121.
10 Imperial culture is the one arena that challenges this generalization: as chapter 4 will indicate, imperial peoples circulated and combined cultural forms – musical, linguistic, ideological – in ways that slowly forged a rim circumventing the imperial centre.
11 Edward Luttwak, in *The Grand Strategy of the Roman Empire*, distinguishes between force (as in Newtonian mechan-

ics, 'consumed in application') and power (which 'works not by causing effects directly, but by eliciting responses – if all goes well the *desired* responses'), pp. 196–7. He further suggests that, '[i]n dynamic terms force and power are not analogous at all, but they are, in a sense, opposites. One is an input and the other an output, and efficiency requires the minimization of the former and the maximization of the latter'; ibid., appendix.

12   S. N. Eisenstadt, *The Political Systems of Empires*, p. 25.
13   R. G. Wesson, *The Imperial Order*, p. 19.
14   Koebner, *Empire*, and M. Duverger (ed.), *Le concept d'empire*.
15   D. B. Abernethy, *The Dynamics of Global Dominance: European Overseas Empires 1415–1980*; M. W. Doyle, *Empires*; P. M. Kennedy, *The Rise and Fall of the Great Powers: Economic Change and Military Conflict from 1500 to 2000*; M. Mann, *The Sources of Social Power: A History of Power from the Beginning to 1740*.
16   Doyle, *Empires*.
17   David Schotter, *Augustus Caesar*, p. 27.
18   J. I. Miller, *The Spice Trade of the Roman Empire, 29 BC to AD 641*, p. 2.
19   The term is used – and discussed occasionally with reference to Rome – in A. Al-Azmeh, *Muslim Kingship: Power and the Sacred in Muslim, Christian and Pagan Polities*, esp. Part I.
20   Greg Woolf, 'Inventing Empire in Ancient Rome'.
21   S. E. Finer, *The History of Government from the Earliest Times*, Vol. 1: *Ancient and Modern Empires*, p. 498.
22   For detailed accounts see H. Bielenstein, *The Bureaucracy of Han Times*; T'ung-tsu Ch'ü, *Han Social Structure*; and chapter 8 of D. Twitchett and M. Loewe (eds), *Cambridge History of China*, Vol. 1: *The Ch'in and Han Empires, 221 BC – AD 220*, pp. 491–519.
23   Twitchett and Loewe, *Cambridge History of China*, p. 511.
24   Finer, *The History of Government*, p. 525.
25   Ibid., p. 502. The comparison with Rome is made in P. Garnsey and R. Saller, *The Roman Empire: Economy, Society and Culture*, p. 20, who in turn derive the figure from Keith Hopkins, 'Models, Ships and Staples', p. 186.
26   E. M. Wood, *Empire of Capital*, p. 27.
27   Finer, *The History of Government*, p. 513.
28   Whether the state happens to be a kingdom, a duchy, a republic, a caliphate or a confederation is immaterial in this context. All these regime types are compatible with both imperial and national forms of state, and what matters here

is how their territorial limits are defined and political space is organized.

29   The use of these terms does of course vary through time and place. R. J. Johnston et al. (eds), *The Dictionary of Human Geography*, state: 'The terms border and frontier are sometimes used as if they were equivalents to boundary, which they are in popular English-language usage. But they seem more "matter of fact" referring to legal or official boundary lines and zonal areas respectively.' See also J. R. V. Prescott, *Political Frontiers and Boundaries*.

30   See for instance P. Chatterjee, *The Nation and its Fragments: Colonial and Postcolonial Histories*.

31   For a good overview of different approaches see 'Empire, Systems and States: Great Transformations in International Politics', special issue of *Review of International Studies*, Vol. 27, December 2001. See also B. Teschke, *The Myth of 1648: Class, Geopolitics and the Making of Modern International Relations*.

32   H. Spruyt, *The Sovereign State and its Competitors: An Analysis of Systems Change*.

33   I. Wallerstein, *The Modern World-System: Capitalist Agriculture and the Origins of the European World-Economy in the Sixteenth Century*, p. 15.

34   M. Hechter, *Internal Colonialism: The Celtic Fringe in British National Development 1536–1966*.

35   L. Colley, *Britons: Forging the Nation 1707–1837*.

Chapter 2   Empire as Space

1   Eric Voegelin, 'World-Empire and the Unity of Mankind', p. 179.

2   In writing this chapter, I have benefited enormously from reading Paul Hirst's last book, *Space and Power: Politics, War and Architecture*.

3   J. S. Romm, *The Edges of the Earth in Ancient Thought: Geography, Exploration and Fiction*, p. 36. See also David Inglis, 'Global Ecumene', unpublished entry for an encyclopaedia, University of Aberdeen.

4   A. Pagden, *Lords of All the World*, p. 19.

5   R. Haley, *Maps and the Columbian Encounter*.

6   A. L. March, *The Idea of China: Myth and Theory in Geographic Thought*, p. 18.

7   See John B. Henderson, 'Chinese Cosmographical Thought: The High Intellectual Tradition'; and Robin D. S. Yates,

'Body, Space, Time and Bureaucracy: Boundary Creation and Control Mechanisms in Early China', and also his 'Cosmos, Central Authority and Communities in the Early Chinese Empire'.

8   Henderson, 'Chinese Cosmographical Thought', p. 213.
9   Yates, 'Body, Space, Time and Bureaucracy', p. 80.
10 A. Waldron, *The Great Wall of China: From History to Myth*, p. 9.
11 Stevan Harrell, 'Introduction: Civilizing Projects and the Reaction to Them', in S. Harrell (ed.), *Cultural Encounters on China's Ethnic Frontiers*, p. 7.
12 Ibid., p. 19.
13 O. Lattimore, *Inner Asian Frontiers of China*, p. 3.
14 Waldron, *The Great Wall of China*.
15 T. J. Barfield, *The Perilous Frontier: Nomadic Empires and China, 221 BC to AD 1757*, p. 3.
16 S. Berthon and A. Robinson, *The Shape of the World*, p. 27.
17 O. A. W. Dilke, 'Maps in the Service of the State: Roman Cartography to the End of the Augustan Era', and C. Nicolet, *Space, Geography and Politics in the Early Roman Empire*, ch. 5.
18 Greg Woolf, 'Inventing Empire in Ancient Rome', p. 317.
19 Ibid.
20 S. R. F. Price, 'The Place of Religion: Rome in the Early Empire', p. 815.
21 See, for instance, chapter 5 of K. Hopkins, *Conquerors and Slaves*.
22 Price, 'The Place of Religion', p. 823, and C. Tadgell, *Imperial Form: From Achamenid Iran to Augustan Rome*.
23 Alan K. Bowman, 'Provincial Administration and Taxation', p. 344.
24 Aurelius Aristides, quoted in C. Nicolet, *The World of the Citizen in Republican Rome*, p. 18.
25 Ibid., p. 20.
26 Nicolet, *Space, Geography and Politics*, ch. VII.
27 Dilke, 'Maps in the Service of the State', p. 210.
28 E. N. Luttwak, *The Grand Strategy of the Roman Empire in the First Century AD*. See also A. Ferrill, *Roman Imperial Grand Strategy*, and D. Williams, *The Reach of Rome: A History of the Roman Imperial Frontier 1st–5th Centuries AD*.
29 F. Millar, 'Government and Diplomacy in the Roman Empire during the First Three Centuries', p. 352.
30 B. Isaac, *The Limits of Empire: The Army in the East*, p. 395.

31 Ibid.; S. P. Mattern, *Rome and the Enemy: Imperial Strategy in the Principate*; Millar, 'Government and Diplomacy'; P. S. Wells, *The Barbarians Speak: How the Conquered Peoples Shaped Roman Europe*; C. R. Whittaker, *Frontiers of the Roman Empire: A Social and Economic Study*.

32 Derek Williams cites a brief passage from the *Augustan History* candidly accepting that '[t]hese four words "by which barbarians and Romans should be divided" are the only Roman Statement of a frontier intention we have'; Williams, *The Reach of Rome*, p. 97.

33 Arther Ferrill, 'The Grand Strategy of the Roman Empire', p. 75.

34 Benjamin Isaac, 'The Meaning of the Terms Limes and Limitanei', p. 134.

35 M. Kunt and C. Woodhead, *Süleyman the Magnificent and his Age: The Ottoman Empire in the Early Modern World*, p. 10.

36 For a highly informative and accessible account of these historiographical debates and the various meanings of the term *gaza*, see H. W. Lowry, *The Nature of the Early Ottoman State*.

37 This view has been presented in Rudi P. Lindner's 1983 revision of Paul Wittek's seminal *The Rise of the Ottoman Empire* (London, 1938) in his *Nomads and Ottomans in Medieval Anatolia*.

38 C. Kafadar, *Between Two Worlds: The Construction of the Ottoman State*, p. 53.

39 See the classic essay by Halil Inaclik, 'Ottoman Methods of Conquest'.

40 Respectively, Christian (mainly Balkan and Caucasian) youths purchased or apprehended as slaves, converted to Islam and trained for service in the Ottoman administration; and descendants of mixed marriages between Ottoman (generally Anatolian) soldiers and Arab women. See A. Tunger-Zanetti, *Le Communication entre Tunis et Istanbul, 1860–1913: province et métropole*, ch. 1.

41 S. Faroqui, *The Ottoman Empire and the Wider World*. See also K. H. Karpat and R. W. Zens (eds), *Ottoman Borderlands: Issues, Personalities and Political Challenges*.

42 A. Hourani, *A History of the Arab Peoples*, p. 226.

43 See J. H. Elliot, *Imperial Spain, 1469–1716*, and A. C. Hess, *The Forgotten Frontier: A History of the Ibero-African Frontier*.

44 Manuel González Jiménez, 'Frontier and Settlement in the Kingdom of Castile (1085–1350)'.

45 Ibid., p. 49.
46 J. H. Elliot, 'The Spanish Conquest', p. 9.
47 Cited in P. Seed, *Ceremonies of Possession in Europe's Conquest of the New World, 1492–1640*, p. 69.
48 Ibid., p. 14.
49 E. R. Wolf, *Europe and the People Without History*, p. 133.
50 Richard M. Morse, 'Urban Development', p. 180.
51 Ibid., p. 188.
52 A. Hennessy, *The Frontier in Latin American History*. See also Silvio Zavala, 'The Frontiers of Hispanic America'.
53 Hennessy, *The Frontier*, pp. 60–8.
54 Ibid., p. 70.
55 See, for instance, F. A. Jabar and H. Dawod (eds), *Tribes and Power: Nationalism and Ethnicity in the Middle East*, and P. S. Khoury and J. Kostiner (eds), *Tribes and State Formation in the Middle East*.
56 Khoury and Kostiner, *Tribes and State Formation*, p. 15.
57 M. Yapp, *The Near East Since the First World War: A History to 1995*, and I. Pappé, *A History of Modern Palestine: One Land, Two Peoples*.
58 G. Shafir, *Land, Labor and the Origins of the Israeli–Palestinian Conflict, 1882–1914*. See also Pappé, *History of Modern Palestine*.
59 B. Larson, *Trials of Nation Making: Liberalism, Race, and Ethnicity in the Andes, 1810–1910*, p. 7.
60 Benjamin S. Orlove, 'Putting Race in its Place: Order in Colonial and Postcolonial Peruvian Geography'.
61 Ibid., p. 301.
62 Larson, *Trials of Nation Making*, p. 150.
63 Orlove, 'Putting Race in its Place', p. 328.
64 Ibid.
65 Larson, *Trials of Nation Making*, p. 166.
66 Mark Thurner, *From Two Republics to One Divided: Contradictions of Postcolonial Nationmaking in Peru*.

Chapter 3 Empire as Market

1 Karl Polanyi, 'The Economy as Instituted Process', p. 255.
2 M. N. Pearson, 'Merchants and States', p. 81.
3 E. R. Wolf, *Europe and the People Without History*, p. 298.
4 See, for instance, J. Abu-Lughod, *Before European Hegemony: The World System AD 1250–1350*, and K. N. Chaudhuri, *Asia Before Europe: Economy and Civilisation of the Indian Ocean from the Rise of Islam to 1750*.

5 See Ralph Davis, *The Rise of the English Shipping Industry in the Seventeenth and Eighteenth Centuries*.

6 Wolf, *Europe and the People Without History*, p. 124.

7 See, for instance, N. Ferguson, *Empire: How Britain Made the Modern World*, pp. 18–19.

8 P. Lawson, *The East India Company: A History*, p. 22.

9 See Davis, *The Rise of the English Shipping Industry*, and P. M. Kennedy, *The Rise and Fall of British Naval Mastery*.

10 G. V. Scammell, *The World Encompassed: The First European Maritime Empires, c.800–1650*.

11 Ibid., p. 44.

12 Ibid., p. 406.

13 Peter Mathias and Patrick O'Brien, 'Taxation in Britain and France, 1715–1810: A Comparison of the Social and Economic Incidence of Taxes Collected for the Central Governments', p. 617.

14 Pearson, 'Merchants and States', p. 92.

15 See C. R. Boxer, *The Dutch Seaborne Empire 1600–1800*.

16 Cited in Geoffrey Parker, 'Europe and the Wider World, 1500–1750: The Military Balance', p. 180.

17 Scammell, *The World Encompassed*, p. 408.

18 Wolf, *Europe and the People Without History*, p. 238.

19 Ferguson, *Empire*, p. 22.

20 Ibid., p. 32.

21 E. M. Wood, *Empire of Capital*, p. 80.

22 Sir John Davies, quoted in ibid., pp. 81–2.

23 See, for instance, Robert Miles, *Capitalism and Unfree Labour*, and, more broadly, Aidan Foster-Carter, 'The Modes of Production Controversy'.

24 R. Blackburn, *The Making of New World Slavery: From the Baroque to the Modern, 1492–1800*, p. 448 and p. 525 respectively.

25 For figures and a broader discussion, see ibid., p. 520.

26 Wolf, *Europe and the People Without History*, p. 196.

27 Blackburn, *The Making of New World Slavery*, p. 388. For a more detailed survey of these figures, see P. Manning, 'The Slave Trade: The Formal Demography of a Global System'.

28 Blackburn, *The Making of New World Slavery*, p. 572.

29 Ibid., p. 542.

30 Patrick O'Brien concluded, in his seminal article 'The Costs and Benefits of British Imperialism' (p. 199), that 'the notion that the empire made any positive long-term contribution to the health of the domestic economy is unlikely to survive systematic economic analysis and statistical testing' (although he has since qualified this view in his 'Imperialism and the Rise

and Decline of the British Economy, 1688–1989'). Michael Edelstein, in direct contrast, in his 'Imperialism: Cost and Benefit', maintains that 'the empire made a significant contribution to the growth in income and output of Great Britain in the nineteenth and early twentieth centuries' (p. 215). See also L. E. Davis and R. A. Huttenback, *Mammon and the Pursuit of Empire: The Political Economy of British Imperialism, 1860–1912*.

31 E. Williams, *Capitalism and Slavery*, p. 64.
32 A. W. Crosby, *Ecological Imperialism: The Biological Expansion of Europe 900–1900*.
33 Most recently, M. Rediker and P. Linebaugh, *The Many-Headed Hydra: Sailors, Slaves and Commoners and the Hidden History of the Revolutionary Atlantic*.
34 See C. E. Bayly, *Indian Society and the British Empire*.
35 See D. Omissi, *The Sepoy and the Raj: The Indian Army 1860–1940*.
36 M. H. Fisher, *Indirect Rule in India: Residents and the Residency System*, p. 8.
37 For a useful recent overview, see Duncan S. A. Bell, 'Empire and International Relations in Victorian Political Thought: Historiographical Essay,' where he discusses, among other recent texts, J. Pitts, *A Turn to Empire: the Rise of Imperial Liberalism in Britain and France*, and Sankar Muthu, *Enlightenment Against Empire*.
38 E. Hobsbawm, *Industry and Empire*, p. 134.
39 M. Barratt Brown, *After Imperialism*, p. 63.
40 A. G. Kenwood and A. L. Lougheed, *The Growth of the International Economy 1820–2000: An Introductory Text*, ch. 2.
41 John Gallagher and Roland Robinson, 'The Imperialism of Free Trade', p. 13.
42 See Kennedy, *The Rise and Fall of British Naval Mastery*, chs 6 and 7.
43 Gallagher and Robinson, 'The Imperialism of Free Trade', p. 3.
44 G. Arrighi, *The Long Twentieth Century: Money, Power and the Origins of our Time*, p. 34.
45 See, for instance, J. Blaut, *The Colonizer's Model of the World: Geographical Diffusionism and Eurocentric History*.
46 P. J. Cain and A. G. Hopkins, *British Imperialism: Innovation and Expansion, 1688–1914*.
47 K. Marx and F. Engels, *The Communist Manifesto: A Modern Edition*, pp. 38–9.

48 E. Hobsbawm, *The Age of Capital, 1848–1875*, p. 54.
49 A good overview can be found in C. B. Davis and K. E. Wilburn Jr. (eds), *Railway Imperialism*. For the Indian case, see I. A. Kerr, *Building the Railways of the Raj, 1850–1900*.
50 For a good overview of the place of indentured labour in the imperial economy, see D. Northrup, *Indentured Labour in the Age of Imperialism 1834–1922*.
51 L. Potts, *The World Labour Market: A History of Migration*, p. 66.
52 Ibid., p. 71.
53 P. Koskiennemi, *The Gentle Civilizer of Nations: The Rise of International Law 1871–1960*.
54 J.-M. Penvenne, *African Workers and Colonial Racism*.
55 V. R. Berghahn, *Germany and the Approach of War in 1914*, ch. 5.
56 'Imperialism' appeared in French for the first time in 1838 and in English twenty years later. For a close narrative of the term's history, see R. Koebner and H. D. Smidt, *Imperialism: The Story and Significance of a Word, 1840–1960*.
57 J. A. Hobson, *Imperialism: A Study*, p. 15.
58 Ibid., p. 46.
59 Ibid., p. 61.
60 Ibid., p. 84.
61 Ibid., p. 85.
62 Anthony Brewer's survey *Marxist Theories of Imperialism* (1980) remains unsurpassed as a clear, comprehensive and judicious guide to these and other postwar Marxist debates on imperialism. See also T. Kemp, *Theories of Imperialism*, N. Etherington, *Theories of Imperialism: War, Conquest and Capital*, and B. Semmel, *The Liberal Ideal and the Demons of Empire: Theories of Imperialism from Adam Smith to Lenin*.
63 V. I. Lenin, *Imperialism: The Highest Stage of Capitalism*, p. 90.
64 Ibid., p. 5.
65 For a detailed and evocative account of the intense connections between war, imperialism and communist strategy at the time, see R. Craig Nation, *War on War: Lenin, the Zimmerwald Left and the Origins of Communist Internationalism*.
66 Karl Kautsky, 'Ultra-Imperialism'.
67 Lenin, *Imperialism*, pp. 92 and 93. Emphasis in the original.
68 *Karl Kautsky: Selected Political Writings*, p. 88.
69 Lenin, *Imperialism*, p. 94.

70   R. Luxemburg, *The Accumulation of Capital*, p. 330.
71   Ibid., p. 332.
72   Brewer, *Marxist Theories*, p. 76.
73   J. A. Schumpeter, *Imperialism and Social Classes*, p. 7.
74   Ibid., p. 84.
75   Ibid., p. 122.
76   Ibid., p. 128.
77   H. Arendt, *The Origins of Totalitarianism*, p. 131.
78   Ibid., p. 132.
79   Ibid., p. 146.
80   Ibid., p. 150.
81   For comprehensive overviews, see C. Kay, *Latin American Theories of Development and Underdevelopment*, J. Larrain, *Theories of Development: Capitalism, Colonialism and Dependency*, and Brewer, *Marxist Theories*. The latter two deal more broadly with the contributions from and on Africa by, among others, Samir Amin, Arghiri Emmanuel, Walter Rodney and Immanuel Wallerstein.
82   Thoetonio Dos Santos, 'The Structure of Dependence', p. 231.
83   B. Warren, *Imperialism: Pioneer of Capitalism*, p. 8.
84   Ibid., p. 10.
85   Paul Bairoch has perhaps carried out the most sustained empirical analysis of Third World underdevelopment, concluding in one summary that, 'While there is no doubt that a large number of structurally negative features of the process of economic underdevelopment have historical roots going back directly to European colonization, colonization has probably contributed very little, if at all, to the success story of the economic development of the West. There is not necessarily a link between the advantages of one partner and the disadvantages to the other in certain kinds of economic relation' (Bairoch, 'Historical Roots of Underdevelopment: Myths and Realities', p. 213). For more methodological and historical critiques, see, respectively, Robert Brenner, 'The Origins of Capitalist Development: A Critique of Neo-Smithian Marxism', and Patrick O'Brien, 'European Economic Development: The Contribution of the Periphery'.

Chapter 4   Empire as Culture

1   R. Miles, *Racism After 'Race Relations'*.
2   D. T. Goldberg, *Racist Culture: Philosophy and the Politics of Meaning*, p. 51.

3 A. Pagden, *The Fall of Natural Man: The American Indian and the Origins of Comparative Ethnography.*

4 See A. W. Marx, *Making Race and Nation: A Comparison of South Africa, the United States and Brazil.*

5 Robert J. C. Young, *Colonial Desire: Hybridity in Theory, Culture and Race,* p. 4.

6 E. Said, *Culture and Imperialism,* p. xxix. For Ortiz's original formulation, see F. Ortiz, *Cuban Counterpoint: Tobacco and Sugar.*

7 R. Bartra, *Wild Men in the Looking Glass: The Mythic Origins of European Otherness,* p. 4.

8 A. Pagden, *Spanish Imperialism and the Political Imagination: Studies in European and Spanish-American Social and Political Theory 1513–1830,* esp. ch. 1, and Pagden, *The Fall of Natural Man.*

9 Cited in L. Hanke, *All Mankind Is One: A Study of the Disputation between Bartolomé de Las Casas and Juan Ginés de Sepúlveda on the Religious and Intellectual Capacity of the American Indians,* p. 82.

10 See Pagden, *Spanish Imperialism,* and A.-E. Pérez Luño, *La polémica sobre el Nuevo Mundo: los clásicos españoles de la Fiolosofía del Derecho.*

11 M. Mörner, *Race Mixture in the History of Latin America,* p. 22.

12 For instance, Mörner in ibid.

13 J. I. Israel, *Race, Class and Politics in Colonial Mexico, 1610–1670,* p. 65. See also J. Kinsbruner, *The Colonial Spanish-American City: Urban Life in the Age of Atlantic Capitalism,* esp. chs 7 and 8.

14 Israel, *Race, Class and Politics,* p. 70.

15 Mörner, *Race Mixture,* p. 62.

16 Cited in ibid., p. 70.

17 The neologism 'pigmentocracy' was coined by the Chilean physiologist Alejandro Lipschütz, in his *El indoamericanismo y el problema racial en las Américas.*

18 For useful introductory overviews, see P. D. Curtin, *The Rise and Fall of the Plantation Complex: Essays in Atlantic History,* and J. K. Thornton, *Africa and the Africans in the Making of the Atlantic World, 1400–1800.*

19 R. Blackburn, *The Making of New World Slavery: From the Baroque to the Modern, 1492–1800,* p. 12.

20 N. L. Stepan, *The Idea of Race in Science: Great Britain 1800–1960,* p. x.

21 Ibid., p. xiii.

22 Young, *Colonial Desire,* p. 102.

23   Cited in M. Banton, *The Idea of Race*, p. 47.

24   Anthony Trollope, cited in Young, *Colonial Desire*, p. 142.

25   K. Ballhatchet, *Race, Sex and Class under the Raj: Imperial Attitudes and Policies and their Critics, 1793–1905*, ch. 1.

26   Ibid., p. 10.

27   Ann Laura Stoler, 'Sexual Affronts and Racial Frontiers: European Identities and the Cultural Politics of Exclusion in Southeast Asia'.

28   Ibid., p. 204.

29   Ibid., p. 211.

30   M. Mamdani, *Citizen and Subject: Contemporary Africa and the Legacy of Late Colonialism*, p. 60.

31   M. Mamdani, *When Victims Become Killers: Colonialism, Nativism and Genocide in Rwanda*, p. 26.

32   P. M. E. Lorcin, *Imperial Identities: Stereotyping, Prejudice and Race in Colonial Algeria*, p. 18.

33   See W. A. Hoisington, Jr., *Lyautey and the French Conquest of Morocco*.

34   See John Ruedy's excellent summary in chapter 4 of *Modern Algeria: The Origins and Development of a Nation* and, for a more detailed account, A. Christelow, *Muslim Law Courts and the French Colonial State in Algeria*.

35   Eric Hobsbawm and Terence Ranger (eds), *The Invention of Tradition*, p. 240.

36   A. Phillips, *The Enigma of Colonialism: British Policy in West Africa*, p. 11.

37   For detailed analyses of these processes in opposite ends of the continent, see Bruce Berman, 'Structure and Process in Bureaucratic States in Colonial Africa', and Peter Geschiere, 'Imposing Capitalist Dominance through the State: The Multifarious Role of the Colonial State in Africa'.

38   Phillips, *The Enigma of Colonialism*, p. 11.

39   B. Comrie, S. Matthews and M. Polinsky, *The Atlas of Languages: The Origin and Development of Languages Throughout the World*, p. 19.

40   For some, like Tzvetan Todorov, language or discourse is *the* principal mechanism of conquest. See his *The Conquest of America: The Question of the Other*.

41   Said, *Culture and Imperialism*, p. xxiii.

42   For similar endeavours, see P. Hulme, *Colonial Encounters: Europe and the Native Caribbean 1492–1897*; B. Parry, *Delusions and Discoveries: India in the British Imagination 1880–1930*; and C. Hall, *Civilising Subjects: Metropole and Colony in the English Imagination, 1830–1867*.

43 Said, *Culture and Imperialism*, p. 97.
44 For a comprehensive illustration and analysis, see J. Nederveen Pieterse, *White on Black: Images of Africa and Blacks in Western Popular Culture*.
45 A. McClintock, *Imperial Leather: Race, Gender and Sexuality in the Colonial Contest*. See also T. Burke, *Lifebuoy Men, Lux Women: Commodification, Consumption and Cleanliness in Modern Zimbabwe*.
46 McClintock, *Imperial Leather*, p. 208.
47 Said, *Culture and Imperialism*, p. xxix.
48 Comrie, Matthews and Polinsky, *Atlas of Languages*, p. 154.
49 L.-J. Calvet, *Linguistique et colonialisme: petit traité de glottophagie*.
50 Ibid., p. 160.
51 M. A. De la Torre, *Santería: The Beliefs and Rituals of a Growing Religion in America*, and D. H. Brown, *Santería Enthroned: Art, Ritual and Innovation in an Afro-Cuban Religion*.
52 E. Carmichael and C. Sayer, *The Skeleton at the Feast: The Day of the Dead in Mexico*.
53 See, for the African case, the discussion in Joseph E. Holloway (ed.), *Africanisms in American Culture*.
54 C. L. R. James, *Beyond a Boundary*.
55 Ibid., p. 56.
56 Ibid., p. 72.
57 Brown, *Santería Enthroned*, p. 33.
58 E. Tarlo, *Clothing Matters: Dress and Identity in India*.
59 Ibid., p. 61.
60 V. J. Fletcher (ed.), *Crosscurrents of Modernism: Four Latin American Pioneers: Diego Rivera, Joaquín Torres-García, Wilfredo Lam, Matta*, p. 187.
61 J. Tomlinson, *Cultural Imperialism: A Critical Introduction*.
62 See M. Featherstone et al. (eds), *Global Culture* and *Global Modernities*, and A. Appadurai, *Modernity at Large: Cultural Dimensions of Globalization*.
63 This is especially true of media consortia such as Mexico's Televisa or Brazil's Globo groups. See John Sinclair, 'Latin American Commercial Television: "Primitive Capitalism"'.
64 Andrew Goodwin and Joe Gore make a sophisticated case for the poverty of the term 'cultural imperialism' when analysing 'world music' in their 'World Beat and the Cultural Imperialism Debate'.

Chapter 5   After Empire

1   The term 'standard of civilization' is used here in the sense given to it by the English school of international relations. See G. W. Gong, *The Standard of 'Civilization' in International Society.*

2   Karl Marx makes a distinction between the 'real' and the 'formal' subsumption of labour to capital in the so-called Part VII of *Capital*, entitled 'Results of the Immediate Process of Production'.

3   W. I. Robinson, *Promoting Polyarchy.*

4   S. E. Ambrose, *Rise to Globalism: American Foreign Policy Since 1939*, p. xi.

5   For an insightful if occasionally over-familiar account of the 'Wisconsin school' of American historians, see the symposium in *Diplomatic History*, 28, 5 (November 2004). See also the introduction to the 1991 edition of E. R. May, *American Imperialism: A Speculative Essay*, and R. J. Maddox, *The New Left and the Origins of the Cold War.*

6   W. LaFeber, *The New Empire: An Interpretation of American Expansion 1860–1898*, p. 417. Italics in the original.

7   W. A. Williams, *The Tragedy of American Diplomacy*, p. 55. Italics in the original.

8   Geir Lundestad, 'Empire by Invitation? The United States and Western Europe, 1945–1952'.

9   Most recently, John Agnew, in his *Hegemony: The New Shape of Global Power.*

10   Robert W. Cox, 'Gramsci, Hegemony and International Relations: An Essay in Method', p. 61.

11   See, among others, S. Gill, *American Hegemony and the Trilateral Commission*; K. Van der Pijl, *The Making of an Atlantic Ruling Class*; O. Holman, *Integrating Southern Europe: The EC and the Transnationalization of Spain*; H. Overbeek, *Neo-Liberalism and Global Hegemony: Concepts of Control in the Global Political Economy*; Robinson, *Promoting Polyarchy*; M. Rupert, *Producing Hegemony*; and B. van Apeldoorn, *Transnational Capitalism and the Struggle over European Integration.*

12   J. S. Nye, *The Paradox of American Power: Why the World's Only Superpower Cannot Go it Alone*, and G. J. Ikenberry, 'American Power and the Empire of Capitalist Democracy'.

13   Some of the principal exponents are collected in A. Colás and R. Saull, *The War on Terrorism and American 'Empire' After the Cold War.*

14   Peter Gowan, 'The Bush Turn and the Drive for Primacy', p. 132.
15   Ibid., p. 146.
16   See, respectively, D. Harvey, *The New Imperialism*, E. M. Wood, *Empire of Capital*, and A. Callinicos, *The New Mandarins of American Empire*.
17   Leo Panitch and Sam Gindin, 'Global Capitalism and American Empire', p. 28.
18   Ibid., p. 33.
19   Ibid., p. 31.
20   M. Mann, *Incoherent Empire*.
21   E. Todd, *After the Empire: The Breakdown of the American Order*.
22   Mann, *Incoherent Empire*, p. 21.
23   Ibid., p. 13.
24   M. Hardt and A. Negri, *Empire*, p. iv. Emphasis in the original.
25   Ibid., p. xii. Emphasis in original.
26   As pointed out by one of the authors themselves, in an interview which sets out some of the context and clarifies parts of the content of the book. See S. Budgen and A. Colás, 'An Interview with Michael Hardt'.
27   Hardt and Negri, *Empire*, p. xvi.
28   For a background account, see S. Wright, *Storming Heaven: Class Composition and Struggle in Italian Autonomist Marxism*.
29   Hardt and Negri, *Empire*, p. 15.
30   Ibid., p. 194.
31   Ibid., p. 190. Emphasis in the original.
32   Ibid., p. 32.
33   Ibid., p. 294.
34   See, respectively, A. A. Boron, *Empire and Imperialism: A Critical Reading of Michael Hardt and Antonio Negri*, and two collections of essays – P. A. Passavant and J. Dean (eds) *Empire's New Clothes: Reading Hardt and Negri*, and S. Aronowitz and G. Balakrishnan (eds), *Debating Empire*.
35   F. Fukuyama, *State-Building: Governance and World Order in the Twenty-First Century*, p. ix.
36   T. P. Barnett, *The Pentagon's New Map: War and Peace in the Twenty-First Century*, p. 121.
37   *State Failure Task Force Report: Phase III Findings*.
38   Ibid., p. 11.
39   Tony Blair, 'Doctrine of the International Community'.
40   Ibid.
41   Tariq Ali, 'NATO's Balkan Crusade', p. 349.

42 R. Paris, *At War's End: Building Peace After Civil Conflict*, p. 5.
43 R. Caplan, *International Governance of War-Torn Territories: Rule and Reconstruction*, and S. Chesterman, *You, the People: The United Nations, Transitional Administrations, and State-Building*.
44 Most notably N. Feldman, *What We Owe Iraq: War and the Ethics of Nation Building*.
45 Toby Dodge, 'Iraq: The Contradictions of State Building in Historical Perspective', p. 190. For a more detailed account, see also his *Inventing Iraq: The Failure of Nation Building and a History Denied*.
46 W. Bello, *Deglobalization: Ideas for a New World Economy*, p. 113.

References

Abernethy, D. B., *The Dynamics of Global Dominance: European Overseas Empires 1415–1980* (New Haven, CT, and London: Yale University Press, 2000).

Abu-Lughod, J., *Before European Hegemony: The World System AD 1250–1350* (Oxford and New York: Oxford University Press, 1989).

Agnew, J., *Hegemony: The New Shape of Global Power* (Philadelphia: Philadelphia University Press, 2005).

Al-Azmeh, A., *Muslim Kingship: Power and the Sacred in Muslim, Christian and Pagan Polities*, 2nd edn (London and New York: I. B. Tauris, 2001).

Ali, T., 'NATO's Balkan Crusade', in T. Ali (ed.), *Masters of the Universe: NATO's Balkan Crusade* (London and New York: Verso, 2000).

Ambrose, S. E., *Rise to Globalism: American Foreign Policy Since 1939*, 7th edn (London: Penguin, 1993).

Apeldoorn, B. van, *Transnational Capitalism and the Struggle over European Integration* (London and New York: Routledge, 2002).

Appadurai, A., *Modernity at Large: Cultural Dimensions of Globalization* (Minneapolis, and London: University of Minnesota Press, 1996).

Arendt, H., *The Origins of Totalitarianism* (San Diego, New York and London: Harcourt, 1966).

Armitage, D. *The Ideological Origins of the British Empire* (Cambridge: Cambridge University Press, 2000).

Aronowitz, S., and Balakrishnan, G. (eds), *Debating Empire* (London and New York: Verso, 2003).

Arrighi, G., *The Long Twentieth Century: Money, Power and the Origins of our Time* (London: Verso, 1994).

Bairoch, P., 'Historical Roots of Underdevelopment: Myths and Realities', in W. J. Mommsen and J. Osterhammel (eds), *Imperialism and After: Continuities and Discontinuities* (London: Allen & Unwin, 1986).

Ballhatchet, K., *Race, Sex and Class under the Raj: Imperial Attitudes and Policies and their Critics, 1793–1905* (London: Weidenfeld & Nicolson, 1980).

Banton, M., *The Idea of Race* (London: Tavistock, 1977).

Barfield, T. J., *The Perilous Frontier: Nomadic Empires and China, 221 BC to AD 1757* (Oxford, and Cambridge, MA: Blackwell, 1996).

Barnett, T. P., *The Pentagon's New Map: War and Peace in the Twenty-First Century* (New York: Putnam, 2004).

Barratt Brown, M., *After Imperialism* (London: Heinemann, 1963).

Bartra, R., *Wild Men in the Looking Glass: The Mythic Origins of European Otherness*, trans. C. T. Berrisford (Ann Arbor: University of Michigan Press, 1994).

Bayly, C. E., *Indian Society and the British Empire* (Cambridge: Cambridge University Press, 1988).

Bell, D. S. A. 'Empire and International Relations in Victorian Political Thought: Historiographical Essay', *Historical Journal*, 49, 1 (2006), pp. 281–98.

Bello, W., *Deglobalization: Ideas for a New World Economy* (London and New York: Zed Books, 2002).

Berghahn, V. R., *Germany and the Approach of War in 1914*, 2nd edn (Basingstoke, Macmillan, 1994).

Berman, B., 'Structure and Process in Bureaucratic States in Colonial Africa', in B. Berman and J. Lonsdale, *Unhappy Valley: Conflict in Kenya & Africa* (Oxford: James Currey, 1992), pp. 140–76.

Berthon, S., and Robinson, A., *The Shape of the World* (London: George Philip, 1991).

Bielenstein, H., *The Bureaucracy of Han Times* (Cambridge: Cambridge University Press, 1980).

Blackburn, R. *The Making of New World Slavery: From the Baroque to the Modern 1492–1800* (London and New York: Verso, 1997).

Blair, T., 'Doctrine of the International Community', speech given at the Economic Club, Chicago, 24 April 1999; http://www.pm.gov.uk/output/Page1297.asp.

Blaut, J., *The Colonizer's Model of the World: Geographical Diffusionism and Eurocentric History* (New York and London: Guilford Press, 1993).

Boron, A. A., *Empire and Imperialism: A Critical Reading of Michael Hardt and Antonio Negri*, trans. Jessica Casiro (London and New York: Zed Books, 2005).

Bowman, A. K., 'Provincial Administration and Taxation', in A. K. Bowman et al. (eds), *The Cambridge Ancient History*, Vol. X: *The Augustan Empire, 43 BC–AD 69*, 2nd edn (Cambridge: Cambridge University Press, 1996), pp. 344–70.

Boxer, C. R., *The Dutch Seaborne Empire 1600–1800* (London: Hutchinson, 1965).

Brenner, R., 'The Origins of Capitalist Development: A Critique of Neo-Smithian Marxism', *New Left Review*, 104 (1977), pp. 25–92.

Brewer, A., *Marxist Theories of Imperialism* (London: Routledge & Kegan Paul, 1980).

Brown, D. H., *Santería Enthroned: Art, Ritual and Innovation in an Afro-Cuban Religion* (Chicago and London: University of Chicago Press, 2003).

Budgen, S., and Colás, A., 'An Interview with Michael Hardt', *Historical Materialism: Research in Critical Marxist Theory*, 1, 3 (2003), pp. 121–52.

Burke, T., *Lifebuoy Men, Lux Women: Commodification, Consumption and Cleanliness in Modern Zimbabwe* (London: Leicester University Press, 1996).

Cain, P. J., and Hopkins, A. G., *British Imperialism: Innovation and Expansion, 1688–1914* (London and New York: Longman, 1993).

Callinicos, A., *The New Mandarins of American Empire* (Cambridge: Polity, 2002).

Calvet, L.-J., *Linguistique et colonialisme: petit traité de glottophagie* (Paris: Payot, 1974).

Caplan, R., *International Governance of War-Torn Territories: Rule and Reconstruction* (Oxford: Oxford University Press, 2005).

Carmichael, E., and Sayer, C., *The Skeleton at the Feast: The Day of the Dead in Mexico* (London: Trustees of the British Museum, 1991).

Chatterjee, P., *The Nation and its Fragments: Colonial and Postcolonial Histories* (Princeton, NJ: Princeton University Press, 1993).

Chaudhuri, K. N., *Asia Before Europe: Economy and Civilisation of the Indian Ocean from the Rise of Islam to 1750* (Cambridge: Cambridge University Press, 1990).

Chesterman, S., *You, the People: The United Nations, Transitional Administrations, and State-Building* (Oxford: Oxford University Press, 2004).

Christelow, A., *Muslim Law Courts and the French Colonial State in Algeria* (Princeton, NJ: Princeton University Press, 1985).

Ch'ü, T'ung-tsu, *Han Social Structure*, ed. J. K. Dull (Seattle and London: University of Washington Press, 1972).

Colás, A., and Saull, R. (eds), *The War on Terrorism and American 'Empire' After the Cold War* (London and New York: Routledge, 2005).

Colley, L., *Britons: Forging the Nation 1707–1837* (New Haven, CT, and London: Yale University Press, 1992).

Comrie, B., Matthews, S., and Polinsky, M., *The Atlas of Languages: The Origin and Development of Languages Throughout the World* (New York: Quarto; London: Bloomsbury, 1996).

Cox, R. W., 'Gramsci, Hegemony and International Relations: An Essay in Method', in S. Gill (ed.), *Gramsci, Historical Materialism and International Relations* (Cambridge: Cambridge University Press, 1993).

Crosby, A. W., *Ecological Imperialism: The Biological Expansion of Europe 900–1900* (Cambridge: Cambridge University Press, 1986).

Curtin, P. D., *The Rise and Fall of the Plantation Complex: Essays in Atlantic History* (Cambridge: Cambridge University Press, 1990).

Davis, C. B., and Wilburn, K. E., Jr. (eds), *Railway Imperialism* (New York, Westport, CT, and London: Greenwood Press, 1991).

Davis, L. E., and Huttenback, R. A., *Mammon and the Pursuit of Empire: The Political Economy of British Imperialism, 1860– 1912* (Cambridge: Cambridge University Press).

Davis, R., *The Rise of the English Shipping Industry in the Seventeenth and Eighteenth Centuries* (London and New York: Macmillan, 1962).

De la Torre, M. A., *Santería: The Beliefs and Rituals of a Growing Religion in America* (Grand Rapids, MI, and Cambridge: William B. Eerdmans, 2004).

Dilke, O. A. W., 'Maps in the Service of the State: Roman Cartography to the End of the Augustan Era', in J. B. Harley and D. Woodward (eds), *The History of Cartography*, Vol. I: *Cartography in Prehistoric, Ancient and Medieval Europe and the Mediterranean* (Chicago and London: University of Chicago Press, 1987), pp. 201–11.

Dodge, T., *Inventing Iraq: The Failure of Nation Building and a History Denied* (New York: Columbia University Press, 2003).

Dodge, T., 'Iraq: The Contradictions of State Building in Historical Perspective', *Third World Quarterly*, 27, 1 (2006), pp. 187–200.

Dos Santos, T., 'The Structure of Dependence', *American Economic Review*, 60, 2 (1970), pp. 231–6.

Doyle, M. W., *Empires* (Ithaca and London: Cornell University Press, 1986).

Duverger, M. (ed.), *Le concept d'empire* (Paris: Presses Universitaires de France, 1980).

Edelstein, M., 'Imperialism: Cost and Benefit', in R. Floud and D. N. McCloskey (eds), *The Economic History of Britain since 1700*, Vol. 2: *1860–1939*, 2nd edn (Cambridge: Cambridge University Press, 1997), pp. 197–216.

Eisenstadt, S. M., *The Political Systems of Empires* (London: Collier-Macmillan, 1963).

Elliot, J. H., *Imperial Spain, 1469–1716* (London: Edward Arnold, 1963).

Elliot, J. H., 'The Spanish Conquest', in L. Bethell (ed.), *Colonial Spanish America* (Cambridge: Cambridge University Press, 1987).

Etherington, N., *Theories of Imperialism: War, Conquest and Capital* (London: Croom Helm, 1984).

Faroqui, S., *The Ottoman Empire and the Wider World* (London and New York: I. B. Tauris, 2005).

Featherstone, M. et al. (eds), *Global Culture* (London: Sage, 1990).

Featherstone, M. et al. (eds), *Global Modernities* (London: Sage, 1995).

Feldman, N., *What We Owe Iraq: War and the Ethics of Nation Building* (Princeton, NJ: Princeton University Press, 2005).

Ferguson, N., *Empire: How Britain Made the Modern World* (London: Penguin, 2003).

Ferrill, A., 'The Grand Strategy of the Roman Empire', in P. Kennedy (ed.), *Grand Strategies in War and Peace* (New Haven, CT, and London: Yale University Press, 1991), pp. 71–85.

Ferrill, A., *Roman Imperial Grand Strategy* (Lanham, MD: University Press of America, 1991).

Finer, S. E., *The History of Government from the Earliest Times*, Vol. 1: *Ancient and Modern Empires* (Oxford: Oxford University Press, 1997).

Fisher, M. H., *Indirect Rule in India: Residents and the Residency System 1746–1858* (Delhi and New York: Oxford University Press, 1999).

Fletcher, V. J. (ed.), *Crosscurrents of Modernism: Four Latin American Pioneers: Diego Rivera, Joaquín Torres-García,*

Wilfredo Lam, Matta (Washington, DC: Smithsonian Institution, 1992).

Foster-Carter, A., 'The Modes of Production Controversy', *New Left Review*, 107 (1978), pp. 47–77.

Fukuyama, F., *State-Building: Governance and World Order in the Twenty-First Century* (London: Profile Books, 2004).

Gallagher, J., and Robinson, R., 'The Imperialism of Free Trade', *Economic History Review*, 6, 1 (1953), pp. 1–15.

Garnsey, P., and Saller, R., *The Roman Empire: Economy, Society and Culture* (London: Duckworth, 1987).

Geschiere, P., 'Imposing Capitalist Dominance through the State: The Multifarious Role of the Colonial State in Africa', in W. van Binsbergen and P. Geschiere (eds), *Old Modes of Production and Capitalist Encroachment* (London: Routledge & Kegan Paul, 1985), pp. 94–141.

Gill, S., *American Hegemony and the Trilateral Commission* (Cambridge: Cambridge University Press, 1990).

Goldberg, D. T., *Racist Culture: Philosophy and the Politics of Meaning* (Oxford, and Malden, MA: Blackwell, 1993).

Gong, G. W., *The Standard of 'Civilization' in International Society* (Oxford: Clarendon Press, 1984).

González Jiménez, M., 'Frontier and Settlement in the Kingdom of Castile (1085–1350)', in R. Bartlett and A. MacKay (eds), *Medieval Frontier Societies* (Oxford: Clarendon Press, 1989), pp. 49–74.

Goodwin, A., and Gore, J., 'World Beat and the Cultural Imperialism Debate', *Socialist Review* [San Francisco], 20, 3 (1990), pp. 63–79.

Gowan, P., 'The Bush Turn and the Drive for Primacy', in A. Colás and R. Saull, *The War on Terrorism and American 'Empire' After the Cold War* (London and New York: Routledge, 2005), pp. 132–54.

Haley, R., *Maps and the Columbian Encounter* (Washington, DC: National Endowment for the Humanities, 1992).

Hall, C., *Civilising Subjects: Metropole and Colony in the English Imagination, 1830–1867* (Cambridge: Polity, 2002).

Hanke, L., *All Mankind Is One: A Study of the Disputation between Bartolomé de Las Casas and Juan Ginés de Sepúlveda on the Religious and Intellectual Capacity of the American Indians* (De Kalb: Northern Illinois University Press, 1974).

Hardt, M., and Negri, A., *Empire* (Cambridge, MA: Harvard University Press, 2000).

Harrell, S. (ed.), *Cultural Encounters on China's Ethnic Frontiers* (Hong Kong: Hong Kong University Press, 1990).

Harvey, D., *The New Imperialism* (Oxford: Oxford University Press, 2003).

Hechter, M., *Internal Colonialism: The Celtic Fringe in British National Development 1536–1966* (London: Routledge & Kegan Paul, 1975).

Henderson, J. B., 'Chinese Cosmographical Thought: The High Intellectual Tradition', in J. B. Harley and D. Woodward (eds), *The History of Cartography*, Vol. 2, Book II: *Cartography in the Traditional East and Southeast Asian Societies* (Chicago and London: University of Chicago Press, 1958), pp. 203–27.

Hennessy, A., *The Frontier in Latin American History* (London: Edward Arnold, 1978).

Hess, A. C., *The Forgotten Frontier: A History of the Ibero-African Frontier* (Chicago and London: University of Chicago Press, 1978).

Hirst, P., *Space and Power: Politics, War and Architecture* (Cambridge: Polity, 2005).

Hobsbawm, E., *Industry and Empire* (London: Penguin, 1968).

Hobsbawm, E., *The Age of Capital, 1848–1875* (London: Weidenfeld & Nicolson, 1962).

Hobsbawm, E., *The Age of Empire, 1875–1914* (London: Weidenfeld & Nicolson, 1995).

Hobsbawm, E., and Ranger, T. (eds), *The Invention of Tradition* (Cambridge: Cambridge University Press, 1983).

Hobson, J., *Imperialism: A Study* (Ann Arbor: University of Michigan Press, 1965).

Hoisington, W. A. Jr., *Lyautey and the French Conquest of Morocco* (London: Macmillan, 1996).

Holloway, J. E. (ed.), *Africanisms in American Culture*, 2nd edn (Bloomington: Indiana University Press, 2005).

Holman, O., *Integrating Southern Europe: The EC and the Transnationalization of Spain* (London and New York: Routledge, 1996).

Hopkins, K., *Conquerors and Slaves* (Cambridge: Cambridge University Press, 1982).

Hopkins, K., 'Models, Ships and Staples', in P. Garnsey and C. R. Whittaker (eds), *Trade and Famine in Classical Antiquity* (Cambridge: Cambridge University Press, 1983), pp. 84–109.

Hourani, A., *A History of the Arab Peoples* (London: Faber & Faber, 1991).

Hulme, P., *Colonial Encounters: Europe and the Native Caribbean, 1492–1897* (London: Methuen, 1986).

Ikenberry, G. J., 'American Power and the Empire of Capitalist Democracy', *Review of International Studies*, 27, Special Issue (2001), pp. 191–212.

Inaclik, H., 'Ottoman Methods of Conquest', *Studia Islamica*, 2 (1954), pp. 104–29.

Isaac, B., 'The Meaning of the Terms Limes and Limitanei', *Journal of Roman Studies*, 78 (1988), pp. 125–47.

Isaac, B., *The Limits of Empire: The Army in the East* (Oxford: Oxford University Press, 1990).

Israel, J. I., *Race, Class and Politics in Colonial Mexico, 1610– 1670* (Oxford: Oxford University Press, 1975).

Jabar, F. A., and Dawod, H. (eds), *Tribes and Power: Nationalism and Ethnicity in the Middle East* (London: Saqi Books, 2003).

James, C. L. R., *Beyond a Boundary* (London: Stanley Paul, 1963).

Johnston, R. J., et al. (eds), *The Dictionary of Human Geography*, 4th edn (Oxford: Blackwell, 2000).

Kafadar, C., *Between Two Worlds: The Construction of the Ottoman State* (Berkeley, Los Angeles and London: University of California Press, 1995).

Kamen, H., *Imperio: La forja de España como potencia mundial* (Madrid: Aguilar, 2003).

Karpat, K. H., and Zens, R. W. (eds), *Ottoman Borderlands: Issues, Personalities and Political Challenges* (Madison: University of Wisconsin Press, 2003).

Kautsky, K., 'Ultra-Imperialism' [Eng. Trans. of *Neue Zeit* article], *New Left Review*, 59 (1967).

Kautsky, K., *Karl Kautsky: Selected Political Writings*, ed. and trans. Patrick Goode (London: Macmillan, 1983).

Kay, C., *Latin American Theories of Development and Under- development* (London and New York: Routledge, 1989).

Kemp, T., *Theories of Imperialism* (London: Dobson Books, 1967).

Kennedy, P. M., *The Rise and Fall of British Naval Mastery*, 2nd edn (London and New York: Macmillan, 1983).

Kennedy, P. M., *The Rise and Fall of the Great Powers: Economic Change and Military Power from 1500 to 2000* (London: Fontana, 1988).

Kenwood, A. G., and Lougheed, A. L., *The Growth of the Inter- national Economy 1820–2000: An Introductory Text*, 4th edn (London and New York: Routledge, 1999).

Kerr, I. A., *Building the Railways of the Raj, 1850–1900* (Oxford and Delhi: Oxford University Press, 2005).

Khoury, P. S., and Kostiner, J. (eds), *Tribes and State Formation in the Middle East* (Berkeley: University of California Press, 1990).

Kinsbruner, J., *The Colonial Spanish-American City: Urban Life in the Age of Atlantic Capitalism* (Austin: University of Texas Press, 2005).

Koebner, R., *Empire* (Cambridge: Cambridge University Press, 1966).

Koebner, R., and Smidt, H. D., *Imperialism: The Story and Significance of a Word, 1840–1960* (Cambridge: Cambridge University Press, 1964).

Koskiennemi, P., *The Gentle Civilizer of Nations: The Rise of International Law 1871–1960* (Oxford: Oxford University Press, 2001).

Kunt, M., and Woodhead, C., *Süleyman the Magnificent and his Age: The Ottoman Empire in the Early Modern World* (London and New York: Longman, 1995).

LaFeber, W., *The New Empire: An Interpretation of American Expansion 1860–1898* (Ithaca, NY, and London: Cornell University Press, 1963).

Larrain, J., *Theories of Development: Capitalism, Colonialism and Dependency* (Cambridge: Polity, 1989).

Larson, B., *Trials of Nation Making: Liberalism, Race, and Ethnicity in the Andes, 1810–1910* (Cambridge: Cambridge University Press, 2004).

Lattimore, O., *Inner Asian Frontiers of China* (New York: American Geographical Society, 1951).

Lawson, P., *The East India Company: A History* (London and New York: Longman, 1993).

Lenin, V. I., *Imperialism: The Highest Stage of Capitalism* (London and Chicago: Pluto Press, 1996).

Lindner, R. P., *Nomads and Ottomans in Medieval Anatolia* (Bloomington: Indiana University Press, 1983).

Lipschütz, A., *El indoamericanismo y el problema racial en las Américas* (Santiago: Editorial Nascimento, 1944).

Lorcin, P. M. E., *Imperial Identities: Stereotyping, Prejudice and Race in Colonial Algeria* (London and New York: I. B. Tauris, 1995).

Lowry, H. W., *The Nature of the Early Ottoman State* (Albany: State University of New York Press, 2003).

Lundestad, G., 'Empire by Invitation? The United States and Western Europe, 1945–1952', *Journal of Peace Research*, 23, 3 (1986).

Luttwak, E. N., *The Grand Strategy of the Roman Empire: From the First Century AD to the Third* (Baltimore and London: Johns Hopkins University Press, 1979).

Luxemburg, R., *The Accumulation of Capital* (London: Routledge, 2003).

McClintock, A., *Imperial Leather: Race, Gender and Sexuality in the Colonial Contest* (London and New York: Routledge, 1995).

Maddox, R. J., *The New Left and the Origins of the Cold War* (Princeton, NJ: Princeton University Press, 1973).

Mamdani, M., *Citizen and Subject: Contemporary Africa and the Legacy of Late Colonialism* (Princeton, NJ: Princeton University Press, 1996).

Mamdani, M., *When Victims Become Killers: Colonialism, Nativism and Genocide in Rwanda* (London: James Currey, 2001).

Mann, M., *The Sources of Social Power: A History of Power from the Beginning to 1740* (Cambridge: Cambridge University Press, 1986).

Mann, M., *Incoherent Empire* (London and New York: Verso, 2003).

Manning, P., 'The Slave Trade: The Formal Demography of a Global System', in J. E. Inikori and S. L. Engerman (eds), *The Atlantic Slave Trade: Effects on Economies, Societies, and Peoples in Africa, the Americas and Europe* (Durham, NC, and London: Duke University Press, 1992), pp. 117–44.

March, A. L., *The Idea of China: Myth and Theory in Geographic Thought* (Newton Abbot: David & Charles, 1974).

Marx, A. W., *Making Race and Nation: A Comparison of South Africa, the United States and Brazil* (Cambridge: Cambridge University Press, 1998).

Marx, K., and Engels, F., *The Communist Manifesto: A Modern Edition* (London: Verso, 1998).

Mathias, P., and O'Brien, P., 'Taxation in Britain and France, 1715–1810: A Comparison of the Social and Economic Incidence of Taxes Collected for the Central Governments', *Journal of European Economic History*, 5, 3 (1976), pp. 601–50.

Mattern, S. P., *Rome and the Enemy: Imperial Strategy in the Principate* (Berkeley: University of California Press, 1999).

May, E. R., *American Imperialism: A Speculative Essay* (Chicago: Imprint Publications, 1991).

Miles, R., *Capitalism and Unfree Labour* (London: Tavistock, 1986).

Miles, R., *Racism After 'Race Relations'* (London and New York: Routledge, 1993).

Millar, F., 'Government and Diplomacy in the Roman Empire during the First Three Centuries', *International History Review*, 10, 3 (1988), pp. 345–516.

Miller, J. I., *The Spice Trade of the Roman Empire, 29 BC to AD 641* (Oxford: Clarendon Press, 1969).

Mörner, M., *Race Mixture in the History of Latin America* (Boston: Little, Brown, 1967).

Morse, R. M., 'Urban Development', in L. Bethell (ed.), *Colonial Spanish America* (Cambridge: Cambridge University Press, 1987).

Motyl, A. J., *Revolutions, Nations and Empires: Conceptual Limits and Theoretical Possibilities* (New York: Columbia University Press, 1999).

Muthu, S., *Enlightenment Against Empire* (Princeton, NJ: Princeton University Press, 2003).

Nation, R. C., *War on War: Lenin, the Zimmerwald Left and the Origins of Communist Internationalism* (Durham, NC, and London: Duke University Press, 1989).

Nederveen Pieterse, J., *White on Black: Images of Africa and Blacks in Western Popular Culture* (New Haven, CT, and London: Yale University Press, 1992).

Nicolet, C., *The World of the Citizen in Republican Rome*, trans. P. S. Fall (London; Batsford, 1980).

Nicolet, C., *Space, Geography and Politics in the Early Roman Empire* (Ann Arbor: University of Michigan Press, 1991).

Northrup, D., *Indentured Labour in the Age of Imperialism 1834–1922* (Cambridge: Cambridge University Press, 1995).

Nye, J. S., *The Paradox of American Power: Why the World's Only Superpower Cannot Go it Alone* (Oxford and New York: Oxford University Press, 2001).

O'Brien, P., 'European Economic Development: The Contribution of the Periphery', *Economic History Review*, 35, 1 (1982), pp. 1–18.

O'Brien, P., 'The Costs and Benefits of British Imperialism', *Past and Present*, 120 (1988), pp. 163–200.

O'Brien, P., 'Imperialism and the Rise and Decline of the British Economy, 1688–1989', *New Left Review*, 238 (1999), pp. 48–80.

Omissi, D., *The Sepoy and the Raj: The Indian Army 1860–1940* (London and New York: Macmillan, 1994).

Orlove, B. S., 'Putting Race in its Place: Order in Colonial and Postcolonial Peruvian Geography', *Social Research*, 60, 2 (1993), pp. 301–36.

Ortiz, F., *Cuban Counterpoint: Tobacco and Sugar*, trans. H. de Onis (Durham, NC, and London: Duke University Press, 1995).

Overbeek, H., *Neo-Liberalism and Global Hegemony: Concepts of Control in the Global Political Economy* (London and New York: Routledge, 1996).

Pagden, A., *The Fall of Natural Man: The American Indian and the Origins of Comparative Ethnography* (Cambridge: Cambridge University Press, 1982).

Pagden, A., *Spanish Imperialism and the Political Imagination: Studies in European and Spanish-American Social and Political Theory 1513–1830* (New Haven, CT, and London: Yale University Press, 1990).

Pagden, A., *Lords of All the World: Ideologies of Empire in Spain, Britain and France c.1500–c.1800* (New Haven, CT, and London: Yale University Press, 1997).

Panitch, L., and Gindin, S., 'Global Capitalism and American Empire', in L. Panitch and C. Leys (eds), *The New Imperial Challenge: Socialist Register 2004* (London: Merlin, 2003), pp. 1–34.

Pappé, I., *A History of Modern Palestine: One Land, Two Peoples* (Cambridge: Cambridge University Press, 2004).

Paris, R., *At War's End: Building Peace After Civil Conflict* (Cambridge: Cambridge University Press, 2004).

Parker, G., 'Europe and the Wider World, 1500–1750: The Military Balance', in J. D. Tracy (ed.), *The Political Economy of Merchant Empires: State Power and World Trade, 1350–1750* (Cambridge: Cambridge University Press, 1991), pp. 161–227.

Parry, B., *Delusions and Discoveries: India in the British Imagination 1880–1930* (London and New York: Verso, 1998).

Passavant, P. A., and Dean, J. (eds), *Empire's New Clothes: Reading Hardt and Negri* (London and New York: Routledge, 2004).

Pearson, M. N., 'Merchants and States', in J. D. Tracy (ed.), *The Political Economy of Merchant Empires: State Power and World Trade, 1350–1750* (Cambridge: Cambridge University Press, 1991), pp. 41–116.

Penvenne, J.-M., *African Workers and Colonial Racism* (London: James Currey, 1995).

Pérez Luño, A.-E., *La polémica sobre el Nuevo Mundo: los clásicos españoles de la Fiolosofía del Derecho* (Madrid: Editorial Trotta, 1992).

Phillips, A., *The Enigma of Colonialism: British Policy in West Africa* (London: James Currey; Bloomington: Indiana University Press, 1989).

Pitts, J. A., *Turn to Empire: The Rise of Imperial Liberalism in Britain and France* (Princeton, NJ: Princeton University Press, 2005).

Polanyi, K., 'The Economy as Instituted Process', in K. Polanyi et al. (eds), *Trade and Markets in the Early Empires: Economies in History and Theory* (Glencoe, IL: Free Press, 1957), pp. 243–70.

Porter, B., *The Absent-Minded Imperialists: Empire, Society and Culture in Britain* (Oxford: Oxford University Press, 2005).

Potts, L., *The World Labour Market: A History of Migration* (London: Zed Books, 1990).

Prescott, J. R. V., *Political Frontiers and Boundaries* (London: Allen & Unwin, 1987).

Price, S. R. F., 'The Place of Religion: Rome in the Early Empire', in A. K. Bowman et al. (eds), *The Cambridge Ancient History*, Vol. X: *The Augustan Empire, 43 BC–AD 69*, 2nd edn (Cambridge: Cambridge University Press, 1996), pp. 812–47.

Rediker, M., and Linebaugh, P., *The Many-Headed Hydra: Sailors, Slaves and Commoners and the Hidden History of the Revolutionary Atlantic* (London: Verso, 2000).

Richardson, J. S., '*Imperium Romanum*: Empire and the Language of Power', *Journal of Roman Studies*, 81 (1991), pp. 1–9.

Robinson, W. I., *Promoting Polyarchy* (Cambridge: Cambridge University Press, 1993).

Romm, J. S., *The Edges of the Earth in Ancient Thought: Geography, Exploration and Fiction* (Princeton, NJ: Princeton University Press, 1992).

Ruedy, J., *Modern Algeria: The Origins and Development of a Nation* (Bloomington and Indianapolis: Indiana University Press, 1992).

Rupert, M., *Producing Hegemony* (Cambridge: Cambridge University Press, 1993).

Said, E., *Culture and Imperialism* (London: Vintage, 1993).

Scammell, G. V., *The World Encompassed: The First European Maritime Empires, c.800–1650* (London and New York: Methuen, 1981).

Schotter, D., *Augustus Caesar*, 2nd edn (London and New York: Routledge, 1995).

Schumpeter, J. A., *Imperialism and Social Classes*, trans. H. Norden (Oxford: Blackwell, 1951).

Seed, P., *Ceremonies of Possession in Europe's Conquest of the New World, 1492–1640* (Cambridge: Cambridge University Press, 1995).

Semmel, B., *The Liberal Ideal and the Demons of Empire: Theories of Imperialism from Adam Smith to Lenin* (Baltimore and London: Johns Hopkins University Press, 1993).

Shafir, G., *Land, Labor and the Origins of the Israeli–Palestinian Conflict, 1882–1914* (Berkeley: University of California Press, 1996).

Sinclair, J., 'Latin American Commercial Television: "Primitive Capitalism"', in J. Wakso (ed.), *A Companion to Television* (Oxford: Blackwell, 2005), pp. 503–20.

Spruyt, H., *The Sovereign State and its Competitors: An Analysis of Systems Change* (Princeton, NJ: Princeton University Press, 1994).

State Failure Task Force Report: Phase III Findings (McLean, VA: Science Applications International Corporation, 2000).

Stepan, N. L., *The Idea of Race in Science: Great Britain 1800–1960* (Hamden, CT: Archon Books, 1982).

Stoler, A. L., 'Sexual Affronts and Racial Frontiers: European Identities and the Cultural Politics of Exclusion in Southeast Asia', in F. Cooper and A. L. Stoler (eds), *Tensions of Empire: Colonial Cultures in a Bourgeois World* (Berkeley, Los Angeles and London: University of California Press, 1997), pp. 198–237.

Symposium on the 'Wisconsin School', *Diplomatic History*, 28, 5 (2004).

Tadgell, C., *Imperial Form: From Achamenid Iran to Augustan Rome* (London: Ellipsis, 1998).

Tarlo, E., *Clothing Matters: Dress and Identity in India* (London: Hurst, 1996).

Teschke, B., *The Myth of 1648: Class, Geopolitics and the Making of Modern International Relations* (London and New York: Verso, 2003).

Thornton, J. K., *Africa and the Africans in the Making of the Atlantic World, 1400–1800* (Cambridge: Cambridge University Press, 1998).

Thurner, M., *From Two Republics to One Divided: Contradictions of Postcolonial Nationmaking in Peru* (Durham, NC: Duke University Press, 1997).

Todd, E., *After the Empire: The Breakdown of the American Order* (London: Constable, 2004).

Todorov, T., *The Conquest of America: The Question of the Other*, trans. R. Howard (New York: HarperPerennial, 1992).

Tomlinson, J., *Cultural Imperialism: A Critical Introduction* (London: Pinter, 1991).

Tunger-Zanetti, A., *Le Communication entre Tunis et Istanbul, 1860–1913: province et métropole* (Paris: L'Harmattan, 1996).

Twitchett, D., and Loewe, M. (eds), *Cambridge History of China*, Vol. 1: *The Ch'in and Han Empires, 221 BC–AD 220* (Cambridge: Cambridge University Press, 1986).

Van der Pijl, K., *The Making of an Atlantic Ruling Class* (London: Verso, 1980).

Voegelin, E., 'World-Empire and the Unity of Mankind', *International Affairs*, 38, 2 (1966), pp. 171–88.

Waldron, A., *The Great Wall of China: From History to Myth* (Cambridge: Cambridge University Press, 1990).

Wallerstein, I., *The Modern World-System: Capitalist Agriculture and the Origins of the European World-Economy in the Sixteenth Century* (New York and London: Academic Press, 1974).

Warren, B., *Imperialism: Pioneer of Capitalism* (London: Verso, 1980).

Wells, P. S., *The Barbarians Speak: How the Conquered Peoples Shaped Roman Europe* (Princeton, NJ: Princeton University Press, 1999).

Wesson, R. G., *The Imperial Order* (Berkeley and Los Angeles: University of California Press, 1967).

Whittaker, C. R., *Frontiers of the Roman Empire: A Social and Economic Study* (Baltimore and London: Johns Hopkins University Press, 1994).

Wittek, P., *The Rise of the Ottoman Empire* (London, 1938).

Williams, D., *The Reach of Rome: A History of the Roman Imperial Frontier 1st–5th Centuries* AD (London: Constable, 1996).

Williams, E., *Capitalism and Slavery* (London: André Deutsch, 1944).

Williams, W. A., *The Tragedy of American Diplomacy*, 2nd edn (New York: Dell, 1972).

Wolf, E. R., *Europe and the People Without History* (Berkeley: University of California Press, 1997).

Wood, E. M., *Empire of Capital* (London and New York: Verso, 2003).

Woolf, G., 'Inventing Empire in Ancient Rome', in S. E. Alcock et al. (eds), *Empires: Perspectives from Archaeology and History* (Cambridge: Cambridge University Press, 2001), pp. 311–22.

Wright, S., *Storming Heaven: Class Composition and Struggle in Italian Autonomist Marxism* (London: Pluto Press, 2002).

Yapp, M., *The Near East Since the First World War: A History to 1995* (London and New York: Longman, 1996).

Yates, R. D. S., 'Body, Space, Time and Bureaucracy: Boundary Creation and Control Mechanisms in Early China', in J. Hay (ed.), *Boundaries in China* (London: Reaktion Books, 1994), pp. 56–80.

Yates, R. D. S., 'Cosmos, Central Authority and Communities in the Early Chinese Empire', in S. E. Alcock et al. (eds), *Empires: Perspectives from Archaeology and History* (Cambridge: Cambridge University Press, 2001), pp. 351–68.

Young, R. J. C., *Colonial Desire: Hybridity in Theory, Culture and Race* (London and New York: Routledge, 1995).

Zavala, S., 'The Frontiers of Hispanic America', in D. J. Weber (ed.), *New Spain's Far Northern Frontier: Essays on Spain in the American West 1540–1821* (Albuquerque: University of New Mexico Press, 1979), pp. 181–97.

Index